Sweeping the German Nation

Domesticity and National Identity in Germany, 1870–1945

Is cleanliness next to Germanness, as some nineteenth-century nation-alists insisted? This book explores the relationship among gender roles, domesticity, and German national identity between 1870 and 1945. After German unification, approaches to household management that had originally emerged among the bourgeoisie became central to Ger-man national identity by 1914. Thrift, order, and extreme cleanliness, along with particular domestic markers (e.g., the linen cabinet) and holiday customs, were used by many Germans to define the distinctions between themselves and neighboring cultures. What was bourgeois at home became German abroad, as "German domesticity" also helped to define and underwrite colonial identities in Southwest Africa and elsewhere. After 1933, this idealized notion of domestic Germanness was racialized even further and incorporated into an array of Nazi social politics. In occupied Eastern Europe during World War II, Nazi women's groups used these approaches to household management in their attempt to "Germanize" Eastern European women who were part of a large-scale project of population resettlement and ethnic cleansing.

Nancy R. Reagin is professor of history and chair of the Department of Women's and Gender Studies at Pace University. She received her Ph.D. from Johns Hopkins University. She previously taught at the University of Texas, Austin. She is the author of *A German Women's Movement: Class and Gender in Hanover, 1880–1933* (1995), and coeditor of *The Heimat Abroad: The Boundaries of Germanness* (2005). She has been awarded fellowships by the National Endowment for the Humanities and the *Deutscher Akademischer Austauschdienst*.

"In a lively and sophisticated study, Nancy Reagin answers the question, 'why did housework and the Hausfrau achieve iconic status in Germany?' Reagin shows how Germans used ideas about women's roles and domesticity to articulate a national identity. She highlights the domestic objects and practices that, along with regional, patriotic, and dynastic symbols, contributed to what it meant to be 'German' in the nineteenth and twentieth centuries. She shows how domestic notions of Germanness were incorporated into social policy after 1918 and into Nazi programs promoting 'German' domesticity at home and in occupied Poland. By using gender as a tool to understand the history of German nationalism and national identity, Reagin has added a whole new dimension to our understandings of these fields. A 'must read' for students of nationalism, German history, social policy, and Nazism. This book will change the meaning of German nationalism."

– Marion Kaplan, *New York University*

Sweeping the German Nation

*Domesticity and National Identity
in Germany, 1870–1945*

NANCY R. REAGIN

Pace University

CAMBRIDGE
UNIVERSITY PRESS

CAMBRIDGE
UNIVERSITY PRESS

32 Avenue of the Americas, New York NY 10013-2473, USA

Cambridge University Press is part of the University of Cambridge.

It furthers the University's mission by disseminating knowledge in the pursuit of
education, learning and research at the highest international levels of excellence.

www.cambridge.org
Information on this title: www.cambridge.org/9780521744157

First published 2007
First paperback edition 2009

A catalogue record for this publication is available from the British Library

Library of Congress Cataloguing in Publication data

Reagin, Nancy Ruth, 1960–
Sweeping the German nation : domesticity and national identity in Germany,
1870–1945 / Nancy R. Reagin.
p.   cm.
Includes bibliographical references and index.
ISBN 0-521-84113-5 (hardback)
1. National characteristics, German – History – 19th century.   2. National
characteristics, German – History – 20th century.
3. Housekeeping – Germany – History – 19th century.   4. Housekeeping –
Germany – History – 20th century.   5. Germany – Social life and customs –
19th century.   6. Germany – Social life and customs – 20th century.   I. Title.
DD76.R33   2007
943.08–dc22   2006007557

ISBN 978-0-521-74415-7 Paperback

For my parents

Contents

vii

Acknowledgments

It is deeply gratifying to thank everyone who helped me and encouraged me while I was working on this study. All scholarly work is produced within at least one community of discussion. I was fortunate in that my research was supported and enriched by my membership in several communities.

Pace University has given considerable support to this book and to my research as a whole. The university has provided an ideal professional environment for me in my efforts to combine good teaching with scholarship. For this project I received some released time from teaching every semester over several years, from both the Provost's office and Dyson College of Arts and Sciences, along with a sabbatical semester in 1998 (which got me started on the project). The university's Interlibrary Loan (ILL) staff also supported my research consistently and efficiently, and they were simply a pleasure to work with. I couldn't have taken my children with me to the New York Public Library, but the ILL staff made that unnecessary, by obtaining loan materials that I could work on at home.

My fellow faculty at Pace provided encouragement and collegial support that would be hard to match anywhere. I count myself very fortunate to have Martha Driver, Karla Jay, Sid Ray, Tom Henthorne, Patricia Pender, and Joan Roland as colleagues. No one could ever ask for better people to work and teach with. This is particularly true when it comes to Karla, who covered my administrative position while

I was on leave, and Martha, who provides almost daily intellectual and emotional sustenance.

My work wouldn't have been possible without the support of fellow German historians. Renate Bridenthal, Bob Moeller, Mary Nolan, and Marion Kaplan wrote letter after letter in support of my grant proposals; and if I hadn't won those, this book would have been still-born. I am very grateful to all of them.

The German Women's History Study Group was by far the single greatest source of intellectual inspiration for this project: the group's members read drafts of almost every chapter in this book and gave the kind of feedback, challenges, critiques, and encouragement that many academics would kill for. My most sincere gratitude goes to Bonnie Anderson, Dolores Augustine, Rebecca Boehling, Renate Bridenthal, Jane Caplan, Belinda Davis, Atina Grossman, Amy Hackett, Deborah Hertz, Young Sun Hong, Marion Kaplan, Jan Lambertz, Mary Nolan, and Krista O'Donnell. Everything I have ever published was enormously improved by their contributions.

Krista O'Donnell deserves special thanks. Her own work is on women in German Southwest Africa, and she shared (no, offered, without my even asking) a huge amount of material that she had amassed during her own research: photocopies of memoirs, newspaper articles, advice literature, and archival documents on women and households in German colonies. It was a staggering gift, and one that deserves my lasting gratitude.

I am also deeply indebted to the anonymous colleagues who read the manuscript for Cambridge University Press, who clearly gave their very best efforts for me. Both their initial and final reports were thoughtful and extremely detailed, and they gave me a great deal to think about. The book improved substantially as a result of their feedback.

My German friends (some of whom are also historians, and some of whom are not) also encouraged and furthered my work in less academic – but also vital – ways. They were willing to spend hours analyzing methods of housekeeping, for one thing, sharing memories of how their own grandmothers did housework, and explaining archaic domestic technology. They put me up in their homes when I did research and coddled and amused me endlessly. I am particularly indebted to Buka and Dietz Denecke and their family, Angelika Doering,

Doris Marquardt, Siegfried Mueller, Anne Rieke-Mueller, and Andreas Schlueter.

My work wouldn't have been possible without the assistance and access granted to me by several archives. I was fortunate to be able to work at the German Federal Archive in Berlin; the Lower Saxony State Archive in Hanover; the State Archive of Northern Rhineland–Westphalia in Muenster; and the State Archive of Bremen. And surely one of the most friendly and interesting archives in the world to work in was that of the Catholic German Women's League in Cologne. The women there provided a truly cordial and encouraging research environment, debating and explaining older methods of household management with me endlessly, and allowing me to rummage through their records at will. Theirs is a friendly and intellectually stimulating institutional culture, one that I greatly enjoyed being part of, if only for a month or so.

Crucial financial support for this project was given to me by the *Deutscher Akademischer Austauschdienst*, which financed my first research trips to Germany for this project, and by the U.S. National Endowment for the Humanities, which gave me the research fellowship that paid for a year's leave in 2002–3, during which I completed the first draft of the manuscript.

During the final stages of writing and revision, I was given daily encouragement, warm and effective, by the members of my online community. They tolerated the posting of daily progress reports on my work, along with lengthy excerpts from chapters, and always persuaded me that they were interested. All of them deserve my thanks, but especially my close friend Camille Trentacoste, and fellow historians Eveline Brugger, Anne Rubenstein, and Birgit Wiedl.

It is customary to close one's acknowledgments by mentioning the family members who supported one's work. I think that it is common to give family the pride of place because it is the children, spouses, and other family members of academics who bear the most intimate burdens associated with research, and who are asked to do the most, to make the work possible.

Certainly, that is true in my case. Bill Offutt, my husband, has been my life's greatest blessing. None of my accomplishments, among them this book, would have happened without him. But because I've already dedicated one book to him, I'd like to dedicate this one to my parents, who helped make me what I am. My debt to them truly can never be repaid, but only acknowledged. In my "choice" of parents (as in so much else in my life) I am one of the most fortunate of women.

Sweeping the German Nation

Domesticity and National Identity in Germany, 1870–1945

Introduction

In the domestic tradition of the German wife and mother, I see a more secure guarantee of our political future than in any of our fortresses.
Otto von Bismarck

This book explores the gendered aspects of what has undoubtedly been the most successful ideology to emerge during the last two centuries: nationalism. Nationalism is sometimes discussed only in terms of its more extreme or vivid manifestations: political organizations that seek independence for an ethnic group, or right-wing movements that attempt to take over a preexisting state. In such older narratives, the nation is presented as a work of men: its origin is told as a story of war, conquest, or revolution. But as historians of cultural nationalism have noted, nationalism can also be expressed in the more everyday forms that help to create and sustain national identity: the shared rituals, values, symbols, and assumptions that bind people together as a nation. Some forms of cultural nationalism (national holidays or symbols such as flags) may be consciously and fervently embraced by some of the citizenry. Other manifestations of nationality have blended into the fabric of daily life, so much so that they are hardly noticed by the nation's citizens. Such quotidian aspects of the nation constitute what Michael Billig calls "banal nationalism," the daily habits of social life, of thinking and of language, that help to reproduce established nations.[1]

In both its obvious and banal aspects, the nation is always a work in progress: national boundaries, symbols, political systems, and identities can and do alter substantially over time. After Italy was welded together out of disparate regions during the 1860s, one of the most prominent Italian nationalist activists, Massimo d'Azeglio, proclaimed, "We have made Italy, now we have to make Italians." Similar to other protonations, the inhabitants of the Italian peninsula, who spoke a plethora of mutually incomprehensible dialects, nonetheless shared a preexisting sense of culture, of peopledom. But many features of the nation were not yet determined and had to be hammered out over decades: what the national language was to be; the nation's boundaries and whether border regions (which were often culturally hybrid) were to be included; and unifying practices such as national rituals, holidays, and symbols. "Invented traditions," created to unify coalescing nations, abounded during the nineteenth century and were usually represented as a revival of "ancient" rituals or symbols of the nation in question.[2]

Like Italy, Germany was a late-forming nation, a state created out of regions that shared a long-standing sense of belonging to Germandom but that also had strong regional and local identities.[3] The unified

---

[1] Michael Billig, *Banal Nationalism* (London: Sage Publications, 1995), 8. Billig argues, "The most endemic image of banal nationalism is not a flag which is being consciously waved with fervent passion; it is the flag hanging unnoticed on the public building."

[2] See Eric Hobsbawm and Terence Ranger, eds., *The Invention of Tradition* (Cambridge: Cambridge University Press, 1983). See also Eric Hobsbawm, *Nations and Nationalism Since 1780: Programme, Myth, Reality* (Cambridge: Cambridge University Press, 1990), ch. 2.

[3] There is a substantial literature of the long-enduring strength of regional loyalties and identities in Germany that sometimes existed in tension with the claims of the nation-state. Some historians argue that German national identity was notable (compared to some European states) for the strength of Germans' regional identities and the resulting federalism in its governmental structure. See particularly Celia Applegate, *A Nation of Provincials: The German Idea of Heimat* (Berkeley and Los Angeles: University of California Press, 1990); Alon Confino, *The Nation as Local Metaphor: Württemberg, Imperial Germany, and National Memory, 1871–1918* (Chapel Hill: University of North Carolina Press, 1997); and Abigail Green, *Fatherlands: State-Building and Nationhood in Nineteenth-Century Germany* (Cambridge: Cambridge University Press, 2001). For a discussion of work published during the last decade on

German nation-state not only had to win citizens' loyalties in a culture where most people had strong preexisting regional allegiances and identities (e.g., as Bavarians or Saxons), but also faced the challenge inherent in the fact that the new German state could not claim to represent all ethnic Germans. The particular geographic boundaries that were established in 1871 were not identical with the world of the German *Kulturvolk*, because millions of German speakers lived in the Hapsburg Empire (where they felt perfectly "at home" and had no loyalty to Germany), scattered across the Russian Empire, and indeed in communities of ethnic Germans around the globe.[4] As in Italy, nationalists therefore faced the challenge of inventing "Germans": a form of national identity compatible with Germany's new boundaries and state developed only slowly, in tension and in conjunction with both strong regional identities and the broader identity of a far-flung *Kulturvolk* that transcended Germany's actual boundaries.

In "inventing" Imperial Germany, nationalists could therefore count on the fact that almost all Germans defined themselves as a people with a shared culture (a *Kulturvolk*), but the process of working out a political national identity that was firmly tied to Germany's specific borders was more difficult and halting. The designation of a national anthem or the establishment of a repertoire of patriotic songs is only one example of how German-speaking Europe's shared culture complicated the creation of an Imperial German nationality. As scholars of German musicology have noted, compared with other contemporary Western nations, "Imperial Germany operated from the start with a deficit of national symbols," and German-speaking Europe's musical

---

this subject, see Nancy Reagin, "Recent Work on German National Identity: Regional? Imperial? Gendered? Imaginary?" *Central European History* 37 (June 2004): 245–71. See also Harold James, *A German Identity, 1770–1990* (New York: Routledge, 1989) for a quite different argument. For the origins and development of Germany as a nation defined by a shared culture, see Otto Dann, "Nationale Fragen in Deutschland: Kulturnation, Volksnation, Reichsnation," in Etienne Francois, Hannes Siegrist, and Jakob Vogel, eds., *Nation und Emotion: Deutschland und Frankreich im Vergleich, 19. und 20. Jahrhundert* (Göttingen: Vandenhoeck and Ruprecht, 1995), 66–82.

4 On the German global diaspora, see Krista O'Donnell, Renate Bridenthal, and Nancy R. Reagin, eds., *The Heimat Abroad: The Boundaries of Germanness* (Ann Arbor: University of Michigan Press, 2005).

canon (although it was illustrious) could not be easily used to remedy this lack.[5] Many important patriotic music pieces could not be simply adopted by late-nineteenth-century German nationalists, because these pieces were celebrating a cultural German nation that differed substantially from the actual political nation established in 1871. Imperial Germany never did adopt a national anthem. Other efforts to create unifying German public rituals, holidays, or symbols have generally been seen by historians as only partially successful.[6]

But although the process was halting, a national identity that many Germans subscribed to was certainly in place by 1914. Over decades, particularist or regional political parties slowly declined in Imperial Germany, as local identities were reconciled with (and sometimes eclipsed by) national identity.[7] Dynastic figures often served as unifying symbols for the nation in their roles within public festivities. And the shared experiences of the wars of German unification formed a basis for the creation of shared public memories and rituals that memorialized the "founding years," with its heroes and battles.[8] As in other nations, print media helped to articulate and solidify a sense of national community that was linked to Germany's actual political borders.

Some of the most successful aspects of the shared national community were those that were rooted in the private sphere. During the late nineteenth century, notions of Germanness expressed within the household became popular and were often more widely shared than many "public" manifestations of German national identity. Thus, Sedan Day failed as a national holiday in Imperial Germany, but Christmas celebrations (both public and private) grew explosively during the same period, as Christmas – with its domestic values and symbols – came to

[5] Celia Applegate and Pamela Potter, eds., *Music and German National Identity* (Chicago: University of Chicago Press, 2002), 16.

[6] For the limited success of attempts to construct national holidays or symbols, see Confino, *The Nation as Local Metaphor*; and also Wolfgang Hartwig, "Bürgertum, Staatssymbolik und Staatsbewusstsein 1871–1914," *Geschichte und Gesellschaft* 16 (1990): 269–95.

[7] The decline of regional particularist parties was widespread by 1900, although, as Abigail Green notes, regional institutions and governments still remained particularly strong in Germany.

[8] See Jean Quataert, *Staging Philanthropy: Patriotic Women and the National Imagination in Dynastic Germany, 1813–1916* (Ann Arbor: University of Michigan Press, 2001).

be seen as *the* German holiday *par excellence*, observed even by some German Jews.

This book argues that the articulation of Germanness came to include a particular domestic identity that was interwoven with the period's dominant notions of gender.[9] The evolution of gender roles in German society during the late nineteenth century produced an ideal of the "German" housewife, household, and domestic practices that became interwoven with Germans' national identity. This ideal was also enshrined in discussions of colonial German households in German Southwest Africa before 1914. These understandings of German domesticity and housekeeping were further articulated and promoted by Germany's large housewives' organizations and increasingly incorporated into public policy after World War I. Under the National Socialists, this domestic ideal of national identity was racialized (a process that had begun before World War I), becoming one part of the mix of racism and misogyny that drove Nazi family policy. It also underlay the housekeeping and consumption practices urged on German women by Nazi women's organizations.

Finally, a particular set of convictions about what made up "German" domesticity helped to inform the work of Nazi women's groups in occupied Poland during World War II. This book discusses briefly how Nazi women participated in ethnic-cleansing campaigns, a topic treated at greater length by Elizabeth Harvey's *Women and the Nazi East*.[10] Although I touch on this, I am more interested in how Reich German women brought to Poland worked to "re-Germanize" hundreds of thousands of ethnic German families who were relocated

---

[9] Until recently, gender was often neglected in the spate of work on European nationalism and nation building inspired by Benedict Anderson's *Imagined Communities: Reflections on the Origins and Spread of Nationalism*, rev. ed. (New York, 1991) although this seems to be changing. Quataert's *Staging Philanthropy* examines how female dynastic figures (especially their involvement in public ceremonies) helped to sustain a "patriotic public" before 1914. For discussions of how particular notions of (generally martial) masculinity helped to shape an understanding of citizenship in Germany before 1871, see Karen Hagemann, *"Männlicher Muth und Teutsche Ehre": Nation, Militär und Geschlecht zur Zeit der Antinapoleonischen Kriege Preussens* (Paderborn: F. Schöningh, 2002); and Svenja Goltermann, *Körper der Nation: Habitusformierung und die Politik des Turnens, 1860–1890* (Göttingen: Vandenhoeck and Ruprecht, 1998).

[10] Elizabeth Harvey, *Women and the Nazi East: Agents and Witnesses of Germanization* (New Haven: Yale University Press, 2003).

en masse from the Soviet Union to German-occupied territories, by teaching metropolitan German patterns of household management to these resettled ethnic German housewives.

But although these domestic notions of Germanness led to unexpected and often vicious actions on the part of Nazi women in occupied Poland, for most of the period covered by this book, domesticity played a seemingly innocuous part in the articulation of German national identity. Before 1914, the most easily identifiable symbols and rituals of nationalism were objects such as the enormous monument to the Teutonic warrior Arminius (the *Hermannsdenkmal*) and the periodic festivities staged by German patriots around the monument, or the public celebrations and rituals surrounding the German monarchs.[11] Organized nationalism was more easily associated with aggressive (and largely masculine) right-wing organizations, such as the Pan-German League or the gymnasts' movement, than it was with housewives' associations and publications.[12] Nationalism was most blatant when it surfaced in national rituals and holidays, gatherings, and anniversaries that provoked surges of patriotism – "conventional carnivals of surplus emotion" – that participants saw as special time, outside the routines of ordinary life.[13]

By contrast, domesticity was one of the most banal aspects of Germanness. Although they may have been dull, this book argues that housekeeping and domesticity were nevertheless enshrined as a crucial site of national identity, especially juxtaposed against widely shared stereotypes about the private lives of people in other national communities. The comparisons that German writers made between their own households and those of foreigners were ubiquitous in nineteenth- and early-twentieth-century household advice literature and were apparently useful in helping these writers (and their readers) to define what was specifically German in the private sphere. During wartime,

---

[11] For the drive to build the Arminius monument, see Charlotte Tacke, *Denkmal im sozialen Raum: Nationale Symbole in Deutschland und Frankreich im 19. Jahrhundert* (Göttingen: Vendenhoeck and Ruprecht, 1995); for the role that rituals celebrating dynastic figures played in building national identity and the "patriotic public," see Quataert, *Staging Philanthropy.*

[12] See Roger Chickering, *We Men Who Feel Most German: A Cultural Study of the Pan-German League, 1866–1914* (Boston: Allen and Unwin, 1984), and Goltermann, *Körper der Nation,* on the gymnasts' movement.

[13] Billig, *Banal Nationalism,* 45.

moreover, the routines of housekeeping were thrown into the national spotlight, as housewives were told that their work and household habits were crucial to the nation's interests.

German national identity was successfully constructed because it was rooted not only in public, but also in private rituals and practices. Ordinary Germans used notions of gender, the household, and family to understand the "imagined" national community and their own identities. What sociologist Pierre Bourdieu called the *habitus* of social life – the routines, predispositions, and practices shared by particular groups – included assumptions and objects that helped to define German identity in ways that were sometimes only half-noticed by Germans. But such banal, domestic Germanness was the other side of the coin to the surges of patriotism provoked by a monarch's public appearance or a visit to the Arminius monument.

Bourdieu argued that one's own *habitus* often only becomes apparent when we are confronted with the norms and mentality of a different social group or culture, which provides a contrast to our own assumptions and habits. Certainly, domestic Germanness was most easily noticed when thrown into relief by exposure to the households and private life of other nations, as it was for Mrs. Alfred Sidgwick, the author of a humorous set of observations about private life in Germany published in 1908, *Home Life in Germany*. Mrs. Sidgwick was a German woman who had married an Englishman. Accustomed to German styles of domesticity, she had to adjust to English approaches to household management after her marriage, and she observed English families with wry amusement. When she first heard a discussion of "English housekeeping," she later wrote, "it was a new idea to me that any women in the world except the Germans kept house at all. If you live among Germans when you are young you adopt this view quite insensibly and without argument."[14] Bourgeois English housewives, Sidgwick wrote, left much of their work to the servants and did not maintain really clean houses.

Although she spent most of her adult life in England, Sidgwick clearly admired and preferred the community of German bourgeois *Hausfrauen* to which her mother, aunts, and cousins belonged. Being part of such a community, and its routines of domesticity, helped

[14] Mrs. Alfred Sidgwick, *Home Life in Germany* (New York: 1908), 113.

to shape Sidgwick's sense of her own Germanness. It was a community that was at least partly imagined, in the sense defined by Benedict Anderson, because most of its members would never meet each other, and yet thought of themselves as belonging to a common group.[15] Reading Sidgwick's work (and earlier literature produced by nineteenth-century bourgeois German women) makes it clear that many considered themselves to be part of a community of German *Hausfrauen*, and that this community – and the template of household management that underlay the community – helped define the national identity of women such as Sidgwick's female relatives and acquaintances.

To Sidgwick, it was indisputable that there was a *German* style of housekeeping, and she seems to have defined this community fairly inclusively, as potentially encompassing all the housewives of her homeland. However, the model of domesticity that she looked back on with such longing was urban and bourgeois in its origins. During the period covered by this book, the home life that Sidgwick envisioned – with a wife who could devote most of her day to housework and child care, some hired domestic help, and a particular level of home décor and accoutrements – was simply beyond the reach of most rural households and the urban working classes. And yet bourgeois domesticity was still relatively successful as a basis for national identity, compared to some of the more overt and deliberately crafted symbols, such as Sedan Day, which were offered by German nationalists and rejected by broad segments of the German public. Unlike national markers or rituals associated with Prussia or the Protestant bourgeoisie, such as Sedan Day, the bourgeois ideal of domesticity was accessible and appealing across regional and confessional boundaries. Ultimately, it was so widely accepted that it could become the foundation for social policy.

---

[15] My discussion of the imagined community of *Hausfrauen* is entirely indebted to Anderson's *Imagined Communities*, esp. pp. 25–6, 37–44, and 67–77. Anderson offers a working definition of such a community as "imagined because the members . . . will never know most of their fellow-members . . . yet in the minds of each lives the image of their communion," *Imagined Communities*, 6. Such imagined communities, Anderson argues, are a precondition for a sense of national identity and national community.

As I will show, particular approaches to housekeeping and domesticity helped to define the community of bourgeois German housewives. These standards and assumptions regarding household management shaped women's roles in their families and formed part of their individual self-identities. But these notions of domesticity were also incorporated into German public life. The patterns of daily life and private households I will discuss were constantly influenced by (and affected) public policies and developments in the workplace; public and private were interwoven and mutually dependent. The distinction between public and private was more prescriptive than descriptive.

In popular discussions of the German home during the late nineteenth or early twentieth centuries, even the most private routines and habits were sometimes seen to have national significance. What could be more private, apparently, than a woman's decisions about how often to wash, what to sew for her children, or what to cook for her family? And what could be more a matter of personal choice? And yet, these decisions were also part of the process of class formation and moved to the heart of discussions of national character by the Imperial period, at the latest. After 1914, the German home was also increasingly the object of attempted interventions by women's organizations, industry, and the state, in the form of home economics education or attempts to change consumers' preferences.

Under the National Socialists, these attempts to influence household management expanded dramatically through a variety of guises and programs: reeducation camps for disorderly families; mandatory domestic service for young women; large-scale campaigns to reshape household consumption; and the introduction of the Mother Cross award, which was distributed to applicants who satisfied not only requirements for fertility, but who also met standards of "proper" housekeeping. Ultimately, these efforts to reshape German domesticity entered the arbitrary and violent campaigns to sort, classify, resettle, and resocialize hundreds of thousands of ethnic Germans in occupied Poland after 1939.

This study examines the myth and the practices of cleanliness and housekeeping. It should be clear from the outset, however, that the Germans are not alone in cherishing a belief that they are "cleaner" than those from other cultures. "Cleanliness" plays a role in the construction of national or ethnic identity and myths of national superiority in a variety of cultures, and certainly throughout the Western World and in European imperialism in the non-Western world. My focus is on development of "cleanliness" (along with such qualities as order, thrift, and time management) and the broader practices associated with domesticity in a single culture. Ultimately, this book traces how a specific style of housekeeping became bound up with German national identity, so much so that it was incorporated, apparently without debate, into the brutal and macabre policies implemented in occupied Poland during World War II.

But the fact that this book limits itself to an examination of domestic norms in a single culture does *not* mean that I am arguing that these values and practices did not exist elsewhere. Undoubtedly they did. This book does *not* seek to demonstrate that German homes were cozier, more orderly, or cleaner than their French, Russian, or British counterparts; such an assertion would be impossible to substantiate. This is a history of self-perception and identity, and of how identity was reflected in both daily life and social policy. Although many German housewives certainly internalized and enacted these standards, I have no reason to believe that a higher percentage did so in Germany than had done so in France, Denmark, or elsewhere.

I have tried, wherever possible, to incorporate evidence about the reactions of actual housewives to this ideal. Certainly, we can find evidence about the norms and goals embraced by some women regarding household management by examining the statements and programs of housewives' organizations. But the aspirations or actual housekeeping of all German women, or even of the "typical" bourgeois German housewife (if she existed), are probably beyond historical reconstruction.

So, although many bourgeois Germans, such as Mrs. Sidgwick, were sure that their housekeeping surpassed that of their foreign counterparts, there is no evidence that they were correct. French women during the late nineteenth century no doubt also thought it a good idea to be very frugal. And similar to the Germans in Southwest Africa, British imperialists thought that they were cleaner than their colonial subjects, and this notion of cleanliness was integral to their racist descriptions of those they ruled over. Many of the attitudes and household standards that Mrs. Sidgwick valued were common among the middle classes in all of the advanced industrial nations of this period, although particular domestic symbols or objects that were venerated (e.g., the German Christmas tree or the institution of British afternoon tea) might vary.

Thus, although bourgeois Germans were sometimes sure that their housekeeping was the best in the world, it most likely was not. And the fact that the German bourgeoisie was able to establish its domestic routines as a model for other classes to emulate was also not unique. The incorporation of the bourgeois model of home life (at least as an aspiration) into German national identity was one more example of the social and cultural accomplishments that David Blackbourne and Geoff Eley argued constituted the silent victories of the German bourgeoisie – the most successful where it was least noticed – in its contest for influence with Imperial Germany's preindustrial aristocratic elites.[16] And as in other Western nations, nothing was more unobtrusive, more taken for granted, and yet less challenged than the fact that an orderly family life and household management were desirable.

Germany did not become a full-fledged parliamentary democracy before 1914, but Germany's bourgeoisie nevertheless achieved a level of economic, cultural, and social influence that paralleled the level enjoyed by their counterparts in other nations during the late nineteenth century. This group was responsible for such developments as the enactment of a German civil code that underwrote bourgeois economic interests; the creation of a host of voluntary organizations and public institutions that made up a large part of the public sphere; and the expansion and reform of higher education and professional certification systems. To this list we can add the construction of a widely shared understanding about the private sphere and what domestic life ought to consist of.

In fact, this bourgeois model had little influence over day-to-day life in aristocratic households (which were generally predicated on preserving claims to standing within that stratum), within working-class families (which generally could not afford to copy the bourgeoisie), or the peasantry. But this ideal of domesticity became what many working-class families at least aspired to realize, in part. And it was incorporated

---

[16] David Blackbourne and Geoff Eley, *The Peculiarities of German History: Bourgeois Society and Politics in Nineteenth Century Germany* (Oxford: Oxford University Press, 1985).

into nineteenth- and early-twentieth-century discussions about what Germanness consisted of, and later into public policies that influenced private households. In all this, the success and influence of the German bourgeoisie mirrored that of its counterparts in other nations. In spite of what Mrs. Sidgwick and her contemporaries believed, in the German domestic sphere there was no strikingly German *Sonderweg*, at least before 1933. As elsewhere, the German bourgeoisie was able to enshrine its ideal of private life as an aspiration for millions who were not bourgeois.

German bourgeois housewives' organizations, along with the advice literature produced for housewives, often mirrored their counterparts in other nations in the pursuit of the standardization of home economics education and the promotion of particular domestic norms and standards. Later, the economic protectionism that was characteristic of German housewives' organizations during the Weimar period could be found elsewhere in the Western world. But after 1933, there was a sharp divergence from practices in other nations in this area, as in so many others, at least in terms of public policy. National Socialist women's organizations carried forward many of the programs and values propagated by Weimar housewives' groups and further racialized them, as well as implementing them on a far broader scale, using more compulsion and violence than their predecessors could ever have dreamed.

Chapter 1 begins with an overview of the norms and practices of domesticity, as they developed among urban middle-strata bourgeois Germans after the middle of the nineteenth century. As in other contemporary nations, specific styles of household management and family life became vehicles for class formation among the bourgeoisie; particular practices and standards for housekeeping helped to form a template for domesticity. Chapter 2 examines how this style of household management was incorporated into the nineteenth- and early-twentieth-century German discourses on national character, both that of Germans and of other nationalities. In scholarly and popular literature, a particular approach to housekeeping, holidays, and domesticity was now seen as a hallmark of Germanness, both within Germany and outside its borders in ethnic German communities in Germany's colonies.

Before 1914, this model of domesticity was not explicitly politicized in any partisan sense and housewives were only loosely organized.

Chapter 3 discusses how the hardships and shortages that World War I imposed on German civilians accelerated the organization of housewives into "professional" associations and drew the state's attention to the importance of housekeeping, because the housewife's use (or misuse) of resources was now linked to the success of the war effort. After 1918, bourgeois housewives' groups continued to expand in number and became explicitly politicized. Their leadership (and grass-roots membership) now overlapped heavily with that of Weimar center-right and right-wing nationalist political organizations. In their work, Weimar leaders of housewives' associations increasingly linked specific practices of housekeeping to a nationalist political agenda. By 1932, the two largest housewives' organizations were part of a broad nationalist electoral coalition that included the National Socialists.

Instead of being dissolved outright (the fate of liberal or feminist women's groups), housewives' associations were largely absorbed into Nazi women's auxiliary organizations after 1933. Chapter 4 examines how the initiatives of Nazi women's groups expanded on many of the programs launched initially by Weimar housewives' organizations, taking small pilot projects that had only existed in a few localities before 1933 (e.g., the proposal to force all young German women to complete a "year of service" doing some sort of domestic work) and reworking them into nationwide programs. Nazi organizations also carried forward many of the norms of housekeeping that had been widespread among the German bourgeoisie before 1933. But Nazi rhetoric and social policy linked particular approaches to housekeeping with "race," making women's membership in the *Volksgemeinschaft* (racial or national community) contingent on orderly housekeeping.

Chapter 5 turns to the Nazi Four-Year Plan (which drove Germany's preparations for World War II) and discusses how housewives were cajoled (or compelled) to change how they shopped, cooked, and sewed in order to support German rearmament. Finally, Chapter 6 focuses on the ways in which Nazi agencies and women activists applied widely shared standards for "German housekeeping" in their work in occupied Poland after 1939, using the metropolitan German notions of domesticity as a yardstick to measure the Germanness of the so-called *Volksdeutschen*, and as the lynchpin of their efforts to "re-Germanize" families whose ethnicity was dubious or shaky.

Throughout this study, I am interested in how domesticity became one component within a "repertoire" of German national identities, in which Germans used not only regional, public patriotic, and dynastic symbols, but also domestic objects and practices to define what it meant to be German. Domestic notions of Germanness were worked into the fabric of daily life, popular culture, and social policy: in the programs of bourgeois housewives' groups; in scholarly and popular discourse regarding national character; in how ordinary people thought of the nation and their place in it; and in the work of Nazi women's groups after 1933.

Symbols rooted in private life were powerful building blocks of national identity and were at least as effective as public ceremonies or rituals, because the practices of private life were usually seen as "unpolitical" and thus more "naturally" and essentially German. They were potentially more inclusive than monuments or holidays, such as Sedan Day, that appealed only to particular political groups. Unlike the Arminius monument, Christmas trees and closets of clean linens appealed to much of the German public (even those who couldn't afford them) and thus could sustain national community powerfully, albeit unobtrusively.[17]

Harold James observed that "there are always, in any society, not one but several storytellers in the invention of nationality, who usually cannot agree even about the general structure of the narrative."[18] Domesticity was a powerful part of the German narrative, but it was only one of several strands that Germans used to weave their story. But the narrative of Germanness (compared to that of other contemporary Western nations) was particularly changeable because Germany was a late-forming nation whose boundaries and political systems fluctuated radically during the period covered by this book. And perhaps it was the unstable nature of the German nation-state – both its geographic boundaries and its form of government – during the late nineteenth and early twentieth centuries that made domesticity even more important as a foundation for national identity.

---

[17] Alon Confino argues in *The Nation as Local Metaphor* that the notion of "Heimat" (home town or locality) was a much more successful unifying symbol than the national holiday (Sedan Day) proposed by German nationalists.
[18] James, *A German Identity*, 8.

In the narratives of nationality that Germans told themselves during the period covered in this book, the practices of private life seemingly stood outside of historical processes, constituting an essential normalcy that allegedly did not change. By using family life and domesticity as one foundation for national community, Germans could draw on a set of symbols and practices to sustain nationality that were "timeless" and private, relatively nonpartisan and hence more universally appealing. These worked effectively to sustain the national community under successive political regimes, even as so many of the other things conventionally used to define a nation – stable geographic boundaries, ruling dynasties, flags, and particular political systems – were refurbished or remodeled during the first half of the twentieth century, or even swept clean away.

I

The *Habitus* of Domesticity

Keep order, love it. Order saves you time and effort.
Popular saying, often embroidered on dishtowels and samplers in
Imperial Germany

Housekeeping, and the broader gestalt of domesticity that household management and family life produce, is the result of a series of choices made by the family members, and particularly by the woman who runs the household. How to decorate the home? How often to clean the rooms, and what standards should one clean to (e.g., is mopping enough, or must the floor be waxed or polished as well)? How often should clothes and linens be washed, or the bed sheets changed? Which items should be ironed after washing? What sorts of foods should be purchased, grown for oneself, canned or preserved, prepared, and eaten, and how often should these actions take place? Should meals be served hot or cold, or should the meal consist of several courses? How often should the family entertain; whom should they entertain; and what should be offered to the guests? What holidays should be celebrated, and how should they be observed? What routines and rules should the children be trained to observe? How much direct supervision should the children receive from their mother, or should she delegate this task to someone else? How should family members be dressed, particularly when they go out in public?

The choices, like the work, are never ending. The allocations made by the housewife using the assets available to her, which include financial assets, but also the more intangible sorts of cultural and social capital that she can draw on, such as help from relatives, domestic skills, training, and "good taste," form the practice of housekeeping. Household management strategies vary from family to family, but generally follow certain norms and patterns within each social group. In Imperial Germany, for example, housewives among the bourgeoisie and the working class were expected to do most of their own sewing, and certainly all of their own mending, as reflected in Clara Geissmar's memoir. Geissmar, a bourgeois Jewish woman, recounted an incident she witnessed during the 1860s:

Once we saw the daughter of a neighbor go by our house, carrying a small package. My mother...spoke to the young woman, and asked her where she was going. The young woman...confessed that she was going to see an old lady who darned stockings for a small sum. She said she had two small children and no servant, and she spent all her time caring for children, cooking, and washing and cleaning, and had no time for mending. And now there was such a pile of socks. My mother became very stern, and said that this was a serious problem...such an action was the first step on a path which would rapidly pull the woman downwards...*no family could get ahead, if a healthy woman paid for things to be done that she could do herself*...[my mother told her] to go home, and never think of such a thing again. The young woman evidently realized that she stood on the brink of a criminal career, and promised to do better in the future. My mother took the package from her, and promised the contrite woman that this once she would do the stockings for her.[1]

The choices made by housewives such as Geissmar's mother and her neighbor (similar to other sorts of social practices) are strongly influenced by what the French sociologist Pierre Bourdieu called *habitus*, as it was expressed in the field of household management. The term was coined by Bourdieu to refer to a set of dispositions, assumptions, values, and norms that are internalized through socialization (usually at the subconscious level) and strongly influence how people act and feel. *Habitus* thus shapes the mentality of individuals within a group and, combined with the assets available to each person – financial assets, but also other sorts of social and cultural advantages, such as personal

---

[1] From Clara Geissmar's memior located in the Leo Baeck Institute Archive in New York; the italics are mine. I am indebted to Marion Kaplan for calling this source to my attention.

connections – determines the practices (habits, rituals, and actions) of both individuals and groups.[2]

A mundane domestic example of how *habitus* influenced household practice was the assumption (common throughout the Western World) that starched and ironed fabrics looked "better" than clean but wrinkled cloth. Among the German bourgeoisie, who usually had the assets – at least one servant, or money for a laundrywoman – to make an exuberant amount of ironing possible, there was an expectation that everything made of fabric (even dishtowels and underwear) should be ironed, precisely folded, and sometimes even tied into bundles with ribbons. Bourgeois table settings were assumed to reflect both a family's wealth and the woman's level of culture or taste, which led to particularly elaborate displays for holidays and entertaining. Other norms were less class-bound and were shared across the social spectrum – for example, that wearing a stained apron meant that a woman was slovenly or even morally suspect – and reflected the belief that what one wore should be spotless, and that the apron was an important indicator of one's level of cleanliness.

Bourgeois norms for housekeeping meant that a family could acquire intangible but real benefits from a "solid domesticity" (respectability, even admiration from acquaintances, and an increased network of social connections), depending on how well the housewife managed her household. And good management also included thrift, which increased the family's savings. If the housewife was skillful and pursued sound strategies, her family's standard of living and social status would be maintained or even enhanced.

The *habitus* of housekeeping shaped bourgeois women's daily work, and was also omnipresent in advice literature, domestic science courses, and in the work of housewives' organizations. Both the mentality and practices could and did alter over time, and across generations,

---

[2] This is a very simplified and abbreviated summary of some of the most basic concepts in Bourdieu's work. For an introduction to these concepts, see Richard Harker, Cheleen Mahar, and Chris Wilkes, *An Introduction to the Work of Pierre Bourdieu. The Practice of Theory* (St. Martin's Press: New York, 1990), 1–25; see also Ingo Mörth und Gerhard Fröhlich, eds., *Das symbolische Kapital der Lebensstile. Zur Kultursoziologie der Moderne nach Pierre Bourdieu* (Frankfurt/Main: Campus, 1994). Some of Bourdieu's most important essays are collected in Pierre Bourdieu, *Language and Symbolic Power* (Cambridge: Cambridge University Press, 1991).

however, as the result of technological changes (e.g., the introduction of new household appliances), a decline in the availability of servants, or as a result of larger economic changes (e.g., those created by the Nazi Four-Year Plan, which created shortages of key domestic products). Both norms for housekeeping and household practice varied significantly across region and by class, as those who tried to reshape housewives' habits (especially their shopping habits and diet) found out during the two world wars. Thus, there was sometimes a gap between the values and practices that advice writers, housewife activists, or domestic science educators tried to promote, and those that actually existed in varying social groups and communities.

The approaches to household management discussed were promoted not only by writers, educators, and organizations, but were also reproduced through simple peer pressure or other sorts of social control. Oral histories of cohorts of German housewives who grew up during the early twentieth century offer persuasive evidence that many housewives from a variety of social backgrounds did internalize the high standards of cleanliness and thrift that I will discuss, and strove to manage their households accordingly.[3] Some women indeed internalized such norms so thoroughly that they even made their families unhappy with incessant cleaning: such a woman was sometimes referred to as a *Putznarr, Putzteufel,* or *Putzfimmel* (none of these terms have English equivalents, but all would translate loosely as "a devil for scrubbing"). Although the technology would alter cleaning processes somewhat over the course of the twentieth century, housewives were still inspecting each other's work – noticing what sorts of foods their neighbors purchased in local shops; how children were dressed when they were sent outside the house; the cleanliness and quality of others' laundry hung out to dry; how often windows and curtains were

---

[3] Bärbel Kuhn and Karen Hagemann have published studies of cohorts of housewives who were born around or after the turn of the century, which make clear the role that socialization and social control played in reproducing the *habitus* of housekeeping and domesticity I discuss here. See Karen Hagemann, *Frauenalltag und Männerpolitik. Alltagsleben und gesellschaftliches Handeln von Arbeiterfrauen in der Weimarer Republik* (Bonn: Dietz, 1990) and Kuhn, *Haus-Frauen-Arbeit 1915–1965. Erinnerungen aus fünfzig Jahren Haushaltsgeschichte* (St. Ingbert: Roehrig Universitaetsverlag, 1994). See also Karen Hausen, "Grosse Wäsche. Technischer Fortschritt und sozialer Wandel in Deutschland vom 18. bis ins 20. Jahrhundert," *Geschichte und Gesellschaft* 13 (1987): 273–303.

cleaned; the state of bedding hung out the window to air, and so forth –
well past World War II.[4] In some small German towns and villages, this
sort of social control is still very effective today.

This chapter discusses the evolution of collective standards among
the German bourgeoisie during the Imperial period regarding household management, housekeeping practices, and the specific symbols
of domesticity that arose out of housework, all of which underlay
such social control. Norms, practices, and symbols helped articulate
a collective identity for bourgeois German women, one which contained both standards for judging individuals within the group (i.e.,
measuring whether a woman was a "good housewife") and a means
of proclaiming one's membership within the group (e.g., maintaining
a well-ordered cabinet of snow white linens). Historians have documented how the household management of middle-class women in a
number of nineteenth-century cultures helped to define and reproduce
class structure and identity.[5] A particular model of domesticity functioned within the German bourgeoisie as a key part of the process of
class formation during the late nineteenth century. But it ultimately
laid the foundations for a gendered national identity that was rooted
in the practices of private life.

We should be clear at the outset, however, that this chapter is concerned with German housewives' norms and self-image, not their actual
housekeeping: available sources make this inevitable. Norms were

---

[4] See Jennifer Loehlin, *From Rugs to Riches. Housework, Consumption, and Modernity in Germany* (New York: Berg, 1999), 138–9.
[5] The use of domesticity to create, define, and reproduce class identity and boundaries is well established for a number of nineteenth-century Western cultures. Notable con-tributions to this rich literature include Leonore Davidoff and Catherine Hall, *Family Fortunes. Men and Women of the English Middle Class, 1780–1850* (Chicago: Uni-versity of Chicago Press, 1987); Jane Rendall, *Women in an Industrializing Society: England, 1750–1880* (Oxford: Basil Blackwell, 1990); Mary P. Ryan, *Cradle of the Middle Class. The Family in Oneida County, New York, 1790–1865* (Cambridge: Cambridge University Press, 1981); Jeanne Boydston, *Home and Work. Housework, Wages, and the Ideology of Labor in the Early Republic* (New York: Oxford University Press, 1990); Bonnie Smith, *Ladies of the Leisure Class: The Bourgeoises of North-ern France in the Nineteenth Century* (Princeton: Princeton University Press, 1984); Marion Kaplan, *The Making of the Jewish Middle Class: Women, Family, and Iden-tity in Imperial Germany* (New York: Oxford University Press, 1991); Phyllis Palmer, *Domesticity and Dirt. Housewives and Domestic Servants in the United States, 1920–1945* (Philadelphia: Temple University Press, 1989); Sibylle Meyer, *Das Theater mit der Hausarbeit. Bürgerliche Repräsentation in der Familie der wilhelminischen Zeit* (Frankfurt: Campus, 1982).

manifested in daily life, certainly. We have abundant evidence that
Clara Geissmar's mother was no anomaly, and that many bourgeois
housewives strove to meet the expectations of their neighbors. But we
cannot measure how compliance with these norms might have varied
from one social group to the next. Nor can we verify whether (as Mrs.
Sigdwick maintained in *Home Life in Germany*) German women really
did keep cleaner houses than their counterparts in other nations: we
only know that many thought that they did so. No doubt many women
from other cultures could match the Germans, however: pressed, pris-
tine bed sheet for bed sheet. I am concerned with self-definition and
with norms so deeply internalized that they were usually taken for
granted and seldom questioned. However, we cannot determine the
realities of housekeeping in Germany as compared to elsewhere. The
idealized standards promoted in German advice literature were important as yardsticks for the organization of identity: on an individual basis
(in helping to determine whether a woman's reputation) and, later, in
the context of national comparisons.

Domestic Practices and Bourgeois Class Formation

Advice literature for German housewives (and the approach to housekeeping promoted therein) emerged gradually during the course of the
nineteenth century, linked to the growing size and internal cohesion
of the German bourgeoisie (*Bürgertum*) and to changes in this group's
household technology and consumption patterns.[6] Germany's rapid
industrialization after 1850 led to an enormous expansion in the number of men employed in administrative, civil service, management,
professional, and other white-collar positions. The wives and daughters of such men were increasingly removed from wage-earning work

---

[6] The literature on the formation and growth of the German bourgeoisie in the
nineteenth century is substantial. Of particular interest for my work here are
Kaplan, *The Making of the Jewish Middle Class*, 13–15; Konrad Jarausch, *Students, Society, and Politics in Imperial Germany: The Rise of Academic Illiberalism* (Princeton: Princeton University Press, 1982), 127–8; Hansjoachim Henning, *Das
westdeutsche Bürgertum in der Epoche der Hochindustrialisierung 1860–1914 Teil
I: Das Bildungsbürgertum in den preussischen Westprovinzen* (Wiesbaden: F. Steiner,
1972); Rudy Koshar, *Social Life, Local Politics, and Nazism: Marburg, 1880–1935*
(Chapel Hill: University of North Carolina Press, 1986), 12–13; Werner Conze and
Jürgen Kocka, *Bildungsbürgertum im 19. Jahrhundert* 4 vols. (Stuttgart: Klett-Cotta,
1985–92).

(or could earn money only in limited ways) and were expected to devote themselves full time to housekeeping and child rearing, with the help of one or more servants. Before the nineteenth century, middle-strata women had almost always combined the physical care of their families (e.g., cooking, clothing production) with income-producing activities: working in artisans' shops, in merchants' businesses, or on farms. Women's tasks varied dramatically, depending on their *Stand* (estate). The withdrawal of women from their families' businesses among the urban bourgeoisie meant that by 1870, women from differing income levels within the bourgeoisie increasingly had more homogenous "job descriptions" than had their grandmothers, and that their working lives converged into the role of the *Hausfrau*.[7] This was true only for the urban bourgeoisie, however. Farmers' wives continued as active partners on their families' holdings because much of agricultural work was defined as "women's work."

Although married women in this class were increasingly classified almost uniformly as "housewives," the German bourgeoisie of the Imperial period was still a varied group, whose members possessed dramatically different levels of income and education. The husbands of bourgeois housewives ranged from lower-level civil servants to well-educated professionals or wealthy businessmen. Their wives might manage large, well-staffed villas, or be struggling to keep up appearances in a small apartment with the help of one "maid for everything." What united the *Bürgertum* above all was a set of shared values, behaviors, and elements of life-style – an emphasis on diligence, self-discipline, conscientiousness, achievement, and thrift – that bound them together into a "moral community."[8] The display of such behavior within the household and family life, as reflected in specific domestic practices, was crucial in securing a family's position among the bourgeoisie. A "solid domesticity" (*solide Häuslichkeit*, denoting thrift, cleanliness, and order in the broadest sense within the home) was as important as income level or occupation in determining social standing. This was particularly true for civil servants' families and the

---

[7] Bonnie Smith makes the same point about nineteenth-century French bourgeois housewives in *Ladies of the Leisure Class*, as do Davidoff and Hall in *Family Fortunes*.

[8] The term *moral community* is taken from Koshar, *Social Life, Local Politics, and Nazism*, 12–13. See also the essay by M. Rainer Lepsius, "Das Bildungsbürgertum als ständische Vergesellschaftung" in Conze and Kocka, *Bildungsbürgertum*, 13.

members of the "educated classes" (*Bildungsbürgertum*), who relied upon social or cultural capital, and not wealth, to secure their status. Indeed, a well-ordered private life was an explicit job requirement for the families of civil servants, who could be reproved or demoted if they or their families led "irregular" lives.[9] The burden of maintaining a certain standard of domesticity, therefore, was carried by bourgeois housewives no matter what their income because it was crucial in anchoring their family's social status.

Advice literature for such housewives – especially "practical" advice, written by and for bourgeois women, which offers evidence as to the norms and household management strategies of this social group – hardly existed before the mid-nineteenth century.[10] But the growth in the number of *Hausfrauen* (especially urban, bourgeois housewives, who formed the main audience for such publications), combined with declining publishing costs after 1850 led to a flood of publications for this market that grew throughout the Imperial period.[11] During

---

[9] See Barbara Beuys, *Familienleben in Deutschland. Neue Bilder aus der deutschen Vergangenheit* (Reinbek bei Hamburg: Rowohlt, 1980), 441; Henning, *Das westdeutsche Bürgertum*, 274–5 and 485–90; Lepsius, "Das Bildungsbürgertum als ständische Vergesellschaftung," 8–13.

[10] Eighteenth-century domestic advice literature, the so-called *Hausväterliteratur* and its offshoot, *Hausmütterliteratur*, largely addressed itself to the *Hausmutter*, a woman who was assumed to run an agricultural estate or farm with her husband. Very little of this literature was concerned with housekeeping in its later sense. Late-nineteenth-century advice literature, by contrast, tended to address urban or small-town housewives. For a discussion of *Hausväterliteratur*, see Inga Wiedemann, *Herrin im Hause. Durch Koch- und Haushaltsbücher zur bürgerlichen Hausfrau* (Pfaffenweiler: Centarus-Verlagsgesellschaft, 1993), 17–27; Sabine Verk, *Geschmacksache. Kochbücher aus dem Museum für Volkskunde* (Berlin: Staatliche Museen zu Berlin, 1995), 8–12; and Marion Gray, "Prescriptions for Productive Female Domesticity in a Transitional Era: Germany's Hausmütterliteratur, 1780–1840," *History of European Ideas* 8 (1987): 413–26 and "Bourgeois Values in the Rural Household, 1810–1840: The New Domesticity in Germany," *The Consortium on Revolutionary Europe, 1750–1850; 1993 proceedings*, 23 (1994): 449–56, who notes that this genre, along with the term *Hausmutter*, declined after 1840.

[11] The overwhelming bulk of the advice literature I discuss here addressed itself to an urban audience, assuming that the reader might possess a small garden at most. Rural housewives developed their own organizations and publications much later and will be discussed in Chapter 3. See Renate Bridenthal, "Organized Rural Women in the Conservative Mobilization of the German Countryside in the Weimar Republic," in Larry E. Jones and James N. Retallack, eds., *Between Reform, Reaction, and Resistance. Studies in the History of German Conservatism from 1789 to 1945*

the eighteenth and early nineteenth centuries, young women from middle-class families had often compiled their own handwritten notebooks about housekeeping. They filled their books with verses, sewing patterns, recipes for homemade medicines, and cooking recipes for dishes that were seldom made or required exact proportions. Recipes often included a notation as to where they came from (Aunt Lina or Frau Dr. B.). These books were often added to over the course of a woman's housekeeping career, and passed on to her daughter. Unless they were married to the owners of agricultural estates, however, they were unlikely to need or use *Hausmütterliteratur*, advice literature produced for women who were married to estate owners.[12]

After 1850, however, bourgeois women could select from the increasing body of publications directed at housewives, including general household advice manuals, cookbooks, domestic science treatises, special columns or supplements in women's magazines, and magazines produced by and for housewives.[13] By the Wilhelmine period, manufacturers had begun to distribute free cookbooks and pamphlets in order to promote their products. Many of the most successful authors or editors of such publications were women from the

---

(New York: Berg, 1993), 375–405; "'Professional Housewives': Stepsisters of the Women's Movement," in Renate Bridenthal, Atina Grossmann, and Marion Kaplan, eds., *When Biology Became Destiny: Women in Weimar and Nazi Germany* (New York: Monthly Review Press, 1984), 153–73; and "Class Struggle around the Hearth: Women and Domestic Service in the Weimar Republic," in Michael Dobkowski and Isidor Walliman, eds., *Towards the Holocaust: Anti-Semitism and Fascism in Weimar Germany* (Westport, CT: Greenwood Press, 1983), 243–64. See also Elizabeth Jones, "Gender and Agricultural Change in Saxony, 1900–1930," (Ph.D. diss., University of Minnesota, 2000).

[12] Wiedemann, *Herrin im Hause*, 40–2.

[13] Advice literature for housewives was addressed to *bürgerliche* housewives and assumed that the reader had at least one servant. A rare exception to this rule was the best-selling advice manual addressed to working-class women, *Das häusliche Glück*. See Bärbel Kuhn, "Und herrschet weise im häuslichen Kreise. Hausfrauenarbeit zwischen Disziplin und Eigensinn," in Richard van Duelmen, ed., *Verbrechen, Strafen, und soziale Kontrolle* (Stuttgart: Fischer, 1990), 238–77. See Annabel Weismann, *Froh erfülle deine Pflicht. Die Entwicklung des Hausfrauenleitbildes im Spiegel trivialer Massenmedien in der Zeit zwischen Reichsgruendung und Weltwirtschaftskrise* (Berlin: Schelzky and Jeep, 1989); Siegfried Bluth, *Der Hausfrau gewidmet. Ein Beitrag zur Kulturgeschichte der Hausfrau* (Weil der Stadt: Hadecke, 1979); Wiedemann, *Herrin im Hause*; and Gisela Marenk and Gisela Framke, eds., *Beruf der Jungfrau. Henriette Davidis und Bürgerliches Frauenverständis im 19. Jahrhundert* (Oberhausen: Graphium Press, 1988).

bourgeoisie forced by circumstances to earn money by writing about what they knew best: housekeeping. Henriette Davidis, a pastor's daughter from a large family, published her famous cookbook in 1844, which ultimately went into sixty-three editions. During the late nineteenth century, it was said that bourgeois households, if they possessed no other books, had at least copies of the Bible and "the Davidis."

Lina Morgenstern, a mother of five who came from a prosperous Jewish family in Berlin, was active in a variety of feminist and charitable organizations and a key figure in the creation of housewives' voluntary organizations. She helped found and led the Berlin housewives' association and edited their widely read magazine, *Die Deutsche Hausfrauen-Zeitung*, for over thirty years.[14] Morgenstern's work and that of her contemporary, Hedwig Heyl, points to the partial overlap between the producers of advice literature for housewives and the activists who created housewives' organizations. After 1870, bourgeois women began to form voluntary organizations for housewives across Germany, and some of the magazines published for housewives were put out by such voluntary organizations.[15]

Before 1890, housewives' associations were formed in a handful of larger German cities. Housewives' groups in Berlin and Königsberg, for example, were among the earliest and largest such groups in Germany, and later played leading roles in housewives' national leagues. During the Wilhelmine period, such organizations proliferated; the first national league of such groups was created in 1908. Housewives' associations before 1914 were primarily concerned with the "servant question," working against servants' unionization, and creating referral bureaus that matched housewife-employers with women seeking

---

[14] Davidis (as an author) and Morgenstern (as an editor and organizer) were both key figures in the development of the imagined community of *Hausfrauen*. For Davidis, see Bluth, *Der Hausfrau gewidmet*, 57 and Framke and Marenk, *Beruf der Jungfrau*. For Morgenstern, see Kaplan, *Making of the Jewish Middle Class*, 206–8; see also Jutta Dick and Marina Sassenberg, eds., *Jüdische Frauen im 19. und 20. Jahrhundert* (Reinbek bei Hamburg: Rowohlt, 1993), 283–6; Heinz Knoblauch, *Die Suppenlina. Wiederbelebung einer Menschenfreundin* (Berlin: Hentrich, 1997).

[15] *Die Frau im Osten* (which addressed bourgeois women in Eastern Prussia) is another example of advice literature produced for housewives by bourgeois women activists. Hedwig Heyl was the author of one of the most widely read cookbooks and household *Ratgeber*, *Das ABC der Küche* 4th ed. (Berlin: Carl Habel Verlag, 1897).

positions. They also offered a variety of vocational training for younger bourgeois women, including specialized cooking courses, infant care courses, and sewing and handicrafts courses. For married women, they offered lectures and demonstrations about issues of consumption and housekeeping, such as advice on purchasing household goods. The imagined community of *Hausfrauen* was thus fostered by women's contact with both literature and organizational life, which were new vehicles for housewives' collective socialization.[16]

Housewives' magazines, courses, and organizations found an audience because they met a need: changes in household technology and class structure meant that there were aspects of housekeeping that a young woman couldn't simply learn by asking her mother, or by looking it up in mother's notebook. Rapid urbanization (and the transfers to which civil servants in particular were often subject) meant that a woman might not be able to easily consult her mother or aunt. If she was attempting to secure a somewhat higher social status for her family than her parents had enjoyed, a bourgeois housewife might use advice literature to learn to entertain her husband's colleagues, to set the table and fold napkins properly. Advice manuals offered elaborate illustrations for novices on how to create the origami-like folded napkins because the properly set table was an important marker of a prosperous and well-run household. For special events, the housewife would often rent extra china or silver and lay it out in carefully proscribed patterns to achieve maximum effect.

Younger women also turned to advice literature to learn how to cook new foods (e.g., tomatoes or bananas) that their mothers had never used. Housewives' organizations and Davidis' cookbook also taught women to use new devices (e.g., a coal range instead of a fireplace, or using the new glass jars and rubber rings to "put up" fruits and vegetables). Bourgeois women also had to learn how to clean and maintain a plethora of household items, including Turkish carpets and

---

[16] For the early history of housewives' associations, see Kirsten Schlegel-Matthies *"Im Haus und am Herd." Der Wandel des Hausfrauenbildes und der Hausarbeit 1880–1930* (Stuttgart: F. Steiner, 1995). See also Bridenthal, "Professional Housewives"; Nancy Reagin, *A German Women's Movement: Gender and Class in Hanover, 1880–1933* (Chapel Hill: University of North Carolina Press, 1995), 226–34. For the role played by publications in creating imagined communities and group identities, see Anderson, *Imagined Communities*, 37–44.

mahogany furniture, which were now more widely owned than in previous generations. Before the Imperial period, visitors to Germany had noted that even in well-to-do households, carpets were rare and furniture was usually simple.[17] More luxurious décor proliferated in bourgeois homes after 1870, however, and such furnishings were more prone to become filthy, as coal-burning stoves spread soot through the house. The growth of industries supplying consumer goods meant that urban housewives now shopped for foods, rather than relying mainly on self-provisioning, which required knowledge of prices and materials. By reading a housewives' magazine, a woman could learn how to detect adulteration in loose goods, and how to evaluate the color and consistency of products such as coffee or cocoa, which were sold at a "colonial goods" store.[18]

Advice literature and housewives' organizations thus met the real needs of a growing group of women, but they also helped to articulate and define the role of the *Hausfrau*, a term that could increasingly be applied to women from all regions of Germany and from different social strata. They promoted collective identity and norms among German housewives, so that many bourgeois women came to see themselves as constituting a distinct social category. After 1900, bourgeois women within such *Hausfrauen* organizations began to argue that they constituted a *Stand* (a corporate estate), that housework was a "profession," and thus that the job of a *Hausfrau* was a well-defined, highly skilled position.[19] Leaders of such associations saw their groups as being analogous to the organizations emerging among other female professionals (e.g., nurses' associations or teachers' organizations). Such bourgeois women volunteers identified strongly with the community of *Hausfrauen*.

---

[17] See Charles Loring Brace, *Home Life in Germany* (New York: C. Scribner, 1860).

[18] See Wiedemann, *Herrin im Hause*, 38–9, 54–5, 60, and 72; Verk, *Geschmacksache*, 57–60. See also Henriette Davidis, *Die Hausfrau. Praktische Anleitung zur selbständigen und sparsamen Führung von Stadt- und Landhaushaltungen* 6th ed. (Leipzig: E. A. Seemann Verlag, 1872); this edition was one of the first (and few) that had some sections addressing rural housewives.

[19] See Schlegel-Matthies *"Im Haus und am Herd"* for the argument by housewives' organizations that theirs was a "profession," see Bridenthal, "Professional Housewives"; Reagin, *A German Women's Movement*, 226–34. See also Brigitte Kerchner, *Beruf und Geschlecht: Frauenberufsverbände in Deutschland, 1848–1908* (Göttingen: Vandenhoek and Ruprecht, 1992), 211–43.

Advice literature directed at housewives and the public work of housewives' organizations reminded bourgeois women across the nation of other bourgeois women, who were doing the same kinds of jobs and occupied roughly the same social position as themselves, thus creating an imagined community among such women. In columns devoted to letters from readers, women's magazines gave readers access to recipes and housekeeping tips from women of whom readers would otherwise never hear.[20] Such publications (and later, housewives' organizations) promoted the collective identity of housewives by making readers aware of the universe of thousands of bourgeois women who had similar roles in their families. The community of *Hausfrauen* was an imaginary one (in the sense defined by Benedict Anderson) because most German housewives would never meet each other, and yet increasingly, many thought of themselves as belonging to a common group.[21]

And this imaginary community was implicitly (and often explicitly) a German one. It was full of cultural references to recipes, holidays, and details of housekeeping that were specific to the German-speaking world. As a result, the body of publications aimed at housewives helped to both define and delimit their group identity. Readers were implicitly encouraged to think about and identify with bourgeois housewives across German-speaking Europe, but not outside of it, a fact reflected in the title of Lina Morgenstern's magazine, *Die deutsche Hausfrauen-Zeitung*.[22] The community of *Hausfrauen* was only one of a number of communities created among the European bourgeoisie after the emergence of what Benedict Anderson calls "print capitalism," which

[20] See, e.g., letters to the editor that appeared in *Die Frau im Osten* between 1910 and 1913.

[21] My discussion of the imagined community of *Hausfrauen* is entirely indebted to Benedict Anderson's *Imagined Communities*, esp. pp. 25–6, 37–44, and 67–77.

[22] I am not aware of any leading domestic science work by a non-German author that was widely read within Germany before 1914. Authors sometimes referred to foreign works (e.g., Catherine Beecher's treatise), but their works reflected local tastes. After 1918, the American trend toward translating Taylorism into the home through "scientific" household management found a following in Germany. See Mary Nolan, *Visions of Modernity. American Business and the Modernization of Germany* (New York: Oxford University Press, 1994), 206–33; Nancy Reagin, "Comparing Apples and Oranges: Housewives and the Politics of Consumption in Interwar Germany," in Susan Strasser, Charles McGovern, and Mathias Judt, eds., *Getting and Spending: European and American Consumer Societies in the Twentieth Century* (Cambridge: Cambridge University Press, 1998).

facilitated the emergence of various vernacular print-languages. Vernacular literature produced for bourgeois readers unified dialects and made readers aware of the universe of thousands of people in their own language and social groups. Fellow readers, Anderson argues, were the "embryo of the nationally imagined community," and the various bourgeois groups who made up these groups of readers were "the first classes to achieve solidarities on an essentially imagined basis."[23]

But because the *Deutsche Hausfrau* was herself imaginary, authors of magazines and domestic science treatises were trying to establish a set of norms and standards that would apply to women from a variety of regions and middle-strata social groups. This was a difficult task. Invariably, there were differences between income groups and across regions in how these norms were observed, and how households were managed. Lina Morgenstern acknowledged the challenge of trying to construct generalizations that could apply equally to the housekeeping of the wife of a Berlin professor, the daughter of a Bremen merchant, and an elderly spinster in Westphalia.[24] Enormous variation – in terms of geography, income level, social obligations, and religion – existed among the German bourgeoisie, and thus among housewives. The ideal of the *Hausfrau* tried to bridge these differences by denying them, setting standardized approaches to housekeeping. Indeed, some cookbook writers consciously tried to collect recipes that would be useable for all German housewives, so that all German women would learn similar recipes, and (as one author remarked) "also become quite familiar with the vocabulary and expressions used in other German regions."[25] But although some practices and especially recipes varied by region, many norms took root during this period (especially those involving household cleanliness, organization, and display) to which bourgeois women across Germany subscribed.

The definition of *German housewife* was therefore simultaneously inclusive, and exclusive, both in terms of class and region. In a formal sense, the editors of housewives' magazines, cookbook authors, and the leaders of housewives' associations were addressing all German housewives. In theory, any woman could join a housewives' group or

[23] See Anderson, *Imagined Communities*, 42–4 and 77.
[24] See Lina Morgenstern's note in *Die Deutsche Hausfrauen-Zeitung* 14 (1887): 368.
[25] Quoted in Wiedemann, *Herrin im Hause*, 30.

purchase "the Davidis." In practice, however, the life-style and assumptions that these groups were predicated upon could not be exported across some social boundaries.

One of the most obvious limitations to this model of housewifery was class and income level. The dues charged by housewives' organizations, and the cuisine and fashions promoted in advice literature (even in the "simple and practical" editions, as opposed to the *gut bürgerliche* versions) were too expensive for working-class budgets.[26] The patterns of consumption that underlay a bourgeois model of housekeeping included the purchase of items that were beyond the reach of poorer households: glass jars and rings for putting up produce; china, cutlery, and linens for entertaining; and porcelain bathtubs, "solid" furniture, and rugs. Thus, much of the advice given by bourgeois women's organizations regarding entertainment, cooking, and how to clean particular objects was inapplicable to working-class lives. And the frugality promoted by such organizations was already a part of poorer households' strategies. Working-class housewives did not form their own organizations before 1914, in part because they were discouraged by the Social Democratic Party (SPD) from forming a group that would be separate from those of other women's occupational groups. Poor women therefore generally appeared in housewives' magazines and organizations' discussions only as the intended beneficiaries of bourgeois reformers' efforts during the Wilhelmine period. The reformers were anxious to teach poor women "proper" methods of housekeeping.[27]

A second important barrier to the widespread adoption of bourgeois housekeeping was the difference in women's work roles in urban and rural households. What urban women understood under the rubric of "housework" was only a small part of the workload shouldered by farmers' wives. Many of the jobs to be done on a medium- or small-sized agricultural holding were specifically classified as "women's

---

[26] The housewives who helped create the first housekeeping schools in late-nineteenth-century cities tacitly acknowledged that most bourgeois advice literature was impractical for working-class housewives and created new *Ratgeber* explicitly addressed to working-class women, such as the best-selling *Das häusliche Glück*.

[27] For the efforts of bourgeois women vis-à-vis working-class housewives, see the discussion in the following text. For the SPD's refusal to permit the creation of a separate housewives' organization, see Hagemann, *Frauenalltag und Männerpolitik*, 133–8. During the Weimar period, working-class housewives did articulate their own concerns in a variety of publications issued by the SPD and the German Communist Party (KPD).

work" in rural German culture: gardening, which included raising fruits and vegetables for the market; feeding pigs, poultry, goats, or rabbits; hoeing and digging root crops such as potatoes or beets, and sorting the resulting harvests; cleaning stalls; and milking, butter and cheese making, and dairy work of all kinds. Unlike bourgeois housewives, farm women did not spend much of their day inside the kitchen and parlor. Instead, they often worked sixteen-hour days, rotating between cellars, stalls, pig pens, laundry rooms, kitchens, gardens, fields, and chicken coops. The pride of a rural family was its fields and stables, and not a "sparkling clean" house or tastefully set table. The farmyard and fields were much more important because they provided the food for the family's survival and secured its reputation in the community.

A healthy younger farm woman was, therefore, not expected to spend most of her waking hours doing what a city woman would have seen as housework. Instead, cleaning and cooking might be left to an older female relative or older child (if the household had such on hand). Indeed, the amount of agricultural work expected of farm women increased after the "agricultural crisis" of the 1870s. As grain prices fell, many smaller farms shifted to intensive cultivation of root crops, livestock, and garden crops. Most of the work in these areas fell to women under the established sexual division of labor in rural communities. During the same period that urban bourgeois housewives were shifting their attention to more elaborate standards and schedules for various sorts of housework, therefore, farmers' wives were shouldering an increased workload in agricultural production. For much of the year, they simply could not aspire to an urban bourgeois model of domesticity, although in the slower winter months they might be able to devote more time to the home. One study of rural households in Saxony found that farm women spent twice as many hours per week on housework in November, compared to June; for most of the year, their work in the fields, garden, and stalls simply took precedence.[28] Housework and child care were therefore jammed into the day's schedule as time allowed, and the domestic standards prevalent in urban bourgeois domestic households were simply inapplicable.

---

[28] For a discussion of the impact of the agricultural crisis on rural women's workloads and an overview of the sexual division of labor in rural communities, see Jones, "Gender and Agricultural Change in Saxony, 1900–1930," 27–31 and 162.

But a domestic template that could seldom be found in the countryside was relatively successful among women of all religious backgrounds. With some variations, bourgeois Jewish and Catholic women could be and were "proper" German housewives. The obvious adaptation that German Jewish housewives made was in the area of cooking, because many still observed the rules of *kashrut*. Mainstream cookbooks often implicitly excluded Jewish housewives, as such publications heavily featured recipes that included lard and pork, along with special dishes for Christmas. But bourgeois Jewish women who wanted to keep kosher could turn to special cookbooks created for a bourgeois Jewish audience. This subgenre promoted a style of household management that – with its emphasis on thrift, order, and cleanliness – largely resembled that of the German bourgeoisie as a whole, while still trying to preserve Jewish religious and ethnic identity in domestic expressions of Judaism. Housewives could express a sensibility that was both Jewish and bourgeois when they set an impressive Sabbath table, for example, or hosted a "proper" bourgeois seder.[29]

Apart from cookbooks, most mainstream advice literature could be used by Jewish women, and organizations created by bourgeois housewives often included Jewish members. Housewives' magazines generally did not include recipes, kosher or otherwise (Lina Morgenstern did not), and focused on topics that would have appealed to Jewish and Christian readers alike: endless embroidery and craft patterns; articles on how to pose children in photographs; advice on how to teach children proper table manners; mild physical exercises for women; household bookkeeping; and servants. Of the magazines surveyed for this study, only the conservative *Kolonie und Heimat* often included recipes that were not kosher.

There was no such dietary barrier for bourgeois Catholic housewives, who in theory could appreciate and join the publications and organizations created by their Protestant counterparts. In practice, however, most of the best-known writers for this audience came from Protestant circles, and the organized housewives' movement (as was

---

[29] See Kaplan, *Making of the Jewish Middle Class*, 72–4; and also a dissertation, "Matzo Balls and Matzo Kleis: A Comparative Study of Domestic Life in the United States and Germany, 1840–1914," soon to be completed by Ruth Abusch-Magder at Yale University.

true for the bourgeois women's movement as a whole) was located largely in Protestant-dominated areas (although Jewish women were certainly also well represented). Catholic bourgeois housewives only began to create their own associations after 1900. When they did so, they organized separately on the basis of confession, a practice that continued until 1933.[30]

The segregation of Catholic housewives' groups mirrored the division between Protestants and Catholics in other sorts of voluntary organizations, as in many other areas of social life during the Imperial period. Although both intermarriage rates and geographical integration between Protestants and Catholics increased during this period, German society was still marked by social and political confessional divisions that had been sharpened by the *Kulturkampf*, a legislative effort by the German government during the 1870s to assert control over the Catholic Church's schools and clergy in Germany, and to curtail the influence of "foreign" Catholic groups such as the Jesuits. Protestant bourgeois parties had generally supported Bismarck's legislative efforts in this area, as they associated Germany unity and national identity with the values of Protestantism. But German Catholics and their Church had bitterly and stubbornly resisted the effort to assert secular control over the Church hierarchy, and the *Kulturkampf*, Helmut Smith persuasively argues, was "an ultimately unsuccessful attempt to create a common national culture across confessional lines."[31]

In the aftermath of the *Kulturkampf*, German Protestants and Catholics had substantial differences in life-style and culture. As groups, they often pursued strategies of self-segregation that were often peaceful – patronizing different shops, taverns, and clubs, for example – but that were sometimes ridden with conflict and disputes. Their differences were particularly acute in what Smith calls "print cultures":

---

[30] Catholic housewives' groups were founded in some cities before 1914, but Catholic housewives did not create a separate national Catholic housewives' league until after World War I, which was affiliated with the *Katholischer Deutscher Frauenbund*. See Chapter 3 for details about Catholic housewives' organizations.

[31] Helmut Smith, ed., *German Nationalism and Religious Conflict. Culture, Ideology, Politics, 1870–1914* (Princeton: Princeton University Press, 1995), 11. See also Jonathon Sperber, *Popular Catholicism in Nineteenth-Century Germany* (Princeton: Princeton University Press, 1984), 226–34. See also Helmut Smith, *Protestants, Catholics and Jews in Germany, 1880–1914* (New York: Berg, 2002).

Catholics and Protestants read different sorts of devotional literature, almanacs, newspapers, and journals. Catholic writers, moreover, were generally excluded from the national literary canon, as defined by Protestant scholars, and the two confessions had sharply contrasting views of German history.[32]

Confessional differences in print cultures certainly spilled over into the domestic sphere as well. Surveys done in Baden in 1889 and 1894 found that Protestant homes typically owned homilies by Luther, hymnals, the Bible, and Protestant devotional literature. Catholic homes generally owned almanacs and novels written by Catholic authors, along with Counter-Reformation works on Jesus or about apparitions of the Blessed Virgin.[33] The walls of Catholic households were apt to feature quite different images from those found in Protestant homes, particularly pictures of the various manifestations of the Virgin.

But the differences between Catholic and Protestant styles of domestic management did not go quite as deep as the statuettes of the Infant of Prague in some Catholic homes might suggest, as bourgeois households of both confessions embraced fairly similar domestic standards for cleanliness, order, and thrift. Similar to Catholic bicyclists' associations and hikers' groups, Catholic housewives' organizations generally held themselves aloof from the Protestant-dominated nondenominational associations. But the concerns and programs that Catholic housewives' groups pursued were, generally speaking, identical to those of their Protestant counterparts.[34] Just like their Protestant counterparts, middle-strata Catholic women had to maintain *standesgemässige* households, and the strategies they used to pursue this end do not seem to have differed appreciably. As Jonathan Sperber notes, Catholics were underrepresented among the German bourgeoisie, and thus formed a smaller minority among that class than in other social groups, one that was influenced by the Protestant majority in some respects. Bourgeois Catholics were more likely to be secularized and were less influenced by the religious revival among lay Catholics during

---

[32] Smith, *German Nationalism and Religious Conflict*, 63–70 and 80–2.

[33] Ibid., 82.

[34] For the identical programs and concerns pursued by bourgeois Protestant and Catholic housewives' groups in Hanover, e.g., during both the Imperial and Weimar periods, see Reagin, *A German Women's Movement*, 60–5 and also Chapter 3.

1850–70 than were other Catholic social groups.[35] Subjected to similar social controls and class standards as their Protestant counterparts, Catholic bourgeois housewives were thus exposed to the same domestic norms.

Although the community of German *Hausfrauen* formally included all German housewives, it was implicitly bourgeois and urban. The model of domesticity espoused by this group could, with a few modifications, transcend religious divisions, but most of it could not be exported across class lines or into farming households in rural areas. This approach to housekeeping had roots in particular strata of German society, but writers and housewives' organizations attempted to promote these norms across regional lines among the German bourgeoisie as a whole, replacing the Babel of cooking and housekeeping styles with a uniform way of approaching household management, at least among the urban bourgeoisie.

Before the mid-nineteenth century, housekeeping was not seen as something to be formally learned in a course, but rather something handed down within families and neighborhoods from older to younger women (e.g., from Aunt Lina or Frau Dr. B.). Styles of housekeeping and cooking were intrinsically local and familial. Standards and judgments regarding women's housekeeping were set locally, varied regionally, and were evaluated within the context of particular households. In rural areas, for example, housework was only one part of a woman's broader job description, and she might be respected locally much more for the consistent quality of the butter she made and sold, than for the whiteness of her linens.

In the process of building the imagined community of *Hausfrauen*, authors and leaders of housewives' organizations were remaking and expanding that part of the older job description that had consisted of housework, even as the self-provisioning and agricultural work that many of their grandmothers had done now dropped out of the urban housewife's job description. At the same time, leaders of housewives' groups were trying to construct uniform standards and schedules that would apply across middle-strata households. They thus established a job description for the *Deutsche Hausfrau*: writers articulated standardized norms, for example, regarding how often curtains should

---

[35] Sperber, *Popular Catholicism*, 281–2.

be washed, and how many times they should be rinsed during washing (ten times, according to Mrs. Sidgwick).[36] The popularity of such publications reflected and furthered the growth of a group of self-identified *Hausfrauen*.

The creation of this imagined community was crucial to the creation and maintenance of bourgeois class identity and class boundaries. As in other Western cultures of this period, specific aspects of housekeeping became markers of class: floors and furniture that housewives (or their servants) frequently scrubbed and polished; clothes (particularly aprons) that were clean, starched and ironed; fixed mealtimes and schedules for family members (especially children); and household management that allowed a family to live within its means and put aside regular savings.[37] This style of housekeeping helped build the "moral community" of the bourgeoisie, bridging income differences within the bourgeoisie and enforcing class boundaries between the middle strata and the working poor. But the bourgeoisie also deployed these standards against working-class housewives. During the late nineteenth century, bourgeois social workers, home economists, and club women increasingly tried to intervene in working-class households and remake poorer housewives through inspection, domestic science training, and the granting or withholding of aid in accordance with these standards of household management.[38]

Thrift – regardless of the cost in labor – was one of the lynchpins of the ideal style of household management articulated in German advice literature and by housewives' organizations in both their missionary efforts vis-à-vis working-class housewives, and in publications directed toward women of their own class. Bourgeois female writers urged the

---

[36] For the attempt to establish uniform schedules, see Bärbel Kuhn, "Und herrschet weise im häuslichen Kreise."

[37] For the ways that bourgeois housekeeping functioned to define class in other nations, see the works cited in note 3. See also Rendall, *Women in an Industrializing Society*, 44ff; Susan Strasser, *Never Done. A History of American Housework* (New York: Patheon Books, 1982).

[38] For German bourgeois women's attempts to remake working-class housewives in their own image, see Reagin, *A German Women's Movement*, 43–98 and Ute Frevert, "Fürsorgliche Belagerung. Hygienebewegung und Arbeiterfrauen im 19. und frühen 20. Jahrhundert," *Geschichte und Gesellschaft* 11 (1985); see also Kathleen Canning, *Languages of Labor and Gender. Female Factory Work in Germany, 1850–1914* (Ithaca: Cornell University Press, 1996), 300–7.

Hausfrau to recycle or make things herself, even when she could purchase commercial substitutes at modest prices. When doing the wash, she should take the time to brew her own batch of starch out of potato peelings or stockpiled candle stubs every week. Even after ready-made tailored suits for men could be easily purchased, some women still sewed their husbands' suits themselves, and almost all bourgeois women produced their own and their children's daily wardrobes well past 1945, hiring a seamstress only occasionally to make the "best" outfits. Indeed, before she married, a bourgeois woman was expected to sew sufficient amounts of table and bed linens, and underclothes to last her entire married life. Long after canned produce was on store shelves, authors expected that housewives would spend weeks every summer and fall, putting up fruits and vegetables for the winter.[39] Germans saved scraps of leftover food to make slop for animals (as elsewhere), but German manuals on housekeeping went further, recommending that the first bucket of water used in washing dishes also be given afterward to animals (if the small-town housewife kept chickens or pets), as it might also contain small bits of food.[40]

In many families, necessity dictated thrift. Civil servants, in particular, earned very little and had to live within their means. At the same time, they had to keep house in a style that was "appropriate to one's station" (*standesgemäss*) and scrape together school fees for their sons and dowries for daughters; they often squeezed the surplus for this out of the food budget.[41] But thrift had long been perceived as a key "bourgeois virtue," also practiced by many of those who could afford to live more expansively. Historian Percy Ernst Schramm, who came from a prosperous Hamburg attorney's family (his father was later elected

[39] Produce preserved at home was also valued because it was seen as being more wholesome, but thrift was an important additional motive. See Kuhn, "Und herrschet weise," 257–60; Wiedemann, *Herrin im Hause*, 118–21; and Bluth, *Der Hausfrau gewidmet*, 78, who comments that "home and cooking advice books were, above everything else, books on how to save money."

[40] See Seminar der Koch- und Haushaltungsschule "Hedwig Heyl," *Lehrgang des Pestalozzi-Fröbel-Hauses II* (Berlin: Carl Habel Verlag, 1905), 89.

[41] Lower-level civil servants' families often lived in extremely straightened circumstances. Their wives might attempt to supplement the family's income by taking in boarders or doing sewing at home, but they risked official reprimands for their husbands if the wife's income-producing activities became too public. See Beuys, *Familienleben*, 446.

mayor during the 1920s) recalled in his memoirs his astonishment, as a child, upon accidentally discovering that his grandfather put butter on his *Zwiebäcke* at breakfast. "We had been told at home that whoever did this, would be put in prison. Indeed, Aunt Emmy went even one step further: she maintained that whoever put marmalade on top of butter was wasteful, and such behavior would lead inexorably to hell!"[42] Hans Fallada, born in 1893 to the family of a well-off higher civil servant (a *Reichsgerichtsrat*) wrote later that his Aunt Gustchen (admired in the family for her thrift) contrived to cook her breakfast egg in the water that was boiling for the morning tea.[43] Family entertainment among the bourgeoisie tended to consist of activities that cost little or nothing: a walk in the park after Sunday dinner; reading aloud to family members in the evening; and making music together on the piano or recorder (mothers who played could teach the children and thus save the cost of music teachers' fees). Visiting English or American authors sometimes commented that the German bourgeois families they observed lived more simply, and spent less on food and clothing, than their English-speaking counterparts.[44]

All expenditures were supposed to be meticulously recorded in housekeeping account books. This meant additional work, but also that husbands could inspect each woman's thrift (or lack of it). In working-class or lower-middle-class families, such economies were often necessary, but writers presented extreme thrift as a virtue for every German housewife, no matter how prosperous. The trade-off was clear: thrift almost always entailed additional labor on the part of women.[45] As one 1910 household advice manual urged, "never spend money on things which you can make or grow yourself. Only purchase what is absolutely necessary."[46] It is impossible to know exactly how many bourgeois women followed this advice, but it is indisputable that many women did, as historians who have done oral histories on the

---

[42] Quoted in ibid., 440–1. For the economic position of civil servants, by contrast, see ibid., 439 and Henning, *Das westdeutsche Bürgertum*, 487–90 and 274–5.

[43] Quoted in Wiedemann, *Herrin im Hause*, 132.

[44] See Brace, *Home Life in Germany* and also Ida A. R. Wylie, *The Germans*, (Indianapolis: Bobbs-Merrill, 1911), 269–78.

[45] See Kaplan, *Making of the Jewish Middle Class*, 29–30.

[46] Quoted in Wiedemann, *Herrin im Hause*, 118.

cohort of housewives born during the Wilhelmine period (and subsequent cohorts) have noted.[47]

Not merely the quest to save money, but also the high standards of cleanliness promoted by housewives' publications and organizations also resulted in labor-intensive housework. Late-nineteenth-century advice literature presented housewives with detailed schedules for cleaning, with days set aside each week and month for washing, ironing, and so forth. Manuals suggested washing floors daily and polishing the stove after every use. A housewife should empty out and clean all shelves and cabinets at least once every eight days. The procedure given by Davidis for the daily cleaning of the bedroom, far too lengthy to reprint here, required that the woman cleaning wear spotless white cotton gloves, an apron, and slippers (to keep from contaminating the room). If followed to the letter, this approach would have rendered the room almost sterile.[48]

She should also take down curtains and wash them every three months, put them through ten separate rinses, and starch and iron them before they were rehung, now "sparkling white" again, because extremely clean curtains were something that were seen and noticed by neighbors.[49] Descriptions of properly cleaned curtains in such literature, similar to other linens, always noted that they should be "snow white" or "sparkling white." Indeed, there are adjectives for white (e.g., *blühendweiss*) that are challenging to translate. German housewives seem to have had as many adjectives for *white* in regards to cleaning, as Eskimos are popularly (and erroneously) believed to have for snow.

The kitchen and the linen cabinet in particular were depicted as sites where a housewife's cleanliness, diligence, skills, and order were on display. The kitchen should be spotless and gleaming after every meal; if any chance visitors glanced into it, they should see a shining stove,

---

[47] See Hagemann, *Frauenalltag und Männerpolitik* and Kuhn, *Haus-Frauen-Arbeit*.

[48] The instructions are reprinted in Marenk and Framke, *Beruf der Jungfrau*, 77.

[49] Extremely high standards for cleanliness, along with a constant round of cleaning, are discussed in Kuhn, "Und herrschet weise," 244–52; Wiedemann, *Herrin im Hause*, 113–18; Bluth, *Der Hausfrau gewidmet*, 75–8. Interviews with housewives done by Kuhn in *Haus-Frauen-Arbeit*, 69, include the details of the elaborate cleaning procedures women followed for curtain cleaning.

floor, and pans. The linen cabinet containing the trousseau should be full of snow white linens: pressed and precisely stacked. Mrs. Sidgwick described the inside of the linen cabinet of a German acquaintance of hers, a professor's wife, whom Sidgwick depicted as typical in this regard:

[She] threw back both doors of an immense cupboard occupying the longest wall in the room. . . . [F]or their happiness they possessed all this linen: shelf upon shelf, pile upon pile of linen, exactly ordered, [and] tied with lemon coloured ribbons.[50]

The linen cabinet thus simultaneously demonstrated order and cleanliness, while reminding the viewer of the Wilhemine housewife's hard work and affluence, as measured by the amount of linens and by how white they were. Much of the work a housewife did, after all, was invisible to the community (e.g., meals and picking up, which had to be done again and again). But the laundry, which included the linens, and the whiteness of her wash was one area in which a woman could produce something that really could be shown off to visitors and neighbors. As one housewife commented, when a woman hung out laundry to dry, or set out bleached and ironed linens for guests to see, "one could really judge how hard-working a housewife was by looking at her linens." The weekly laundry, neatly mended, spotless, and hung out in well-organized rows (it was supposed to be sorted and hung by category and size) thus was seen as public proof of a housewife's diligence, thriftiness, sense of order, degree of domestic skill, and overall capability.[51]

Besides the daily round of sweeping, straightening, dusting, polishing, and cooking, at least once a week (often Fridays), women had a special cleaning day when floors were waxed and special chores done. Saturday mornings were also days when extra cleaning was done: "Saturday was usually cleaning day," one woman who grew up in Southern Germany before World War I later recalled, "a woman who

---

[50] Sidgwick, *Home Life in Germany*, 135–6. For an additional discussion of the symbolic importance of "snow white" linens, see Wiedemann, *Herrin im Hause*.

[51] Quote taken from the interviews done with early-twentieth-century housewives in Kuhn, *Haus-Frauen-Arbeit*, 31.

didn't have her house all sparkling and polished by early Saturday afternoon, was considered lazy and slow."[52]

On Saturday afternoons, housewives would prepare "better" weekend foods and often bake a cake for Sunday afternoon. The Sunday coffee and cake would be served later, after the main midday meal, which often featured the "Sunday roast" or other more expensive meat entree. The overall menu for the week was to be planned on the woman's *Küchenzettel* (a small list or chart that contained a week's meal plan), which could help her track the various ingredients she needed to purchase and stay within budget.[53]

Other models of housekeeping, which might have stressed fine cooking or offered a schedule that allocated a greater amount of time to be spent with children (or even more time for community involvement or hobbies), were thus eclipsed.[54] Historians of American domesticity point to a somewhat different distribution of the housewife's workload. Phyllis Palmer, for example, argues that by the mid-nineteenth century, American housewives no longer produced goods as much as they had in earlier generations. Instead, she concludes, much of the cleaning and cooking was left to servants, as the housewife was expected to spend much of her time overseeing the household's shopping and consumption, supervising her children's moral and intellectual development, assuring her husband's comfort, maintaining the family's network of social connections, and engaging in charitable and community welfare work. Some American advice books even recommended prioritizing romance and companionship within the marriage, even if it meant leaving the dinner dishes unwashed for the evening!

That is a substantially different model than the "job description" for German housewives contained in the advice literature examined. Even in families with relatively modest incomes among the middle strata, it was assumed that the *Hausfrau* would hire low-paid "help" to watch the children while she oversaw (and did much of) the cleaning

---

[52] Ibid., 66.

[53] The recipes in advice literature and ingredients lists in model *Küchenzettel* often listed prices for each ingredient, so the housewife could calculate the cost of each dish. See Wiedemann, *Herrin Im Hause*, 29.

[54] See Palmer, *Domesticity and Dirt*, 5–6 and 36–8.

and cooking.[55] The pressure to clean was undoubtedly linked to rising standards for personal and household cleanliness (e.g., how often bed sheets had to be changed). Overall, as homes became somewhat larger in some classes and filled with more objects, the amount of time required for cleaning also rose.[56]

The imperative to maintain a "spotless" table and household indeed sometimes trumped other considerations, such as practicality. Advice literature often denounced *Wachstücher* (waxed table coverings, forerunners to today's vinyl table cloths that could be easily wiped clean). Bourgeois housewives held them in low regard precisely because of their convenience. One 1900 housekeeping manual disparagingly remarked that "nothing leads so easily to uncleanliness and carelessness at mealtimes as these convenient waxed tablecloths, which can be simply wiped off." A "sparkling" white tablecloth, the author concluded, would train family members to be clean.[57] *Convenience* was thus literally a dirty word. Advice manual writers acknowledged, however, that the frequent bleaching and bluing required in order to maintain a "snow white" appearance was damaging to the fabric, shortening its life. The alternative – allowing linens to become slightly yellowed or dingy over time – simply did not enter the discussion.[58]

Various media of popular culture promoted the norms of snow white cleanliness, relentless thrift, and the maintenance of good household

---

[55] For an emphasis on extreme cleanliness as a marker of upward mobility (common in Western cultures in this period), see Kuhn, "Und herrschet weise"; and Robert Frost, "Machine Liberation: Inventing Housewives and Home Appliances in Interwar France," *French Historical Studies* 18 (1993): 115.

[56] The rise in standards for cleanliness and the increased amount of time spent cleaning during the nineteenth century have been noted by historians who have studied housewifery in a number of Western nations. For this development in Ireland, see Joanna Bourke, *Husbandry to Housewifery. Women, Economic Change, and Housework in Ireland 1890–1914* (Oxford: Clarendon Press, 1993), 206–35; for the United States, see Boydston, *Home and Work* and Strasser, *Never Done*; for Britain, see Caroline Davidson, *A Woman's Work is Never Done. A History of Housework in the British Isles, 1650–1950* (London: Chatto and Windus, 1982) and Jane Rendall, *Women in an Industrializing Society*, 89; for France, see Smith, *Ladies of the Leisure Classes*.

[57] Wiedemann, *Herrin im Hause*, 77.

[58] Ibid., 117. During World War II, when soap, bleach, etc. were in short supply (as was new fabric), officials in the housekeeping division of the National Socialist *Deutsches Frauenwerk* debated whether to urge housewives to omit bleaching in order to spare the fabric. They concluded, however, that housewives would never accept such advice and that dingy linens would lead to bad morale.

order. Sometimes writers presented these characteristics as specifically
"German" domestic virtues. Excerpts from treatises by eighteenth-
century authors such as Schiller, Goethe, and Campe (which had been
originally written for a narrower eighteenth-century audience of "the
educated") urging that young women be trained to order, cleanliness,
and thrift, were now widely reprinted in household advice manuals
and cookbooks.[59] Late-nineteenth-century housewives' magazines and
books also frequently quoted and excerpted the section of Schiller's
1800 poem, "The Song of the Bell" (enormously popular among the
bourgeoisie, and reprinted in numerous school textbooks and antholo-
gies during the nineteenth century) that listed the duties of the housewife. Schiller urged the housewife

> to rule wisely, in the domestic circle, and teach the daughters, and guard the
> sons, and employ without ceasing, your industrious hands, to increase the
> [family's] prosperity, with a sense for order.... And collect in a clean polished
> cabinet, the gleaming wools, the snow white linens.... [60]

Women also embroidered couplets from Schiller's poem, along with
other sayings promoting these "domestic virtues," on framed wall-
hangings and *Überhandtücher* (literally: "towels that hang on top").
These last were pressed, decorative linens with embroidered sayings,

---

[59] For eighteen examples of treatises on sex roles (*Geschlechtscharakter*) that stress
the domestic "bourgeois" virtues that later characterized housewives' advice literature, see Paul Münch, *Ordnung, Fleiss, und Sparsamkeit. Texte und Dokumente zur
Entstehung der "bürgerlichen Tugenden"* (Munich: DTV, 1984), 210–16, 260–71,
and 341–3. Münch argues that "order, industry, and thrift, which are closely linked
to the ideals of cleanliness and purity, form the center of the ... 'bourgeois' book of
virtues. They have also long determined the self-image of Germans, and their stereotypes of foreigners in a peculiar fashion." For the development of gender roles and sexual stereotypes during the Enlightenment more generally, see Karin Hausen, "Family
and Role Division: The Polarization of Sexual Stereotypes in the Nineteenth Century
– An Aspect of the Disassociation of Work and Family Life," in Richard Evans and W.
R. Lee, eds., *The German Family* (London: Croom Helm, 1981), 51–83. For the popularization of these Enlightenment authors in nineteenth-century household advice
manuals, see Weismann, *Froh erfülle deine Pflicht*, 215–17. For the increasing emphasis on bodily cleanliness among the German bourgeoisie during the late eighteenth and
early nineteenth century, see Manuel Frey, *Der reinliche Bürger. Entstehung und Verbreitung bürgerlicher Tugenden in Deutschland, 1760–1860* (Göttingen: Vandenhoek
and Ruprecht, 1997).

[60] "The Song of the Bell" (*das Lied der Glocke*) is reprinted in Friedrich Schiller,
Gedichte/ Schiller (Berlin: Aufbau Verlag, 1980), 244. This translation and all others
in this book, unless otherwise noted, are my own.

which covered and concealed slightly rumpled dishtowels – not even
a dishtowel could be seen in a wrinkled condition – or were used to
conceal corners containing brooms and mops, sewing machines, bread
baskets, ironing boards, laundry baskets, table tops, and even water
facets. These textiles gained popularity after 1870, first among the
upper-middle-class and then spreading downward. They were common
in working-class homes by 1914 and had indeed become a marker of the
lower-middle and working class by the 1920s (as they fell out of fashion
among wealthier families). Many of these linens bore the same cliché of
"home, sweet home" found in the English-speaking world (e.g., *Eigner
Herd ist Goldes wert* and *Trautes Heim, Glück allein*), while others celebrated the "domestic virtues" of order, thrift, and cleanliness. Popular
examples included *Halte Ordnung, liebe sie. Ordnung spart dir Zeit
und Müh'; Reinlichkeit der Küche Zierde*; and *Sauberkeit ziert.*[61] By
the Wilhemine period, some of these embroidered decorations explicitly claimed these domestic virtues as the particular provenance of the
German *Hausfrau*. A typical example was an embroidery pattern for
a linen cabinet decoration from 1913 that proclaimed:

[S]weet smelling, soft, and snow white, protected lies herein, the most beautiful
linens, rewarding the industry of the faithful hands of the German housewife –
her ornament and glory![62]

The typical bourgeois home was thus filled by the late nineteenth century with objects preaching cleanliness, order, and thrift, sometimes
claiming these virtues for German women especially. The linen cabinet in particular seems to have become a national domestic symbol in
trivial forms of popular culture.

Holidays were also an important part of domesticity. Christmas –
celebrated with a variety of rituals, practices, and symbols – became
a crucial part of domestic life (as opposed to being primarily a religious holiday) among the German bourgeoisie during the nineteenth

---

[61] These sayings, translated in order, are: "One's own hearth is worth gold," "Dear
home, source of all happiness," "Keep order, love it. Order saves you time and effort,"
"Purity is the kitchen's decoration," and "Cleanliness is an ornament."

[62] Quoted in Weismann, *Froh erfülle deine Pflicht*, 220. Weismann's collection of sayings
embroidered on textiles includes a number of other references praising the "German
housewife." Some editions of Davidis offered similar embroidery patterns.

century.[63] Christmas trees began to appear in well-off urban homes in the late eighteenth century, and had become common in bourgeois homes across Germany a century later. Poorer and rural Germans did not adopt these practices until the twentieth century. By the mid-nineteenth century, the tree was laden with wax candles, gilded nuts, glass balls, flowers and ribbons, and marzipan and chocolates, while the parlor and other "public" rooms were decorated with a growing variety of holiday objects. On Christmas Eve, the tree's candles were lit; the household's children were allowed to enter the room where the tree stood; and the family exchanged gifts, sang songs, or listened to the children recite poems. Elaborate meals with special holiday dishes also accompanied the holiday.

These new Christmas practices were supported and spread by the same structural shifts that had made possible the broader culture of bourgeois domesticity of which Christmas was such an important part: the rise of print culture, which made possible elaborate popular "Christmas books" with their songs, poems, and stories; the growth of consumer culture, which fostered the many products associated with the holiday; the expansion of the bourgeoisie; and the sentimental, even sacralized notions of the home and family life that Christmas reinforced.[64] This version of Christmas was one of the most successful "invented traditions" of the century. Ultimately, the tree and many of the associated practices spread from Germany throughout the English-speaking world.

Christmas was also successful as a German national holiday. By 1900, contemporaries spoke of a "German Christmas," and widely shared the belief that Christmas was better celebrated in Germany than anywhere else, as its values were particularly consonant with German national character. Visiting English and American authors were often persuaded to share this view, even as they publicized and

---

[63] I am indebted here to the analysis of how Christmas observance became interwoven with German national identity offered in Joseph Perry, "The Private Life of the Nation: Christmas and the Invention of Modern Germany" (Ph.D. diss., University of Illinois at Urbana-Champaign, 2001). See also Ingeborg Weber-Kellermann, *Das Weihnachtsfest: Eine Kultur- und Sozialgeschichte der Weihnachtszeit* (Munich: C. J. Buchner, 1987); and Klaus-Dieter Dobat, "O Tannenbaum, O Tannenbaum...." "Wie der Siegeszug eines deutschen Weihnachtssymbols begann," *Damals* 21 (1989): 1093–101.

[64] See Perry, "Private Life of the Nation," 29–41.

promoted this version of the Christmas celebration in their own countries. Ida Wylie, an Englishwoman who lived in Karlsruhe for six years, later wrote that "Germany without Christmas – or better – Christmas without Germany! For me the one state is as unthinkable as the other...there is no country in the world...where Christmas is so intensely 'Christmasy,' as in the Fatherland."[65] Indeed, Christmas was able to become *the* national holiday, because it was far more attractive and inclusive than Sedan Day (which was observed primarily among the Protestant bourgeoisie), or other holidays that tried and failed to cement a national community. Even German Jews found the tree and its associated practices hard to resist: more secularized Jewish families might exchange Hanukkah presents under the tree. German Christmas indeed became a holiday in which sentimental domestic customs helped to create a shared feeling of national identity.[66] Scholarly and popular publications spread the (false) belief that German Christmas – particularly the tree and lights – were rooted in pre-Christian "Germanic" tribal customs. In many families, Christmas trees were decorated with small national flags or hung with glass ornaments in the shape of Bismarck's head.[67] Christmas thus succeeded as a national holiday in part because its domestic nature made it an attractive forum for the articulation of national identity.

The bourgeois model of domesticity – how to clean, cook, and celebrate holidays – were acquired not only through advice literature and training in the home and neighborhood, but increasingly in formal domestic science education, starting in the late nineteenth century. Before 1933, educational policy on domestic science varied between different regions, but the national trend toward introducing home economics instruction (both in popular private courses and as a mandatory part of the public school curriculum) was unmistakable. In the decades before World War I, young women from better-off families were often sent to the household of a relative or friend for domestic training, or

---

[65] Wylie, *The Germans*, 85; Maggie Browne, *Chats About Germany* (London: Cassel and Co., 1884), 18; see the promotion of "German Christmas" by an American author in Brace, *Home Life in Germany*, 221–2; for the popularization of "German Christmas" throughout the English-speaking world in the late nineteenth century, see Perry, "Private Life of the Nation," 30.

[66] Ibid., 22.

[67] Ibid., 82–9; see also Dobat, "O Tannenbaum," 1094–6.

even spent a year at special boarding schools that specialized in home economics for bourgeois girls. Bourgeois women's organizations and employers offered evening courses in the domestic arts, which were often oversubscribed, for working-class women.[68]

After 1900, many provinces and cities began to introduce mandatory courses in cooking, cleaning, infant care, general household management, knitting, and various sorts of sewing. In Munich, for example, an eighth grade was added to girls' schools (the *Volksschule*, which working-class children attended) in 1896, and the additional grade was made mandatory in 1913; much of the curriculum for this year was devoted to various aspects of domestic science. One Bavarian school inspector justified the extra needlework instruction by arguing that "A woman who can mend her clothing, who can keep in use for years every scrap of lining material and every button, is a pearl for the house." Another inspector claimed that the new domestic science courses taught "those virtues that should adorn every housewife: cleanliness and orderliness, thriftiness and industriousness, simplicity and good taste."[69]

Conclusion

By the beginning of the twentieth century, a particular approach to household management and domesticity had reached full flower among the German bourgeoisie. It was primarily urban in its origins and assumptions, but was generally accessible to Jewish, Catholic, and Protestant bourgeois women alike. After 1890, housewives' organizations, public schools, and employers began to promote a simplified version of this model of domesticity among young working-class women. Domestic science education for the lower classes recognized

---

[68] For the spread of home economics instruction, see Reagin, *A German Women's Movement*, 74–80 and 232–3; see also Schlegel-Matthies, *Im Haus und am Herd*, 222; Katherine D. Kennedy, "Lessons and Learners: Elementary Education in Southern Germany, 1871–1914" (Ph.D. diss., Stanford University, 1981), 333–45 and "Domesticity (Hauswirtschaft) in the *Volksschule*: Textbooks and Lessons for Girls, 1890–1914," *Internationale Schulbuchforschung* 13 (1991): 5–21; Kerchner, *Beruf und Geschlecht*, 212 ff. Formal instruction in domestic science became increasingly popular in many Western nations after the turn of the century.

[69] The first quote is taken from Kennedy, "Domesticity in the *Volksschule*," 12; the second quote comes from Kennedy, "Lessons and Learners," 345.

that working-class housewives couldn't afford all the accoutrements of a bourgeois household, certainly, but still attempted to instill the norms of domestic cleanliness, order, and thrift across class lines using courses, advice literature, the work of housewives' organizations, and the more informal mechanisms of peer pressure and social control.

Certain idealized practices, symbols, and objects had come to represent this vision of bourgeois domesticity. Among them were the celebration of "German Christmas"; "snow white" linens and curtains; the Sunday cake and roast; and orderly household accounts and the *Küchenzettel*, which documented household thrift. All these symbols were outgrowths of the practices dominant among the Wilhelmine bourgeoisie. But what was merely bourgeois at home became German abroad, when such practices were placed into a comparative context. And such everyday objects and approaches to household management would become key symbols in discussions of German national character. In the discourse on national character, the ways in which German national identity was rooted in the household management strategies of the bourgeois private sphere would become clear: cleanliness was next to Germanness.

2

Domesticity and German National Character

Polish management.
It looks like the Hottentots live here.
> *Popular sayings, used to describe sloppiness or chaos, as in household management*

The preservation of Germanness demands a clean home. The drive to scrub, innate in our *Volk*, has a moral and national value."
> *Käthe Schirmacher, a leading conservative German feminist, 1917*

Clara Brockmann, a journalist and lecturer, went to German Southwest Africa for a lengthy visit during 1907–9, to study the lives of German women in the colony. After returning to Germany, Brockmann wrote and lectured widely about the need for more German women in German Southwest Africa. More women were needed in German colonies, she argued in a 1910 publication, because without their home-making skills, newly settled farms would not become true German homes:

[W]ithout the presence of a *Hausfrau*...a [colonial] farm cannot become *heimisch*, because only [her presence] secures German ways and customs, and a German family life.... [I knew a bachelor farmer in Southwest Africa] whose animals throve but whose house and rooms were in terribly neglected condition.... [T]he farmer's study presented a picture of impressive disorder.... [T]he desk had not been dusted for six months.... [After his bride arrived from Germany] the unkempt dwelling was transformed into an inviting rural home. In the kitchen and courtyard everything was well-organized . . . the rooms now resembled the comfortable abodes of the homeland.[1]

Brockmann was drawing upon an understanding of what "German" ways and life-styles included, which was widely shared by her bourgeois contemporaries by the turn of the century. It was an understanding of Germanness that had developed alongside the model of domesticity that it incorporated, a set of assumptions about what it meant to be German that gradually spread among the urban bourgeoisie in the decades after German unification.

Like Italians after their nation's unification, Germans had to be "invented." Legal, national, and cultural definitions of what it meant to be German – which were revisions of earlier notions of Germanness, but now linked to the particular state and boundaries established in 1871 – developed gradually during the decades before World War I. The new nation had to create laws that established criteria for citizenship, decide whether or how to organize national institutions (e.g., a centralized railroad or postal system), and struggle to establish symbols for the German nation (e.g., a flag, national anthem, or national holiday). As we have seen, Imperial Germany never did designate an official national holiday or anthem, and only adopted a national flag in 1892. Even the postal and diplomatic systems were not merged before 1918; only in Weimar Germany were "German" (instead of Prussian or Saxon) stamps introduced.[2]

Although the unification of national institutions and establishment of national symbols was halting and incomplete, preexisting regional loyalties were gradually complemented by or even overshadowed (in most areas of Germany) by a growing allegiance to Germany as a whole, as a shared German national identity was consolidated before 1914. German national identity drew heavily upon preexisting regional and confessional identities, and was anchored in the long-shared

---

[1] Clara Brockmann, *Die deutsche Frau in Südwestafrika. Ein Beitrag zur Frauenfrage in unseren Kolonien* (Berlin, 1910), 3–6.

[2] For the difficulties and delays in establishing a national holiday and unified postal, railroad, diplomatic systems, etc. see Confino, *The Nation as Local Metaphor* and Green, *Fatherlands*; for the debates over establishing criteria for German citizenship in the new nation, see Howard Sargent, "Diasporic Citizens: The Persistent Problem of Germans Abroad in German Citizenship Law, 1815–2000," in O'Donnell, *The Heimat Abroad.*

sense – which went back at least to the eighteenth century – that the inhabitants of all the German states shared an overarching culture. At the same time, the coalescing sense of Imperial German national identity was implicitly challenged by competing or contradictory visions of what it meant to be German. German national identity was still a work in progress during the Imperial period (and beyond), as the Protestant bourgeoisie struggled to assert its vision of Germanness in opposition to competing understandings, which arose across the divides of class, religion, and region.[3]

Millions of ethnic Germans, for example, still lived throughout Central and Eastern Europe, usually in states where they felt perfectly "at home" (and thus did not necessarily look toward Imperial Germany as their "natural" allegiance).[4] Within Germany, conservative nationalists and anti-Semites increasingly argued that the only "real" Germans were those who shared ethnic German ancestry. Simultaneously, members of some religious minority groups (e.g., German Jews or German Catholics) certainly considered themselves to be "good Germans," but also developed their own diverse understandings of the national community. After 1890, settlers who immigrated to Germany's new colonies also asserted their place within an expanded, imperial nation.[5] Conflicting and competing visions or definitions of the German national community were possible because – like all nations – it was a community that was at least partly imagined. Because this national bonding was generated through the imagination, conflicting or minority interpretations of what it meant to be German were certainly possible.

[3] For a discussion of recent work on the development of German national identity during the nineteenth century, including competing understandings of Germanness, see my review essay, "Recent Work on German National Identity," 245–71.

[4] For the identities and allegiances of ethnic Germans in the Hapsburg Empire, see Pieter Judson, "Inventing Germans: Class, Nationality and Colonial Fantasy at the Margins of the Hapsburg Monarch," *Social Analysis* 33 (1993): 47–67; and "Frontiers, Islands, Forests, Stones: Mapping the Geography of a German Identity in the Habsburg Monarchy, 1848–1900," in Patricia Yaeger, ed., *The Geography of Identity* (Ann Arbor: University of Michigan Press, 1996), 382–406.

[5] For a discussion of the place of German colonists in the national community, see Krista O'Donnell, "Home, Nation, Empire: Domestic Germanness and Colonial Citizenship" in O'Donnell, *The Heimat Abroad*. For the variations of German identity developed by members of different religious confessions, see Helmut Walser Smith, ed., *Protestants, Catholics and Jews in Germany, 1880–1914*.

The evolution of the imagined German national community was dependent on communication using print media, especially (although not exclusively) as shared among the German bourgeoisie. Journals, newspapers, magazines, and books (which were written in High German and assumed that their readers shared a common national identity) were read by increasing numbers of educated Germans across the nation (and in the colonies). This shared discourse helped to consolidate the imagined national community and to articulate a common identity. Bourgeois Germans debated and wrote a great deal about Germanness during the late nineteenth century: what it meant to be German; who was included in the community; and what were the core behaviors, values, and symbols that defined being a German. Although the understandings of Germanness proposed in these discussions were usually implicitly bourgeois, there were regional and confessional variations, as Protestant and Catholic German writers debated which literary works, for example, ought to be included in a national canon of German literature.[6]

Germans also wrote about other cultures, defining their own community and values through comparison and contrast with others. Although almost all Europeans who wrote on national character during the nineteenth century tended to define their own communities through contrast with other nations, German scholars and authors were, perhaps, particularly prone to self-definition opposition to or comparison with other cultures.[7] But their preoccupation with the "innate" character of people from other cultures was not unique. The discussion of national character was a flourishing genre throughout the West in the nineteenth century, both in scholarly publications and in the popular press. Academics and popular writers produced a steady stream

---

[6] For debates between Catholic and Protestant writers – almost all of them bourgeois – over what the German literary canon should include, or over what modern historians would call the "master narratives" of German historiography, see Smith, *German Nationalism and Religious Conflict*, 22–34.

[7] See James, *A German Identity*, 15, who writes that particularly in Germany, "an extreme willingness to make comparisons went hand in hand with ever more aggressive German nationalism." For a discussion of how travel literature shows a pan-European tendency to define one's own nationality through contrast, see Marjorie Morgan, *National Identities and Travel in Victorian Britain* (Palgrave: New York, 2001).

of cultural or "moral" histories of other cultures (both ancient and contemporary), travel literature, and entertainment pieces for popular magazines, which drew upon, expanded, and elaborated on earlier national stereotypes about the customs and "typical" personality traits of Germans and other Europeans. More adventurous authors traveled outside of Europe, and published books describing American life and the life-styles and mentality of "backward" peoples in the non-Western world (generally colonial subjects).[8]

Like their counterparts in other Western nations, German geographers, historians, literary critics, and other academics produced a voluminous literature that compared the "innate" virtues and traits of Germans with those of other nationals.[9] Even in the eighteenth century, German writers such as Campe argued that order and cleanliness were particular German virtues. Nineteenth-century authors on national character before 1870 often argued in general terms that German housewives kept cleaner houses. A typical example was the well-known geographer Hermann Daniel, who noted in passing in 1865 that "it can hardly be calculated how long the cleaning festival that a German

---

[8] Many modern historians have examined the genre of national character discussed here. For an introduction to this literature in Germany, see Jürgen Link and Wulf Wülfing, eds., *Nationale Mythen und Symbole in der zweiten Hälfte des 19. Jahrhunderts. Strukturen und Funktionen von Konzepten nationaler Identität* (Stuttgart: Klett-Cotta Verlag, 1991). See also Charlotte Tacke, *Denkmal im sozialen Raum*, 44–51 and "Nation und Geschlechtscharaktere" in Frauen and Geschichte Baden-Württemberg, eds., *Frauen und Nation* (Tübingen: Silberberg, 1996), 35–48; Alexander Schmidt, *Reisen in die Moderne. Der Amerika-Diskurs des deutschen Bürgertums vor dem Ersten Weltkrieg im europäischen Vergleich* (Berlin: Akademie Verlag, 1997); Ulle Siebert, "Reise. Nation. Text. Repräsentationen von 'Nationalität' in Reisetexten deutscher Frauen, 1871–1914" in *Frauen und Nation*, 49–65.

[9] See James, *A German Identity*, and the numerous articles on "national character" in Link and Wülfing, *Nationaler Mythen und Symbole*. See also Kirsten Belgum, "A Nation for the Masses: Production of the German Identity in the Late-Nineteenth-Century Popular Press" in Scott Denham, Irene Kacandes, and Jonathan Petropoulos, eds., *A User's Guide to German Cultural Studies* (Ann Arbor: University of Michigan Press, 1997), 163–80 and *Popularizing the Nation. Audience, Representation, and the Production of Identity in* Die Gartenlaube, *1853–1900* (Lincoln: University of Nebraska, 1998). For a description of a 1850s museum exhibition on German national character in daily life, which included a "Frauenhalle" on domestic objects, see Annelore Rieke-Müller and Siegfried Müller, "Konzeptionen der Kulturgeschichte um die Mitte des 19. Jahrhunderts: Das Germanische Nationalmuseum in Nürnberg und die Zeitschrift für Deutsche Kulturgeschichte," *Archiv für Kulturgeschichte* 82(2) (2000): 345–75.

housewife would immediately begin, would last, if she entered an Italian home."[10]

Women's roles and status, along with life-style and family life, were often discussed in comparative European works on national character. Some writers indeed claimed that women's position was a sort of yardstick for the overall "progress" of the culture as a whole, and pointed to such practices as concubinage, polygamy, child marriage, suttee, and foot binding as proof that non-Western cultures were barbaric and degraded.[11] German authors also discussed gender roles and private life in their surveys of national character, although they seemed to be less interested in the sexual enslavement of non-Western women, compared to their British and American counterparts.[12] Instead, domesticity assumed a prominent role in many German works on national character, particularly those written by bourgeois women.

During the nineteenth century the model of domesticity that developed among the German bourgeoisie along with its attendant symbols and practices – sparkling white, pressed linens; immaculate rooms; the Sunday roast and cake; a carefully kept household account book; a generally labor-intensive style of housekeeping; and the German Christmas tree – became a yardstick for measuring other nations' households and for defining German identity through domestic contrasts. A particular approach to domesticity, which had begun as a project of class formation, now became a commonplace vehicle for the articulation of national identity. Similar to other debates over German identity, such as those about the national literary canon or "master themes" of German historiography, the discourse on household management and Germanness was implicitly bourgeois. But within the bourgeoisie, this understanding of Germanness had considerable success and ultimately attracted support across religious and regional boundaries.

---

[10] In his *Handbuch der Geographie* 4 vols., 2nd ed. (Leipzig: O. R. Reisland, 1865–8), quoted in Link, *Nationaler Mythen*, 50.

[11] For a discussion of how non-Western women were usually depicted as being degraded and sexually enslaved by Western authors during this period, see Nancy Cott, *Public Vows: A History of Marriage and the Nation* (Cambridge, MA: Harvard University Press, 2000) 116–18.

[12] For the comparatively lesser importance of sexuality in establishing Western superiority in German colonial texts, see Krista O'Donnell, "The Colonial Woman Question: Gender, National Identity, and Empire in the German Colonial Society Female Emigration Program, 1896–1914," (Ph.D. Diss., SUNY Binghamton, 1996).

Domestic Practices in Other Cultures: National Stereotypes and German Identity

After 1870, national identity became increasingly prominent in discussions of German domesticity and advice literature for housewives. This "nationalized" domesticity was only one of the many projects of nation building promoted by the German bourgeoisie during this period.[13] In German discussions of domesticity, as in other aspects of nation building, identity was articulated through opposition with imagined others. In the same texts where writers of advice literature articulated their ideal of housewifery and the *Hausfrau*, they also asserted that German women kept house in a fashion that was different from and superior to the housekeeping of women from other cultures. Articles and stories about women from around the world were staples in nineteenth-century German women's magazines, interspersed with sewing patterns and child-rearing tips. An examination of stereotypes about what kind of housekeepers *other* women were (e.g., the recurring cliché that English women left all their work to servants, or that French women were disproportionately interested in fashion and socializing) reveals how the self-understanding of bourgeois German housewives was constructed in opposition to imagined foreign housekeeping. Bourgeois discussions of housekeeping are an example of the conflation of national and class identity and symbols that was so common among the European bourgeoisie of this period. They are also examples of a popular variant of the widespread discussion of national character.

Women's magazines frequently ran articles on women and the family in foreign cultures. Some focused on the lives of women in other Western nations (especially Britain, France, and the United States), while others examined women in more "exotic" cultures (e.g., Mongol, "Gypsy," Arab, Chinese, Ceylonese, Mexican, Egyptian, Burmese, Turkish, Indian, West African, and Eskimo women). Authors described the wedding customs of foreign women and their approaches to housekeeping, sickbed nursing, child rearing, cooking, and clothing

---

[13] For discussions of nation building among the German bourgeoisie as a whole, see George Mosse, *Nationalization of the Masses: Political Symbolism and Mass Movements in Germany from the Napoleonic Wars through the Third Reich* (Ithaca: Cornell University Press, 1991) and Confino, *The Nation as Local Metaphor.*

production.[14] Some pieces were written by German women who had lived with their families in these societies; others were allegedly written by German women who had worked as governesses abroad, which purported to show the workings of foreign households from an insider's standpoint. Collectively, these pieces constituted a genre, a kind of travel literature for housewives.

In discussing the shortcomings of foreign housekeepers, writers defined, by implication or explicit contrast, the alleged virtues of German housekeeping in much more concrete terms than had the male academics who wrote on national character during the same period. In the process of doing so, these authors linked German national character to the specific practices of bourgeois housekeeping discussed in Chapter 1, creating a pan-German vision of domesticity that was relentlessly bourgeois, represented by particular domestic symbols such as the linen cabinet and the scrubbed kitchen floor.

These articles were not all negative in tone; however, they often treated their subjects as interesting or exotic. Authors found much to admire in foreign housewives. They praised the precision with which Dutch housewives organized their households, the lovely jewelry worn by Arab women, and the beautifully embroidered curtains made by Swedish housewives. But authors almost invariably found foreign households lacking in comparison with an idealized "German" household. Most shortcomings were derived from the fact that foreign housekeeping (as depicted) was less labor intensive.

It was a truism in German women's publications, for example, that English bourgeois women left all their work to servants, rarely setting

---

[14] The articles discussed in this paper were taken from a survey of the following periodicals: *Die Deutsche Hausfrauen-Zeitung, Die Frau im Osten* (which addressed women in the eastern provinces of the Empire), *Fürs Haus. Praktisches Wochenblatt für alle Hausfrauen,* and *Die Welt der Frau,* the women's supplement to the enormously popular illustrated family magazine *Gartenlaube.* The first two magazines show the overlap between housewives' organizations and their advice literature because both were published by leaders of bourgeois women's associations. These two periodicals were edited by women, and almost all of their contributions came from women. The latter two publications were edited by men, although many of the pieces I cite from those publications were written by women. For each periodical, I selected at least five years from the period between 1885 and 1914 (depending upon availability of sources) and read through all issues from the chosen volumes.

foot inside a kitchen (where – lacking the oversight of a mistress – enormous wastage of food and hence money allegedly occurred).[15] French women, on the other hand, spent more time in the kitchen, but were sometimes depicted as being overly concerned with fine food and fashion at the expense of other household concerns.[16] They were elegant and chic, but also often coldhearted and less concerned about their families (i.e., less hard working) than their German counterparts. This recurring stereotype of Frenchwomen surfaces, for example, in a 1905 poem published in the *Praktische Berlinerin* (a magazine for middle-strata Berlin housewives), which contrasted Parisian women with Berlin women. The Parisian was castigated as a "fashion queen"; the Berlin *Hausfrau*, by contrast, was "a woman for real life [*die Frau fürs Leben* or a woman to go through life with]." The poem concluded with a promise that the magazine would instruct "all who want to make a home and hearth according to German custom and nature."[17]

The strengths associated with French women (cooking and fashion) are linked to sociability and public display, precisely those characteristics associated with the French in German academic and popular literature on national character. The French were often depicted by nineteenth-century German writers as frivolous, sociable, quick in action and thought, and "light" (in a moral sense). One widely published German pedagogue reflected this common stereotype when he observed that although French women were graceful, charming, and fashionable, "the duties observed daily by a [German] mother and spouse, the sacrifices that she gladly and willingly undertakes...these are all unknown to most French women...the restrictions [i.e., thrift and hard work] observed in a German household are unknown to French housewives and would be absolutely rejected by them." Many

---

[15] See "Das Dienstbotenproblem in England," *Die Welt der Frau* 39 (1909), where the assertion about leaving all the work to servants is simply presented as an established fact. See also "Kinderleben in England," *Die Deutsche Hausfrauen-Zeitung* 15 (1888) Nr. 1; see the same assertions that British housewives lacked frugality, and left all their housework to their servants in Sidgwick, *Home Life in Germany*.

[16] See, e.g., "Erlebnisse einer deutschen Erzieherin in Frankreich, 1870–1871," in *Die Deutsche Hausfrauen-Zeitung* 13 (1886) Nr. 26.

[17] Quoted in Wiesmann, *Froh erfülle deine Pflicht*, 229.

French marriages were marriages of convenience, he concluded, where both spouses tolerated adultery.[18]

France was often coded as feminine and as morally suspect, while German authors on national character depicted Germany and England as masculine. In this literature, academics contrasted French frivolity and public sociability with Germans' supposed patience and preference for traditional values; Germans were also alleged to prefer their own homes.[19] The poem in the *Praktische Berlinerin* faithfully mirrored these stereotypes, firmly linking the German housewife to home and hearth.

A series of articles in *Die Deutsche Hausfrauen-Zeitung* depicted Dutch housewives as being equal to German women in terms of cleanliness and organization (they even had proper linen cabinets), but they were insufficiently thrifty and hard working: Dutch women supposedly reached these standards only by contracting out much of their work.[20] In another magazine article, which was otherwise largely positive, one author nevertheless concluded that an Italian woman

puts little value on scouring her cooking pots, and keeping them gleaming, but does like to keep her own person [body] clean ... "working from dawn 'til dusk" is not to her taste. She would never agree to get down on her knees, in order to properly wash the floor.[21]

No one, it seemed, worked as hard as German housewives. When describing foreign women who were attractive in some respects, but less industrious than Germans, writers sometimes compared their subjects to the lilies described in the New Testament: "they labor not, nor do they spin."[22] Writers invariably employed only the better known,

---

[18] Gotthold Kreyenberg, *Mädchenerziehung und Frauenleben im Aus- und Inlande. Neudruck der Ausgabe Berlin 1872 mit Einleitung von Ruth Bleckwann* (Paderborn: Hüttemann Verlag, 1990), 230.

[19] See Ute Gerhard and Jürgen Link, "Zum Anteil der Kollektivsymbolik an den Nationalstereotypen" in Link and Wülfing, *Nationale Mythen und Symbole*, 22–30.

[20] See the multipart series on Dutch housewives that began in *Die Deutsche Hausfrauen-Zeitung* 14 (1887) Nr. 30.

[21] From "Italienische Dienstboten" in *Die Welt der Frau* (1909) Nr. 16.

[22] For the biblical passage, from Luke 12: 27–28, on the lilies of the field, which was used to describe women as diverse as New York housewives and East African women, see "Unsere Schwestern in Deutsch-Ostafrika," in *Die Welt der Frau* (1908) Nr. 39., and "Daisys Budget," in *Die Deutsche Hausfrauen-Zeitung* 22 (1895) Nr. 36. This metaphor was also invoked when discussing women who lived in harems.

short version of this passage (Luke 12:27–28), to evoke the concept of a beauty that is linked to leisure. The ideal "German" housewife, defined in contrast to the idle lilies, resembled the virtuous wife of Proverbs 31:15–27, whose price is "far above rubies.... She rises while it is yet night and provides food for her household and tasks for her maiden.... She puts her hands to the distaff, and her hands hold the spindle.... She looks well to the ways of her household and does not eat the bread of idleness."

Most non-Western women were depicted as inferior housekeepers almost by definition. Many, such as "Gypsies" and African women, did not have homes in European-style buildings at all, and thus supposedly could not keep them clean to begin with. Others, such as Slavic women or Mexican housewives lived in buildings that they did not keep as clean as Germans, although the authors praised these women's cooking, embroidery, and sewing.[23] In these articles, housekeeping thus served to draw racial and national boundaries. African women in particular did not keep house or cook in any meaningful sense of the word, according to one article in *Die Welt der Frau*, but rather lived as innocents in the Garden of Eden:

Nature freely (that is, without much work on part of these people) offers an excessive array of foods.... Thus one can hardly blame the native population, which has such simple needs and tastes, for never having really learned the meaning of work.... [T]he making of meals is a downright primitive affair. The men sit crouched around a small fire..., a large basket of fruit is picked off of the nearest banana tree, and each person simply roasts his fruit himself over the open fire. The black housewife can thus take care of dinner by simply obeying the command of her lord and master when he tells her: "light the fire!"[24]

African women would only learn to do "real" housework when they were compelled to work as servants in Europeans' homes.[25]

---

[23] See "Die Frau im Norden und die im Süden der neuen Welt," in *Die Deutsche Hausfrauen-Zeitung*, 23 (1896) Nr. 27; "Unsere Schwestern in Deutsch-Ostafrika," in *Die Welt der Frau* (1908) Nr. 39; "Die Wanderzigeuner Siebenbürgens," in *Die Welt der Frau* (1909) Nr. 15; "Von den Frauen des Ostens," *Die Welt der Frau* (1913) Nr. 17.

[24] See "Unsere Schwestern in Deutsch-Ostafrika," in *Die Welt der Frau* (1908) Nr. 39.

[25] For Africans as servants, see the discussion of German colonial homes on pages 63–5 of this chapter.

Articles on women in the United States appeared regularly in women's publications, both during the Imperial period and later.[26] The descriptions of American housewives were uneasy and ambivalent at best, although they often commented admiringly on some aspects of American women's lives. American women were seen as practical, well-educated, often athletic, independent, and involved in community affairs; but they were hardly seen as "domestic." Indeed, one woman who wrote for the German family magazine *Gartenlaube* concluded in a defensive tone that American women were so well-educated and professional that they must eventually come to look down on German women, "because from their standpoint, we are too industrious, too conscientious in little things, too domestic, and too thrifty."[27]

And yet, American women's virtues cut both ways; although they were better educated and more civic-minded, American women were supposedly inferior homemakers. They were so practical that their homes were not *gemütlich* (cozy and comfortable), and they spent too much time shopping, which signified a lack of both industry and thrift.[28] Some writers argued that American women's distaste for housework caused them to abandon the concept of the home entirely, leading them and their families to take up residence in boarding houses, which German observers bemoaned as a widespread phenomenon in late-nineteenth-century America. As with French housewives, the depictions of American women echoed the broader discussions of American national character among German academics who saw the United States as possessing a vibrant civic culture, but as lacking traditional European family structures and true *Kultur*.[29]

---

[26] For discussions of how Germans perceived American society more generally, see James, *A German Identity*, 26–7 and Schmidt, *Reisen in die Moderne*. For the 1920s, see also Nolan, *Visions of Modernity*, 109 and 206–34.

[27] Quoted in Schmidt, *Reisen in die Moderne*, 195.

[28] For descriptions of American housewives before World War I, see "Die Frau im Norden und die im Süden der neuen Welt," in *Deutsche Hausfrauen-Zeitung* 23 (1896) Nr. 27; "Daisys Budget," in *Deutsche Hausfrauen-Zeitung* 22 (1895) Nr. 36; and "Will die Amerikanerin sich wirklich von Mann, Haushalt, und Kind losreissen?" in *Die Frau im Osten* 8 (1914) Nr. 20. For the same stereotypes in Weimar publications, see Lissy Sysemihl-Gliedemeister, "Über amerikanische Frauentätigkeit" in the *Jahrbuch des Reichsverbandes Deutscher Hausfrauenvereine* (1929), 141–55; "Hausfrau und Volkswirtschaft. Das Fiasko der Konsumfinanzierung in Amerika," in *Die Deutsche Hausfrau* 12 (1927), 74; and Heinz Potthoff, "Erwerbstätigkeit und Hausfrauengeist," in *Die Deutsche Hausfrau* 13 (1928), 50–2.

[29] See Schmidt, *Reisen in die Moderne*, 190–216.

Thus in the end, although women from foreign cultures had their own talents and charms, they simply refused to get down on their knees and scrub like a German housewife, or keep such well-organized household account books and linen cabinets. In many ways, this insistence on German cleanliness and thrift was a feminine extension of the discourse on German *Qualitätsarbeit* (quality work), the widely shared belief in the superiority of German industrial design and workmanship. By emphasizing their own hard work, bourgeois housewives could thus connect themselves to the larger contemporary project of nation building. The symbols and practices they chose to emphasize were generally implicitly limited to the urban bourgeoisie, but this was true of most of the Germans who contributed to discussions of German national identity.

German Domesticity Abroad: National Identity and Colonial Housekeeping

The "Germanness" (and inherent superiority) of specific domestic symbols and approaches to housekeeping also featured prominently in depictions of German colonial housewives in colonial magazines and memoirs that circulated among the bourgeoisie in Wilhelmine Germany, and later during the Weimar period. Similar to the broader genre of housewives' magazines and advice literature, popular literature on women in the German colonies was largely (but not entirely) written by bourgeois women. Most of these authors promoted German women's immigration to the colonies; some had actually resided in German Southwest Africa and wrote about their experiences after returning to Germany. Many writers were affiliated with the Women's League of the German Colonial Society, whose organ was the popular weekly illustrated magazine *Kolonie und Heimat*, which circulated far beyond the circles of those who actually belonged to colonial booster groups.[30] The Herero rebellion of 1904–5 had greatly increased public interest and awareness of Germany's colonies, and helped increase the sales of all sorts of colonial publications, including those written by and for bourgeois women.[31] These publications were generally aimed at

[30] For the popularity of *Kolonie und Heimat*, see Joachim Warmbold, *Germania in Africa. Germany's Colonial Literature* (New York: Peter Lang, 1989), 91 and 241.
[31] Bourgeois women also had access to other sources of information about Germans in Africa, such as the newspaper accounts and novels written by men for a broader

the metropolitan audience with the exception of *Kolonie und Heimat*, which also circulated within Germany's colonies.

Magazine articles and memoirs written by or for colonial housewives addressed the same audiences as did more general housewives' advice literature, but had a somewhat different function and goals. They were intended to entertain and to educate, but also to promote support for Germany's colonies and imperial projects, and to recruit new immigrants among female audiences. The Women's League in particular had embarked on a project of promoting women's immigration to Southwest Africa. At the same time, however, much of the material in women's memoirs and in *Kolonie und Heimat* did focus on housekeeping advice for colonial housewives or would-be female immigrants. Large sections of *Kolonie und Heimat*, in particular, strongly resembled the "women's page" of German newspapers, offering information about colonial fashions, recipes, gardening, and general housekeeping questions. Memoirs by colonial housewives also offered future immigrants detailed advice on the preparation and storage of food and clothing, household routines, and gardening.

In some respects, publications by or about colonial housewives thus resembled the larger body of housewives' advice literature and

bourgeois audience (e.g., the best-selling 1906 novel *Peter Moors Fahrt nach Südwest*), but these publications paid comparatively little interest to questions of domesticity and housekeeping. For memoirs and travel literature written by women who had been to Africa, see Brockmann, *Die deutsche Frau in Südwestafrika*; Else Sonnenberg, *Wie es am Waterberg zuging. Ein Beitrag zur Geschichte des Hereroaufstandes* (Berlin: W. Süsserott, 1905); Ada Cramer, *Weiss oder Schwarz. Lehr- und Leidensjahre eines Farmers in Südwest im Lichte des Rassenhasses* (Berlin: Deutscher Kolonial-Verlag, 1913); Margarethe v. Eckenbrecher, Helene v. Falkenhausen, Stabsarzt Dr. Kuhn, and Oberleutnant Stuhlmann, *Deutsch-Südwestafrika. Kriegs- und Friedensbilder* (Leipzig: E. S. Mittler, 1907); Helene v. Falkenhausen, *Ansiedlerschicksale. Elf Jahre in Deutsch-Südwestafrika 1893–1904* (Berlin: Dietrich Reimer, 1905); Margarethe v. Eckenbrecher, *Was Afrika mir gab und nahm. Erlebnisse einer deutschen Frau in Südwestafrika*, rev. ed. (Berlin: E. S. Mittler, 1940); and Maria Karow, *Wo sonst der Fuss des Kriegers Trat. Farmerleben in Südwest nach den Kriege* (Berlin: E. S. Mittler, 1909). For a discussion of German colonists in popular Wilhelmine and Weimar fiction, see Warmbold, *Germania in Africa*, and Sibylle Benninghoff-Lühl, "'Ach Afrika! Wär ich zu Hause!' Gedanken zum Deutschen Kolonialroman der Jahrhundertwende," in Renate Nestvogel and Rainer Tetzlaff, eds., *Afrika und der Deutsche Kolonialismus. Zivilisierung zwischen Schnapshandel und Bibelstunde* (Berlin: Dietrich Reimer, 1987), 83–100. For a broader history of the migration of women to German Southwest Africa, see Krista E. O'Donnell, "The Colonial Woman Question"; see also Lora Wildenthal, *German Women for Empire, 1884–1945.* (Durham, NC: Duke University Press, 2001); Florence Hervé, ed., *Namibia. Frauen mischen sich ein* (Berlin: Orlanda Frauenverlag, 1993).

magazines. They offered German female audiences an imperial variation on the housekeeping template presented in Davidis and in housewives' magazines. They introduced metropolitan readers to Germany's
colonies and colonial subjects, and presented the bourgeois housewife
as a key part of the imperial project. But these depictions of colonial
housewives also served as a mirror for metropolitan readers, reflecting back an "essence" of German housewifery, thrown into relief by a
foreign setting.[32]

Colonial depictions highlighted how German housewives (and their
practices of domesticity) helped to reproduce nationality and ethnicity. Their roles resembled those analyzed by Nira Yuval-Davis and
Floya Anthias in the case of women in other ethnic groups. As Yuval-
Davis and Anthias note, women often function to establish boundaries for ethnic or national groups (because their relations with men
of other groups are controlled), as well as to transmit the symbols,
languages, and customs that help to define the group's identity.[33] In
the colonial literature discussed, German housewives filled all of these
roles.

As in more general housewives' magazines, colonial publications
defined "German" styles of housekeeping through contrast with imagined others: in this case, African housewives. Whether they were
Herero, Damara, or Khoi, Africans were invariably described as
ill-clad, dirty, and malodorous (at least until they came under the
control of whites). They were infested with vermin, and smeared
themselves with a paste made out of oil and dirt.[34] German female
authors described African homes as "huts" or "hovels," which lacked
the doors, windows, and separate rooms for different activities that

---

[32] I am more concerned here with metropolitan perceptions of colonial housekeeping
than with the reality of women's work in the German colonies.

[33] From Nira Yuval-Davis and Floya Anthias, eds., *Woman-Nation-State* (New York:
St. Martin's Press, 1989), 8–10.

[34] Comments on the poor personal hygiene of Africans were ubiquitous in travel lit-
erature and memoirs. See, e.g., Karow, *Wo sonst der Fuss*, 33–4 and Brockmann,
Die deutsche Frau in Südwestafrika, 25–8. See Timothy Burke, *Lifebuoy Men and
Lux Women. Commodification, Consumption, and Cleanliness in Modern Zim-
babwe* (Durham and London: Duke University Press, 1996), 24–5; see also Jean and
John Comaroff, "Homemade Hegemony: Modernity, Domesticity, and Colonialism
in South Africa," in Karen T. Hansen, ed., *African Encounters with Domesticity* (New
Brunswick, NJ: Rutgers University Press, 1992), 37–74; Nancy Rose Hunt, "Colo-
nial Fairy Tales and the Knife and Fork Doctrine in the Heart of Africa," in Hansen,
African Encounters, 143–71.

characterized European homes. Maria Karow, who kept house for her invalid sister in Southwest Africa for two years, published a memoir later that described the life-style and character of her sister's servants in some detail. She wrote that the homes of all Africans resembled "molehills," without proper doors or ventilation.[35] Margarethe v. Eckenbrecher, who published a memoir about her work as a teacher in Southwest Africa, also compared the typical African home to "an enormous, grey-brown molehill." Eckenbrecher did add later, however, that these homes were kept tolerably clean, an admission that set her apart from almost all other writers on the subject.[36]

Because of the shortage of German brides, many colonists had supposedly been "forced" to marry African or mixed-race women. German memoirists stigmatized such women as wasteful, inferior housekeepers.[37] Helene v. Falkenhausen's characterization of African housewives was typical: "What a tragic life is led [by the settlers] who have married a native born woman! These women are generally too lazy to pay sufficient attention to the household, and too stupid to learn how to do so."[38] Colonial authors repeatedly stressed that it was almost impossible to teach African women "real" (German) housekeeping. This alleged incapacity of African housewives helped to establish domestic racial difference and hierarchies in situations where an individual's "race" was often unclear or problematic (e.g., "Europeanized" mixed-race *Bastards* in Southwest Africa).[39] Settlers who married local women were often referred to as *verkaffert* ("kaffirized") because they adopted the allegedly poor standard of living and morals of their wives. Colonial boosters argued that the increased immigration of German women would "rescue" German men from the necessity of marrying such women. German women would thus help to maintain the "purity" of

---

[35] Karow, *Wo sonst der Fuss*, 154 and 33.

[36] Eckenbrecher, *Was Afrika mir gab und nahm*, 27 and 32.

[37] For a discussion of why German settlers might have preferred to marry local women, see O'Donnell, "The Colonial Woman Question," 46–9.

[38] In Eckenbrecher et al., *Deutsch-Südwestafrika*, 27. See also the disparaging remarks about the housekeeping of African or *Bastard* women in Brockmann, *Die deutsche Frau*, 25–8; see also "Die Frau und die Kolonien," in *Deutsche Kolonialzeitung*, May 30, 1905, 122.

[39] The "race" of individuals who came to German Southwest Africa from the Cape Colony, or the *Bastard* community, was sometimes the subject of heated controversy. See O'Donnell, "The Colonial Woman Question," 48.

the German race, as their presence would help prevent the formation of yet more marriages that produced mixed-race children.

As Krista O'Donnell notes, colonial boosters (especially the Women's League of the Colonial Society) argued that if German women were urged to immigrate to the colonies, they would not only help establish racial boundaries, they would also create a "German" way of life within their new households.[40] Similar to Clara Brockmann, popular writers about German colonial households generally insisted that when a settler married and brought a German housewife to his farm, she immediately introduced metropolitan domestic standards. Indeed, the cleanliness and order described by these authors would have been remarkable in German peasant households, and sometimes sounded suspiciously bourgeois. Painstaking cleanliness, above all, was both a marker of ethnic identity abroad and a reminder of the homeland. Maria Karow wrote that when she visited the homes of several artisans who had migrated to Africa,

[t]heir wives greeted me and showed me with pride their households, in which everything was so clean that it gleamed. If the African servants had not been there, I would have thought myself in Germany.[41]

Several authors described how a German housewife began almost immediately to outfit her home with the objects that symbolized good urban bourgeois housekeeping at home, especially white curtains and embroidered, framed proverbs on the walls. One writer wrote that as soon as a woman arrived,

there begins a hammering and washing...muslin curtains and pure white linens give the house the stamp of a German home...now the wash is conscientiously scrubbed twice with soap, boiled, and bleached on the lawn; after being ironed, it is put – now snow white – in the linen cabinet.[42]

Other writers noted how women hung white curtains and *Andenken* (framed sayings) as one of their first acts after arriving. Considering the difficulties of maintaining an urban metropolitan standard of hygiene in Southwest Africa (where there was a lack of running water – or often any clean water – amidst extremely dusty conditions, along with

[40] Ibid.
[41] Karow, *Wo sonst der Fuss*, 128.
[42] Emmy Möller, "Die deutsche Frau in der Südsee," *Kolonie und Heimat* 3 (1910): 6–7.

an abundance of apparently ferociously aggressive termites) one may be skeptical about such claims.

The linen cabinet, the pride of the German housewife, was mentioned by other writers. Margarethe v. Eckenbrecher described how British soldiers searched her linen cabinet for contraband during World War I in a scene that juxtaposed images of domesticity, gender, and nationality. She described how the Englishmen (who had occupied German Southwest Africa) "opened the cabinet, which looked very pretty and orderly inside. The sweaty soldiers' hands seemed to shrink back when confronted with so much snow white linen. They reached for the front stack only hesitantly."[43] Because the soldiers shrank from disturbing the perfect, white stacks of sheets, they never discovered the weapons she had hidden behind her linens: a small victory for German domesticity.

Writers repeatedly claimed that German housewives were thriftier than African or mixed-race women, keeping orderly household accounts and writing a *Küchenzettel* (menu plan) for each week. Several memoirists noted that each Sunday, as in Germany, they prepared a roast and *Sonntagskuchen* (the cake eaten on Sunday afternoons with coffee).[44]

Taken collectively, these accounts thus presented metropolitan readers with before and after pictures, showing the impact of German housewives. German bachelors were shown living with (and often like) natives, in distressing disorder, their connection to German culture slowly unraveling. When the housewife narrator entered the story, readers saw the colony through her eyes and were introduced to local agricultural practices and terrains, local cuisines (e.g., Southwest African melons and beverages), and the economic value of the colony. The housewife then worked to establish German domestic symbols

---

[43] Eckenbrecher, *Was Afrika mir gab und nahm*, 208.

[44] For the thrifty management of German colonist housewives, see Brockmann, *Die deutsche Frau*, 14–15; Antonie Brandeis, "Die deutsche Hausfrau in den Kolonien," *Kolonie und Heimat* 1(4) (Nov. 10, 1907): 12; Anonymous, *Aus Südwestafrika*, 53. For the maintenance of the tradition of the Sunday cake and roast, see Karow, *Wo sonst der Fuss*, 115–16 and Brockmann, *Die deutsche Frau*, 11–12. *Kolonie und Heimat* regularly featured proposed *Küchenzettel* for settler women, which incorporated some local ingredients but maintained the basic patterns and structure of German bourgeois cuisine. See, e.g., M. Rädnitzer, "Zwei unentbehrliche Freunde der Farmersfrau," in *Kolonie und Heimat* 1(19) (June 6, 1908).

and practices within the household: the cabinet full of snowy linens (in spite of dust and termites); the Sunday cake; and the orderly account book. She thus "Germanized" the household within a colonial context: demarcating colonists from the colonized, linking housework to empire building, and enlisting metropolitan women's support for German imperialism.[45]

Making "German" homes in a colonial context, housewives thus contributed to the creation of communities of Germans in Africa that resembled the idealized, orderly small towns of the homeland, at least in literature for metropolitan audiences. In the best-selling novel *Peter Moor's Journey to Southwest Africa* (one of the most popular novels of the Wilhelmine period), the narrator links the domesticity of the homeland with that of the colony in emotionally laden descriptions of the care given to their families by German housewives. When Peter tells his mother that he is leaving home to join the Navy, "she went quietly into the kitchen and said nothing more about it to me. In the fall [before he departed] she gave me a set of linens, everything pure, clean, and mended, as was proper." He contrasts this cleanliness and supply of appropriate linens with the filth and partial nudity of the Africans he encounters in the colony. When, after weeks of fighting Africans in the desert, his patrol comes across a German settler family, their farm is depicted as a sort of domestic paradise: "There, in the shadow of the veranda, stood a German woman . . . how we rejoiced to see her bright, clean dress, and her pure, friendly face."[46]

In popular literature about the German colonies, the colonial house-wife thus symbolized the model of domestic life and practices that writers associated with the German home. The details that authors incorporated into their descriptions, however, were often more typical of bourgeois metropolitan households than of colonial homesteads, which lacked all the amenities of urban life. Rural colonial farms required an entirely different sort of wife and "helpmeet" for the Ger-man settler. This fact helps to explain why male colonists repeatedly rejected the "fine ladies" that they feared the Women's Colonial League would sponsor as immigrants, and instead sometimes insisted on

---

[45] For an analysis of how domesticity and cleanliness served to define German colonial identity, see O'Donnell, "The Colonial Woman Question," 226.

[46] Quoted in Sibylle Benninghoff-Lühl, "'Ach Afrika! Wär ich zu Hause!'," 85–9.

marrying African or mixed-race brides. Such wives could not make properly "German" homes, in the eyes of metropolitan colonial boosters, but they had agricultural skills and local connections that were clearly more valuable in the eyes of some male colonists.[47]

In the eyes of colonial boosters, however, German housewives eclipsed any locally born settlers' wives, therefore maintaining metropolitan domestic standards and thus Germanness within an African setting. The towns these colonials had founded resembled those of the homeland. Travel writers and novelists described German colonial towns laid out with straight, wide streets, clean public spaces, and homes in good repair, contrasting German settlements with "dirty" British-ruled Mombasa (in Kenya) and Zanzibar. In his 1900 survey of German colonies, *Auf deutschem Boden in Afrika*, Paul Kollmann compared German-ruled Dar-es-Salaam with British Zanzibar:

Viewed from the harbor, the city . . . gives the impression of a development of German villas . . . [with] pretty houses, built mainly of sparkling white lathe and plaster. . . . What a difference between Dar es Salaam and Zanzibar! Like day and night! . . . [in Zanzibar]. Everywhere dilapidated houses . . . everywhere dirt in the streets . . . in harsh contrast to what we see on *German* territory . . . *here* cleanliness prevails to the extreme; tree-lined streets, all the buildings with their decorative exteriors [and] solid and cozy furnishings.[48]

Germans were not alone in using cleanliness, hygiene, and domestic order as markers to draw the boundary between themselves and their colonial subjects. European-style domesticity helped to define racial identity and justify European hegemony throughout the colonial world, as Ann Stoler and other historians have made clear.[49] But as the

---

[47] See O'Donnell, "The Colonial Woman Question," 46–9.

[48] Paul Kollmann, *Auf deutschem Boden in Afrika. Ernste und heitere Erlebnisse* (Berlin, 1900), quoted in Warmbold, *Germania in Africa*, 158; italics in original. See Warmbold, 158–63 for other writers' descriptions of the exceptional cleanliness of German colonies.

[49] See, e.g., Ann L. Stoler, "Carnal Knowledge and Imperial Power: Gender, Race, and Morality in Colonial Asia," in Micaela di Leonardo, ed., *Gender at the Crossroads of Knowledge. Feminist Anthropology in the Post-Modern Era* (Berkeley: University of California Press, 1991); Ann L. Stoler and Frederick Cooper, eds., *Tensions of Empire. Colonial Cultures in a Bourgeois World* (Berkeley: University of California Press, 1997); Margaret Strobel, *Western Women and the Second British Empire* (Bloomington: Indiana University Press, 1991); Burke, *Lifebouy Men and Lux Women*; Hansen, *African Encounters with Domesticity*; and Antoinette Burton, *Burdens of History. British Feminists, Indian Women, and Imperial Culture,*

comparison of British Zanzibar and German Dar-es-Salaam indicates, for many of those who wrote about or participated in German colonization in Africa, extreme cleanliness and a certain approach to domestic management signified not merely whiteness, but Germanness. Just as these writers would have agreed that within Europe, German homes were cleaner and better run than English homes, so too did they see German colonies as being characterized by superior hygiene.

Conclusion

Descriptions of domesticity abroad, which focused on both the private lives of foreigners (to draw comparisons with German family life) and on the housekeeping of colonial Germans (juxtaposed against the inferior domesticity of African cultures), abounded during the late nineteenth and early twentieth centuries. These descriptions were probably largely imaginary, telling us more about German stereotypes than about the actual housekeeping of non-Germans. German writers were doubtless overlooking, for example, the housekeeping of poor and rural women of their own culture (who lacked the servants, time for housework, and running water that many bourgeois urban housewives had), and instead blithely insisted that the household management of women in their nation surpassed that of other cultures, across the board.

Although they were indulging in sweeping generalizations, there is little doubt that the stereotypes such writers were propagating about the quality of German domesticity compared to that of foreigners had a certain currency in daily life and ordinary conversations, especially among the bourgeoisie. When such assumptions about foreign family life formed a backdrop to the actual day-to-day practices and norms of German domesticity described in Chapter 1, the net effect must have been to reinforce the imagined community of German housewives: the propensity of bourgeois housewives to define their own national identity using such gendered terms, and the tendency within German culture as a whole to construct a national identity that was partially rooted in domestic symbols and practices.

1865–1915 (Chapel Hill: University of North Carolina Press, 1994). In the United States, Protestant middle-class housewives also used the concepts of "clean" and "pure" to help define the role and image of white housewives in America, compared to "dirty" black or immigrant women. See Palmer, *Domesticity and Dirt*, 16.

Certainly, the abundant assumptions about foreign domesticity helped to shape how German women thought of themselves *as housewives* compared to the women of other nations. The influence of such stereotypes is clear in an anecdote offered by Mrs. Sidgwick, the native German woman who married an Englishman. In 1908, she reported a conversation between two older well-off German women:

"My son Karl is in England," you hear a German mother say. "I am uneasy about him. I fear he may marry an Englishwoman.... It would break my heart. The women of that nation know nothing of housekeeping. They sit in their drawing rooms all day, while their husband's hard-earned money is wasted in the kitchen.... [An English wife] would give him cold mutton to eat, and he would die of indigestion"[50]

The hypothetical English daughter-in-law gave Karl's mother a yardstick for understanding and evaluating her own housekeeping and, by extension, her own identity and worth.

Descriptions and stereotypes about the housekeeping of foreign women, and of German women in the colonies, must have reassured bourgeois German readers about the essential Germanness of such qualities as cleanliness, order, and well-organized household management. The persistence of symbols such as the linen cabinet in such depictions, and the broader domestic customs and practices they were linked to, showed how such characteristics allegedly were maintained, even in the African bush. In a general sense, the belief that cleanliness and order were "German" virtues had been growing in popularity since the eighteenth century, but the discussions of German domesticity presented were much more detailed and concrete in their layered descriptions of home life than earlier generalizations.[51]

These depictions of foreign housewives and of colonial German households thus could be, and were, used as a mirror by Germans at home, to reflect what they saw as the essence of their national

---

[50] Sidgwick, *Home Life in Germany*, 113–14.

[51] See Münch, *Ordnung, Fleiss, and Sparsamkeit*, who traces how cleanliness, order, and thrift (which were seen as bourgeois values in earlier periods) were redefined as "German" virtues during the eighteenth century. Since then, Münch argues, these "virtues" have "helped to determine both the self-image of Germans and their impressions of others, in a unique fashion," 12–13.

character, and this character was often defined in gendered terms. Women – especially in their roles as housewives – served as vehicles for the expression and maintenance of German identity, an identity that was ostensibly pan-German in a global sense, although it was still implicitly urban and class-based. The appeal of this approach to defining Germanness may have been somewhat limited by its inherently bourgeois nature. But it was still much more successful than other Protestant bourgeois approaches to this problem (e.g., Sedan Day, or celebration of the Hohenzollern dynasty) because "German" domesticity was a basis for identity that could often transcend confessional and regional divisions.

The awareness of "German" housekeeping, contrasted with the inferior domesticity of other cultures, would be taken up and carried forward by Nazi theorists and policy makers. But in a quieter, more constant way, these assumptions about German domesticity helped to shape German national identity throughout the nineteenth and twentieth centuries.

3

The Politicization of Housework

Even in autumn, the fruit of our homeland, the apple, is unreasonably neglected [by housewives] and in its place many sorts of [foreign] oranges are consumed in astonishing quantities.

From a 1927 article in The German Housewife

By the turn of the century, a particular approach to housekeeping, holidays, and domesticity had become an integral part of how Germans saw themselves and others. But the promotion of domesticity or particular practices of housekeeping was of little interest to the state before 1914, except for the spread of domestic science instruction in the public schools. And although housewives had begun to organize themselves during the late nineteenth century, forming quite large associations in some cities, housewives' organizations were not politicized in any partisan sense. The coming of World War I changed this – as it did every other aspect of social life – and drew the state's attention to women's housekeeping practices and their importance to the nation. Housework and domesticity become entangled with the national interest, which accelerated the organization of bourgeois housewives, and boosted their claims to being a *Beruf*, a formal profession. Along with the expansion of bourgeois housewives' organizations came their explicit politicization after 1918, as housewives' associations gained influence in right-wing Weimar political parties.

This chapter turns from the analysis of how national identity was articulated using the practices and symbols of domesticity in various genres and social venues before 1914, to an examination of how house-wives were mobilized on behalf of the nation after 1914, and their daily housekeeping thus politicized both during and after the war. Many of the traits established in German public discussions before 1914 about their own and others' domesticity – especially stereotypes about German housewives' thrifty and labor-intensive approaches to housekeeping – were on display in the political campaigns mounted by German housewives during the Weimar period. But now these domestic practices were put increasingly into service of nationalist causes and interest groups.

At the same time, changes in household technology during the 1920s entered the discussion about what styles of domesticity were appropriate for Germany, and became the focus of much of the work of housewives' groups. The political developments of the Weimar period, and material interests of bourgeois leaders of German housewives' associations, simultaneously drew housewives' organizations steadily toward the right. Thus, the dual thrust of Weimar housewives' groups was to modernize and "professionalize" housework, while also mobilizing housewives for goals beloved of the right wing. By the end of Weimar, the major housewives' leagues were strongly allied with right-wing, nationalist parties, and their leaders pursued a campaign of economic nationalism and agitation against Weimar's parliamentary system, while they also worked to modernize and rationalize the housewife's role.

German Households under Siege

The World War I, which transformed German society and deeply affected private life, provided the impetus for the enormous expansion of housewives' organizations, and thus set the stage for the politicization of housework. The war's demands on the German "home front" indeed led to the rapid expansion not only of housewives' groups, but of the German women's movement across the board. Women's organizations stepped in to fill a vacuum because the German government had not undertaken the kind of detailed planning for the civilian economy required for a long war.

The German army had based its overall planning on the premise of a fast, overwhelming attack on France, similar to its successful strategy during the Franco-Prussian War in 1870–1. The German general staff planned to force the surrender of Belgium and France and then to transport most of its forces rapidly to the Eastern Front to confront the Russian army (which faced some delays in mobilization). Of course, the master plan failed: Germany did not knock France out of the war, and was instead committed to a very long two-front war. But the government had not given much thought to the effect that a drawn-out war would have on civilians, nor created any schedules for the mobilization of the domestic economy.

The immediate result was chaos, when millions of households lost their chief "breadwinners" to the military mobilization. The Allies imposed a fairly complete naval blockade of German ports soon thereafter, which threw still more families into poverty, as the shortage of raw materials and the conversion of the industrial sector to wartime production led to the closure of factories and workshops. The textile industries (which employed a heavily female workforce) were particularly hard hit.

Because of the shortage of materials and foodstuffs, the German government introduced rationing and pursued an unsuccessful policy of autarky. The overall goal was to make Germany – which, with its large population, had been dependent on substantial food imports for decades – self-sufficient in terms of the production of food and raw materials. Autarky proved to be impossible to sustain, however. Germany lacked sufficient sources of fertilizer and fodder, for example, to even maintain a prewar level of food production. The nation also suffered from persistent shortfalls of fats and fuels, along with many raw materials needed for basic consumer goods (e.g., cotton, wool, and leather for clothing). The results for civilians included food shortages, widespread malnutrition, and increased mortality rates in every age group because poor nutrition undermined resistance to disease.[1]

As the war continued, the home front for many women literally ran right through their kitchens. By 1916, many housewives had to devote

---

[1] For the terrible impact that the war had on civilians' diet and health, see also Anne Roerkohl, *Hungerblockade und Heimatfront* (Stuttgart: F. Steiner, 1991). And for an analysis of the politics of food consumption in World War I, see also Belinda Davis, *Home Fires Burning: Politics, Identity, and Food in World War I Berlin* (Chapel Hill: University of North Carolina Press, 2000).

an enormous amount of time and effort simply to keep their household economies functioning. It often took considerable initiative and resourcefulness simply to obtain a minimum of foodstuffs and fuels for heating and cooking. In addition, housewives had to navigate around government attempts to regulate household economies. Marie-Elisabeth Lüders, who was one of the leading organizers of the women's movement's attempts to support the war effort, recalled later that the state's attempts to intervene in the domestic economy

were expanded week by week. In the end, the production and distribution of all materials and objects one needed for daily life were regulated by laws and decrees. . . . [Civilians' lives were] characterized by confiscation, prohibitions regarding the sale and use of materials, by collection drives, and by attempts to save or produce substitutes for raw materials.[2]

The "war-related materials" on Lüders' list, which the state collected, processed, and recycled, included the most varied detritus of domestic life: coffee grounds, wine corks, women's hair, gramophone records, and fruit pits.

Both potato and grain harvests declined sharply during the war, and the shortage of animal fodder led farmers to feed part of their harvests to their livestock, making cereal shortages worse. Prices for both bread and potatoes (which formed the bulk of the diet for much of the German population) rose steadily, and the government mandated the addition of potato additives and rye grain (which grew better in Germany than did wheat) to wheat flour, to produce what was called *K-bread*, which was touted as the patriotic bread choice. The K in *K-bread* stood for both *Krieg* (war) and *Kartoffel* (potato). Consumers loathed K-bread, with its additives, grayish color, and soggy crust, but poorer shoppers had no other choices; as the war progressed, even K-bread was often in short supply.[3]

Housewives might be issued ration coupons for milk, bread, or potatoes, but this did not mean that they could find stores that had these products in stock. Children, for example, were given ration cards that entitled them to one liter of milk per week (a very modest allotment),

[2] Marie-Elisabeth Lüders, *Das unbekannte Heer. Frauen kämpfen für Deutschland, 1914–1918* (Berlin: E. S. Mittler and Sohn, 1936), 186.
[3] For a detailed discussion of grain shortages and the ingredients of K-bread, see Davis, *Home Fires Burning*, 25–30.

but their mothers often could not find any to purchase, as the milk supply available to consumers dropped to 20 percent of its prewar level by 1916.[4] Those who could afford to do so hoarded food and coal, and black markets in food and consumer goods flourished; but black market prices were often so high that only the well-to-do could buy there. The winter of 1917 was popularly known as the "turnip winter" because only turnips seemed to be widely available, and malnutrition became widespread in German cities. Turnips had previously been used as an animal fodder crop, and their diversion to feed urban civilians only worsened the shortage of livestock.

Consumers responded with street riots, strikes in the workplace, and bitter, widespread criticism of the government. Women, who often waited for hours in vain in food lines, were particularly likely to participate in food riots. These, along with related consumer protests undermined the Wilhelmine state, and a heated discussion developed within and outside of government circles about what constituted an equitable distribution of foodstuffs. Such widespread rejection of the state and its authority ultimately prepared the way for political revolution after Germany's defeat in 1918.

Rural or small-town populations had to cope with heavy-handed government regulations, and shortages of crucial supplies of fertilizer, labor, and machinery. Malnutrition wasn't usually as bad in rural areas, however, because people in these areas often had their own gardens or small livestock. But urban consumers found less and less food available in the stores.

Early on during the war, government propaganda attempted to persuade consumers that sufficient food was available, as long as housewives were thrifty with food and no one ate to excess. An often-used slogan assured shoppers that "no one needs to starve, but all must save." Federal and local authorities encouraged women and children to go into the woods, to collect wild fruits and foods such as rose hips, dandelion greens, nuts, thistles, and wild berries to supplement their rations. But even the Imperial War Food Office (*Kriegsernährungsamt*) came to the conclusion that the calories expended in such efforts probably exceeded the nutritional value of what was gathered. The government also organized regular collections of what would have been

[4] Ibid., 162–4.

thrown away as garbage even in the most frugal household before, to replace the raw materials that Germany had previously imported and needed for wartime production. But the constant admonitions to recycle, gather and forage, and contribute to scrap collections did not help a great deal. One agronomist indeed argued that collection and recycling efforts couldn't make a substantial difference, and concluded that the propaganda to do so was yet another symptom of what he called "war time psychosis."[5]

The bourgeois women's movement (in its wartime form, the National Women's Service) became the main vehicle through which the German government tried to mold housewives' shopping and cooking habits to meet the needs of the wartime economy. The National Women's Service distributed recipe booklets and the model menus (*Speisezettel*) published in newspapers to adjust civilians' diets to match available ingredients. These menus stressed foods that would be featured in government discussions throughout the next thirty years: potatoes, dark bread (particularly K-bread), substitutes for bread spreads such as butter and margarine, little meat, and substitutes for cooking with fat, as all sorts of dietary fats were in short supply.

The National Women's Service also helped found housewives' associations in most German cities. With the support and promotion of the National Women's Service and local authorities, the number of chapters of housewives' organizations and their combined membership grew explosively during the war. By the end of the war in 1918, housewives' associations had indeed become some of the largest organizations within the women's movement. The new housewives' groups developed a variety of services to help housewives cope with shortages of every type of product. Housewives' associations offered courses on cooking (to promote *ersatz* ingredients) that taught ordinary women how to cook with substitutes for eggs, butter, flour, and meat. Other classes taught women how to create substitutes for scarce commodities; how to wash clothes and dishes without proper soap; how to repair their own shoes; and (when leather became impossible to obtain) how to plait straw soles for worn-out shoes. In some localities, urban housewives' associations established consumer cooperatives in conjunction

---

5 For recycling and foraging propaganda, see Roerkohl, *Hungerblockade*, 51–7 and 179–81.

with rural housewives' organizations.[6] These urban housewives' associations created a national organization, which changed its name after
the war to the National League of German Housewives' Associations.[7]
Farmer's wives organized into a sister association, the National Federation of Agricultural Housewives' Associations.

Housewives' Associations and Weimar Politics

Housewives' groups had thus been initially created in some areas (or
expanded in cities where they already existed) under wartime conditions, with a focus on consumer issues and reshaping household practices to meet state needs. The privations suffered during wartime had
highlighted the national importance of housewives – in wartime propaganda, within the women's movement, and in state policy – as those
whose shopping and cooking choices could exacerbate or cushion the
impact of a crisis. Käthe Schirmacher, a prominent conservative feminist, reflected the new view of housewives when she observed in 1918
that "the world war has taught us that cooking and homemaking are
service to the country, defense of the country, and a form of citizenship.
Not only the sword is a weapon – in the 'hunger war', the cooking
spoon is equally important."[8] Leaders of housewives' groups would

[6] See ibid., 205–10. For a description of housewives' associations in one locality, see
Nancy Reagin, *A German Women's Movement: Class and Gender in Hanover, 1880–
1933*, 187–202. Renate Bridenthal gives a politically sophisticated analysis of rural
housewives' organizations in "Organized Rural Women in the Conservative Mobilization of the German Countryside in the Weimar Republic," in Larry E. Jones and
James N. Retallack, eds., *Between Reform, Reaction, and Resistance. Studies in the
History of German Conservatism from 1789 to 1945* (New York, 1993), 375–405. See
also Barbara Guttmann, "'in nie erlebter Leibhaftigkeit zum 'Volke' vereint': Frauenbewegung und Nationalismus im Ersten Weltkrieg," in *Frauen und Nation*, 204–13.
[7] The National League was largely Protestant and almost entirely bourgeois. For an
analysis of the league during the Weimar period, see Renate Bridenthal, "'Professional Housewives': Stepsisters of the Women's Movement," 153–73. See also Kirsten
Schlegel-Matthies, *"Im Haus und am Herd." Der Wandel des Hausfrauenbildes und
der Hausarbeit 1880–1930*, 191–228. Working-class housewives' organizations were
established in only two cities because the Social Democrats rejected the idea of creating a separate housewives' organization within the labor movement. Most socialist
housewives' activism was expressed within the labor movement's very successful chain
of consumer cooperatives. See Hagemann, *Frauenalltag und Männerpolitik*, 133–48.
[8] Käthe Schirmacher, *Völkische Frauendienstpflicht* (Charlottenberg: Augustin and Co.,
1917), 6, quoted in Raffael Scheck, *Mothers of the Nation: Right-Wing Women in
Weimar Germany* (New York: Berg, 2004).

repeatedly invoke the metaphor of the cooking spoon as a "women's weapon" for the nation after 1918.

Housewives' associations were to a certain extent the wartime off-spring of the bourgeois women's movement, and they continued to grow, while remaining affiliated with the women's movement through 1932. By 1922, the urban housewives' league had more than two hundred and fifty thousand members, and its sister organization, the rural housewives' league, reached one hundred thousand members by the late 1920s. The steady growth of the urban and rural housewives' organizations meant that by 1929, they were the first and third largest associations within the umbrella league of the bourgeois women's movement. [9] But both housewives' leagues soon found other political allies.

Finally, the German Catholic Women's League created an affiliate group for housewives during the war, the smaller Catholic Housewives' Union. In many respects, the Catholic Housewives' Union pursued almost exactly the same policies as the urban National League of German Housewives' Associations. The main difference seemed to be in the two groups' political affiliations. While the largely Protestant National League of German Housewives' Associations (e.g., the rural house-wives' league) was closely linked to the *Deutschnationale Volkspartei* (DNVP) and *Deutsche Volkspartei* (DVP), the Catholic Housewives' Union strongly supported the Catholic Center Party.

The fact that Catholic housewives chose to organize themselves separately speaks to the ways that the larger Weimar parties often chose to organize their own separate constituencies and not to any meaningful differences in Weimar bourgeois Catholic and Protestant housewives' approaches to household management. Certainly, there was nothing to choose between the two groups in their economic protectionism, and their interest in "rationalizing" and modernizing housework. The Catholic group's publications even promoted the same streamlined vision of "modern," rational house décor. The photos of "ideal" homes

---

[9] For membership figures for these groups, and the relative size of the housewives' groups within the umbrella League of German Women's Associations, see Briden-thal, "Organized Rural Women," 390; "Class Struggle Around the Hearth," 246; and Hiltraud Schmidt-Waldherr, *Emanzipation durch Professionalisierung? Politische Strategien und Konflikte innerhalb der bürgerlichen Frauenbewegung während der Weimarer Republik und die Reaktion des bürgerlichen Antifeminismus und des Nationalsozialismus* (Frankfurt: Materialis, 1987), 176–7.

and advice regarding home décor offered in its publications didn't even include the small religious statues and framed prints found in many Catholic homes during the early twentieth century. Indeed, the leaders of the ostensibly nonconfessional National League of Housewives' Associations often complained bitterly when their Catholic counterparts were given a seat alongside the urban housewives' group on government advisory committees. The National League argued that it represented *all* German housewives, and that the identical policies pursued by the Catholic group meant that a separate representative from their group was unnecessary. But the Catholic Center Party ensured in many regions that its housewives' affiliate group continued to be represented in such forums.

The National Federation of Agricultural Housewives' Associations, however, defined itself rather differently than its Catholic and urban housewives' counterparts. Most of its member organizations had been founded just before or during the war as producer cooperatives, and the rural league as a whole continued to define itself largely as an association of agricultural producers, and not homemakers, throughout the Weimar period. Like the urban housewives' groups, however, the rural league supported economic protectionism and was affiliated with the DNVP.

From their inceptions, therefore, all three housewives' leagues had links (which became stronger over time) to the world of conservative partisan politics. The war had led to rapid growth of all conservative women's organizations, promoted closer links and networks among such nationalist women's groups, and resulted in close links between conservative women's associations and their male counterparts.[10] Rural housewives' associations had been loosely affiliated with the right-wing agrarian pressure group *Bund der Landwirte* before 1914 (some of the housewives' groups' leaders were married to right-wing agrarian activists). In 1921, the Agricultural Housewives' Associations league formally joined the agrarian league's successor organization, the *Reichslandbund*. Indeed, in many rural areas, rural housewives'

---

[10] For the growth of conservative women's organizations during the war, and the networks that developed among them, see Andrea Süchtig-Hänger, *Das 'Gewissen der Nation.' Nationales Engagement and politisches Handeln konservativer Frauenorganisationen 1900 bis 1937* (Düsseldorf: Droste Verlag, 2002).

groups came to be perceived as female auxiliaries to the *Reichsland-bund*. The *Reichslandbund* offered the Agricultural Housewives' Associations league office space, funding, and political support in winning government recognition and subsidies. In return, rural housewives' associations supported the *Reichslandbund's* antirepublican agenda and worked to elect nationalist "black-red-white" candidates in the 1924 and 1925 elections.[11] The Agricultural Housewives' Associations league was also closely linked to the DNVP: a party on the right wing of the Weimar political spectrum – consistently hostile to the nation's parliamentary system and to the center and left parties that founded the Weimar Republic – that grew steadily stronger in the late Weimar period. Many of the rural housewives' leaders (e.g., Elisabet Boehm and Countess Margarethe v. Keyserlingk) also sat on the DNVP's women's committee (indeed, Elisabet Boehm, a strong anti-Semite, was a founding member of the DNVP).[12]

The National League of German Housewives' Associations was not formally affiliated with any masculine pressure group, and its own statutes mandated that the housewives' organization was supposed to stay neutral with regard to partisan politics. In practice, however, many of its leaders (e.g., Countess Margarete v. Keyserlingk, Martha Voss-Zietz, Leonore Kuhn, Bertha Hindenberg-Delbrück, Charlotte Mühsam-Werther, Clara Mende, and Franziska Wiemann) played leading roles in or even held parliamentary seats for the DNVP or the center-right DVP. Judging from internal organization discussions, most of its members voted for or belonged to center-right or right-wing political parties. In order to preserve peace within the organization, the leadership was supposed to avoid endorsing any particular conservative party (although local chapters might work for electoral coalitions of center-right parties).[13] But the overlap between the leadership of both

---

[11] See Bridenthal, "Organized Rural Women," 389–401.

[12] For overlap between the membership of the DNVP and the RLHV (the agricultural housewives' league), see ibid., 400; see also Raffael Scheck, "German Conservatism and Female Political Activism in the Early Weimar Republic," *German History* 15 (1997): 34–55.

[13] While the leadership of the urban National League of Housewives' Associations was overwhelmingly conservative, women who belonged to more liberal political parties were found among the membership in some chapters. For an example of a local chapter that promoted political "neutrality," yet explicitly conservative policies (which

housewives' leagues and the executive committees and parliamentary delegations of both the DVP and DNVP was substantial and striking.[14]

The housewives' leagues thus simultaneously made up the conservative wing within the Weimar bourgeois women's movement, and were also influential constituencies and sources of female activists for the major center-right and right-wing Weimar political parties. For most of the Weimar period, there was little contradiction between these two sets of affiliations. Although Germany's military collapse and civilians' suffering had led to widespread rejection and the ultimate collapse of the Imperial government – which opened the way for Germany's socialist and left-wing parties to establish a parliamentary democracy – much of the middle class remained unreconciled to the nation's military defeat and new political system. Many bourgeois Germans were deeply skeptical of the legitimacy and efficacy of the new political system. Although some voted for the socialist or liberal parties in the first rounds of elections out of fear of a Communist takeover, middle-class voters drifted to the right after 1920, a tendency that was exacerbated by the disastrous hyperinflation of the early 1920s.

Women voters among the bourgeoisie tended to skew toward the religious conservative parties. A number of electoral studies done on the impact of women's enfranchisement have shown that Weimar female voters tended to support parties that had strong religious platforms (e.g., the DNVP and Catholic Center Party) and also (compared to men of the same class) that women tended to prefer parties that

---

ultimately drove out Jewish and liberal members, as the chapter president intended) see Reagin, *A German Women's Movement*, 240–1.

[14] The intricate and extensive linkages between the two housewives' leagues, the DNVP and DVP, are explored in a painstaking and intelligent analysis by Scheck, *Mothers of the Nation*. A few examples of the overlap between housewives' groups and these two parties (drawn from Scheck's study) must serve here. Maria Jecker, chair of the urban housewives' league after 1927, also sat on the women's executive committee of the DVP; Clara Mende, who represented the DVP in the German Reichstag from 1920–8, also played a leading role in the urban housewives' movement; Elisabet Boehm, first chair of the rural housewives' league, was also a member of the women's executive committee of the DNVP; Else von Sperber, active in rural housewives' associations, also represented the DNVP in the Reichstag from 1924–8; the DNVP was represented by two housewife-activists in the Prussian state parliament, Elsa Hielscher-Panthen and Therese Deutsch, for most of the Weimar period; and Milka Fritsch, a leading housewife activist, also represented the DVP in the Reichstag in 1923–4.

were less radical.[15] Thus, working-class women tended to prefer the Social Democrats to the Communists, and bourgeois women skewed toward those conservative parties that also championed religious values. Women voters tended to shun parties they perceived as radical, such as the Communist Party and (up through 1930) the Nazi Party. Instead, Protestant women voted disproportionately for the DVP and DNVP: both parties drew the majority of their votes from women, and the number of female votes that the DNVP received approached 60 percent of the party's total in some elections. Catholic women formed the bulk of the Catholic Center Party's voters, consistently providing 60 percent of that party's votes. Without the mobilization of female voters by female activists in the DNVP, DVP, and Catholic Center parties, Weimar Germany's ruling coalitions would have been considerably further to the left.[16] The overlap between the leadership of housewives' organizations and that of the DNVP and DVP – even though the housewives' associations also belonged to the women's movement – was therefore not as surprising as it might initially seem. And this overlap ensured that housewives' interests would be well represented within both right-wing parties.

Housewives' Leagues, Consumption, and the "Rationalization" of the Household

The consumer politics pursued by all three national housewives' leagues (urban, rural, and Catholic) reflected the broader conservatism of the parties with which they were affiliated. Generally speaking, all three housewives' groups tended to support the same economic policies and goals. All three groups attempted to fuse the rationalization of housework (a self-consciously "modern" stance) with economic nationalism, which stressed a protectionist approach to consumer issues. In a broader sense, all three housewives' leagues argued that "traditional" German family life and roles had been undermined by the stresses of the war, and by the subsequent growth of "immorality" under the socialist-led Weimar Republic. All of the housewives' groups

[15] Julia Sneeringer, *Winning Women's Votes: Propaganda and Politics in Weimar Germany* (Chapel Hill: University of North Carolina Press, 2002), 5.

[16] Scheck, *Mothers of the Nation*, 19–20; and Sneeringer, *Winning Women's Votes*, 5–6.

were thus vocal about trends that they saw as threatening traditional family life. These included a perceived increase in the number of women working outside the home, a decline in the status of housewives, and the steady drop of the German birth rate.[17]

Some of the most conservative leaders of the housewives' league (those who were also active in the DNVP) even compared house-wives to Cinderella, neglected and overworked, and cast professional women – who were more often profiled in popular culture as the New Women – as Cinderella's stepsisters. Bertha Hindenberg-Delbrück, who was prominent in the urban housewives' league in Lower Saxony, reflected the concerns of many housewife leaders when she wrote:

It is on of the regrettable trends of our time that so many German women, out of ignorance of housekeeping and child-rearing, seek to avoid the happiness that a healthy woman receives from [bearing] a child. When one observes today's woman, who is externally masculine, with short hair and cigarettes...one might well fear for the future of the German people.... [Such women are responsible] for the destruction of unborn life [abortions], which are per-formed in such numbers that these losses now exceed all the deaths in the Great War.... [Housewives] must wish that their fellow women would not work in offices so much, but rather should be trained for their real profession as housewives and mothers.[18]

But at the same time, the consumer politics of these Weimar house-wives' organizations (particularly the urban and Catholic housewives' leagues) were strongly influenced by the "rational" model of house-wifery and consumption offered by American home economists such as Christine Fredericks. They hoped that the "rationalization" of house-work could reduce housewives' workload, and also improve their image, by recasting them as professional, indeed scientific, house-hold managers. The combination of "rationality," a desire to uphold

---

[17] For more on the broader politics of housewife leaders and other female activists within the DNVP and DVP – which focused on "threats" to the social fabric and family life, and urged a return to religious and nationalist values – see Scheck, *Mothers of the Nation.*

[18] From a report on a speech given by Hindenberg-Delbrück, dated Sept. 15, 1926, in NH Hann 320 I, no. 22. For other examples of the Cinderella motif used to describe housewives compared to working women, see the letter from Hindenberg-Delbrück to Franziska Wiemann, dated Nov. 22, 1926, in NH Hann 320 I, no. 45; also see her article, entitled "Die Hausfrau," in the Sonder-Beilage of the *Hannoverscher Kurier,* May 5, 1929.

women's role as housewives, and economic nationalism would gener-
ate an often complex response to consumer policy questions, and to
broader questions of domesticity and family life.

American home economist Christine Fredericks (who was translated into German) and her German disciples, especially Dr. Erna
Meyer (author of the best-selling advice manual *The New Household*) attempted to apply Taylorism – especially in the form of time
and motion studies – to the household, by teaching "scientific management" to housewives.[19] Advice literature (in magazines, books,
and government publications) and the emerging discipline of home
economics thus publicized the American model of housework and
consumption within Germany. Members of German housewives' organizations also traveled to America during the 1920s to observe U.S.
households firsthand, and published accounts of their experiences.
These first-person reports indeed became something of a genre in
housewives' groups' publications during the 1920s.[20] Their reaction
to rationalized American housework was generally positive, but they
were sometimes made uneasy by consumption patterns that they perceived in American housewives, which they felt could undercut German
notions of domesticity.

---

[19] For the ways that Germans perceived America during the 1920s, and how the American model influenced German rationalization, see Nolan, *Visions of Modernity. American Business and the Modernization of Germany*. For the movement to rationalize
German housekeeping in general during this period, see Schlegel-Matthies, "Im Haus
und am Herd," 153–90; Hiltraud Schmidt-Waldherr, "Rationalisierung der Hausarbeit in der zwanziger Jahren," in Gerda Tornieporth, ed., *Arbeitsplatz Haushalt.
Zur Theorie und Ökologie der Hausarbeit* (Berlin, 1988), 32–54; Barbara Orland,
"Emanzipation durch Rationalisierung? Der 'rationelle Haushalt' also Konzept institutionalisierter Frauenpolitik in der Weimarer Republik," in Dagmar Reese et al.,
eds., *Rationale Beziehungen? Geschlechterverhältnisse im Rationalisierungsprozess*
(Frankfurt: Suhrkamp, 1993), 222–50.
[20] Housewives' organizations published numerous accounts by these observers in their
yearbooks and magazines, as did professional home economists. Some examples
include Lissy Susemihl-Gliedemeister, "Über amerikanische Frauentätigkeit," in the
1929 *Jahrbuch des Reichsverbandes Deutscher Hausfrauenvereine*, 141–55; articles
in *Die Deutsche Hausfrau* 12 (1927): 74 and 13 (1928): 17, 52, 88, and 122; articles
in *Hauswirtschaftliche Jahrbücher* 2 (1929): 23; 3 (1920): 65; and 4 (1931): 104.
For a discussion of the ways in which the United States was seen as a model for the
future of German consumption, particularly with regard to appliances, see Martina
Hessler, "Die Einführung elektrischer Haushaltsgeräte in der Zwischenkriegszeit –
Der Angebotspush der Produzenten und die Reaktion der Konsumentinnen," *Technikgeschichte* 65 (1998): 297–311.

To German home economists, government officials, and housewives' organizations, *rationalization* was defined primarily as the rearrangement of the workplace and reform of work methods according to time-and-motion studies. The housewife's workplace was above all her kitchen, the production site for meals. Housewives' associations and home economists urged that German kitchens be reduced in size and reorganized, to save the housewife from unnecessary steps and motions and to make cleaning easier. Examples of the new, smaller kitchen were depicted and propagated repeatedly in housewives' magazines, in special exhibits, and in home economics journals. Much of the new, government-sponsored housing built during the 1920s included such kitchens, and housewives' groups worked together with architects, government officials, city planners, and interior decorators to design new public housing and promote "reformed" home décor for the middle and working classes (which Germany invested in more heavily than did the United States during this period).[21] Experts also studied housewives' work methods (in dusting, mopping, etc.), and the government's National Productivity Board published booklets and posters that showed easier, simpler, and more efficient ways for women to accomplish these tasks.[22]

Most supporters of rationalization agreed that the new homes and kitchen/workplaces would not include the consumer durables (washing machines, vacuum cleaners, electric or gas stoves, refrigerators) that were allegedly ubiquitous in American households as a core component of American domestic rationalization. German industrialists and government officials argued that Germany was simply too poor

---

[21] See the article on the Frankfurt kitchen exhibition in *Die Deutsche Hausfrau* 12 (1927): 68; Schlegel-Matthies, *"Im Haus und am Herd,"* 155–73; Nancy Reagin, "Die Werkstatt der Hausfrau: Bürgerliche Frauenbewegung und Wohnungspolitik im Hannover der Zwanziger Jahre," in Adelheid v. Saldern and Sid Auffahrt, eds., *Altes und neues Wohnen: Linden und Hannover im frühen 20. Jahrhundert* (Hanover: Seelze-Velber, 1992), 156–64. For the alliances between housewives' groups and other cadres of experts, see Adelheid v. Saldern, "Social Rationalization of Living and Housework in Germany and the United States in the 1920s," *History of the Family* 2 (1997): 73–97. The "rationalization" of domestic architecture, and of the kitchen in particular, had also long been promoted within the context of cooperative housing arrangements by socialist feminists (e.g., Lily Braun) and socialist architects.

[22] These time-and-motion studies were sponsored and publicized by the Home Economics Group of the National Productivity Board.

to copy the comparatively high wages and widespread ownership of durable goods that characterized American society.[23] The majority of households (i.e., working-class families) simply could not afford these appliances, although many bourgeois housewives could. A 1928 study of Berlin found only 45 percent of all households had electricity; of these, 56 percent had electric irons (by far the most popular of the "new appliances" nationally), 28 percent had vacuum cleaners, and only 0.5 percent had washing machines. In America, by contrast, 76 percent of homes with electricity had irons, 30 percent had vacuum cleaners, and 26 percent had washing machines.[24] The German version of domestic rationalization – at least, the version intended for the working class – with its reorganized kitchens and dearth of labor-saving appliances, has been called an "austere vision of modernity," certainly a fitting characterization for urban working-class households.[25]

Certainly, a lavish "modernization" of the household was not in the cards for most rural housewives. A decline in the availability of maids during this period to work in the dairies, gardens, and homes of rural households meant that agricultural housewives were even more over-burdened than they had been during the prewar period. Rural house-wives' associations therefore assumed that members were interested in household rationalization only insofar as time saved on housework proper could be freed up for more work in the fields and dairy. But as in working-class homes, the modernization involved was to be done on the cheap. Most male heads of rural households were unwilling to invest in electrical appliances (and the cost of the electricity to run them) that would be used only in the kitchen, although the farm might be able to acquire machinery for the fields.

---

[23] Nolan, *Visions of Modernity*, 216; Schlegel-Matthies, "*Im Haus und am Herd*," 171–3.

[24] The results of the entire study are given in Schlegel-Matthies, "*Im Haus und am Herd*," 173. For the popularity of irons in particular, see Herrad U. Bussemer, Sibylle Meyer, Barbara Orland, and Eva Schulze, "Zur technischen Entwicklung von Haushaltsgeräten," in Gerda Tornieporth, ed., *Arbeitsplatz Haushalt. Zur Theorie und Ökologie der Hausarbeit* (Berlin: Dietrich Reimer Verlag, 1988), 122. The spread of ownership of appliances was hindered not only by their cost, but by the high price of electricity. Still by the late 1930s, a percentage of homes that owned vacuum cleaners and irons had increased substantially. See Hessler, "Die Einführung elektrischer Haushaltsgeräte," 300.

[25] Nolan, *Visions of Modernity*, 207.

The 1930–2 diary of Marianne Lantzsch, the daughter of a prosperous farm family outside Dresden, reflects these priorities. Her family's farm did have electric lighting and a powered water pump, but no electric stove or kitchen appliances for the women of the family. The main cleaning tools that she and her female relatives used were buckets, rages, brushes, and water. In fact, like their Wilhelmine predecessors, they spent relatively little of their time doing "housework," as an urban woman would have defined it. Instead, they spent most of their waking hours doing dairy and livestock work, or working in the fields and garden, along with some baking, mending, and food production (e.g., producing sausages) for the household. Her farm did acquire a radio (which could be enjoyed by all family members) in 1930.[26]

The sorts of housework rationalization offered to farmwives by the rural housewives' league therefore tended to focus on time-motion studies and the reorganization of rooms in order to save steps and effort, rather than on the acquisition of new household appliances. The time saved was clearly supposed to be devoted to increasing agricultural production and the farm's income. And the courses offered to members generally focused on their work as agricultural producers, not as homemakers. Although cooking courses for young rural women were popular (as indeed they seem to have been throughout Germany, both before and after the Weimar period), the bulk of the courses and programs offered by the agricultural housewives' federation tried to train rural women as producers, not consumers: courses on sorting and packing fruits and vegetables; programs on the quality control and pricing of eggs; along with a great deal of information on gardening and poultry work.[27]

The more upscale vision of household rationalization, that marketed to more affluent households the lavish household exhibitions discussed in the following text, was implicitly bourgeois and urban. But in these consumer exhibitions, new products were enlisted to help realize a version of urban modernity that was still based on older norms of cleanliness and order. The rational urban household was filled with products designed to make it possible to reach high levels of cleanliness, without the support of a domestic servant: linoleum floors; a lack

[26] Jones, "Gender and Agricultural Change," 212–17.
[27] Ibid., 193–8.

of "dust catching" knick-knacks or elaborate furniture trim; sectioned mattresses (which could be more easily removed for frequent beating) produced in standardized sizes; and smaller "work kitchens," which were designed to save time and effort in cleaning and cooking. German industries worked with housewives' groups and the National Productivity Board to create standardized utensils and canning products, so that housewives could stock their pantries with their own preserves and produce more easily. And these new products were supposed to be acquired in addition to the goods that had always signaled bourgeois domesticity: china, cutlery, and a full cabinet of linens.

Housewives' associations advocated more expensive goods and consumer durables for their (bourgeois) members, while endorsing a variety of smaller "rationalized" products for all households. These included the standardized products that were promoted by the National Productivity Board and the German Standards Committee, ranging from pots and utensils to mattresses, which were designed to be more efficient, easier to clean, or more durable. Housewives' groups also helped popularize products with "modern" design or materials, such as the new Jena glass cookware, along with the sleek, simplified furniture and interior design developed by the Bauhaus movement and others during the 1920s.[28]

The Americanized vision of household modernity – both austere and expansive versions – assumed tangible form for consumers in hundreds of large and small exhibits mounted by housewives' associations during the late 1920s. The largest, such as the massive 1928 shows "Home and Technology" (Munich) and "Nutrition" (Berlin) were created in conjunction with government, business, and industry, and were reviewed and publicized in newspapers and magazines nationwide. Parts of both exhibits were subsequently combined to create a "traveling exhibit" that visited a series of German cities. Even a mid-sized exhibit, such as the "Blue Apron" show created by Düsseldorf women's associations in 1930, could attract fifteen thousand visitors in a month. In smaller cities and towns, local housewives' associations created their

---

[28] See, e.g., Klara Neundörfer, *Haushalten* (Königstein im Taunus: Verlag der Eiserne Hammer, 1929); Ludwig Neundörfer, *Wie Wohnen?* (Königstein im Taunus: Verlag der Eiserne Hammer, 1928; "Gute und schlechte Formen im Haushalt," *Frauenland* 20 (1927): 78. For the work of National Productivity Board, see Nolan, *Visions of Modernity*, 214–15.

own shows, or contracted with firms that specialized in producing these exhibits. In return for the housewives' endorsement, promotion, and donated materials, these firms organized the shows using their own exhibits (along with material from local businesses) and gave the local housewives' association a share of the proceeds.[29]

These exhibits showcased every aspect of household rationalization, including model kitchens, living rooms, bedrooms, and bathrooms. For households with different income levels the largest exhibits would provide several models for every room. Visitors could see demonstrations of the new household appliances that used electricity or gas, along with information on the cost of using these products. In some shows, entire kitchens or laundry rooms from the United States stood alongside German models. Bedrooms and living rooms reflected the new style of interior decoration. In many shows, visitors could also purchase the displayed appliances and furniture. Most shows also stressed rational nutrition, which urged the consumption of more fruits and vegetables, and included cooking demonstrations offering visitors a taste of these healthier dishes and distributing recipe booklets. Other rooms might include materials on rationalized methods of housework or shopping.[30]

Exhibits on the "new household" were usually organized by housewives' groups, but other women's associations (e.g., confessional or teachers' organizations) would hold annual conventions in conjunction with such exhibits to offer their members special tours of the shows. In many cities, pupils from domestic science classes toured the exhibitions. City dwellers came by the thousands, attracted by free food samples, discount coupons, and opportunities to buy the latest gadgets. One critic remarked that the atmosphere of the exhibits often resembled annual fairs.[31] These shows ensured that many (if not most) urban housewives would have been exposed to the vision of the modern

---

[29] See *Der Haushalt als Wirtschaftsfaktor. Ergebnisse der Ausstellung Heim und Technik* (Munich, 1928); *Frauenwirken in Haus und Familie. Die Ausstellung der Düsseldorfer Frauenverbände. Rückblick und Ausblick* (Düsseldorf, 1930). *Die Deutsche Hausfrau* also regularly carried reports on these shows, large and small, from all over Germany. See the correspondence between housewives' associations and firms specializing in these shows in Niedersächsisches Hauptstaatsarchiv (hereafter, NH) Hann 320 I no. 47, and in the archive of the Katholischer Deutscher Frauenbund (hereafter, AKDFB), files 1–74–4 and 1–74–5.

[30] See *Frauenwirken in Haus und Familie* and *Der Haushalt als Wirtschaftsfaktor.*

[31] See the critical article in *Deutsche Hauswirtschaft* 21 (1936): 114.

household, even if their daily reality did not include its technology. Rationalized housekeeping was also incorporated into domestic science classes during this period, both those offered in public schools (in increasing numbers) and those offered by private employers to female employees.[32] This trend in home economics education ensured that the new approach to housekeeping would be transmitted to the younger generation.

The rational shopping habits that housewives' organizations advocated, however, reflected the ambivalence that these associations felt toward mass production and the American model of the consumer society. Housewives' associations had class investments that led them to defend small retailers and artisans (the backbone of the middle class – and key constituencies of the conservative parties) from the threat posed by department stores, one-price stores, consumer cooperatives (affiliated with the socialist labor movement), and chains of larger retailers. Many members of housewives' associations were married to small businessmen or craftsmen. Housewives' associations therefore often denounced the "cheap" quality of mass-produced goods (*Dutzendwaren*), and reminded their members that small retailers could give better advice and more personalized service. Articles that their magazines published on consumer issues also showed strong distrust and dislike of the advertising and promotion that accompanied mass production. Similar to home economists, housewives' associations stressed repeatedly that "the most expensive product is still the cheapest" over the long run, because it would last longer, and advised readers to buy the best quality that they could possibly afford (which implicitly meant buying from craftsmen).[33]

Although they rejected department stores, housewives' groups still sought to empower the housewife/consumer in her dealings with retailers and artisans through increased knowledge about commodities (*Warenkunde*). The housewife's skill at shopping, the result of detailed education about the qualities and attributes of products, would help equalize the relationship between merchants and consumers, and

---

[32] For the increase in the number of rationalized home economics courses offered by employers, see Nolan, *Visions of Modernity*, 216–18.

[33] The saying "the best is still the cheapest" apparently predated World War I and was picked up on by housewives' organizations; the strong preference for "quality" in consumer goods is still very much evident in German discussions today.

housewives' organizations tried to educate their members in meetings and publications. Because housewives did not always have the time to acquire this knowledge, however, housewives' associations went further. The urban National League of German Housewives' Associations created a center to test consumer products in 1925. Producers could submit their products, which were tested for durability, cost of operation, and ease of use. Those that the center judged worthy could carry the League's symbol (a sun stamp) on their products and advertising. Home economists and housewives' magazines advised women to "look for the sun symbol" when shopping.[34] In many larger cities, housewives' organizations established advice centers with permanent exhibitions on the "new household," where consumers could obtain information about new products. The largest and most elaborate was the so-called *Heibaudi*, which advised over fifty thousand consumers in 1932.[35] Housewives' organizations and home economists also emphatically and consistently warned housewives against the use of credit or buying on time. Paying cash, they argued, put the housewife/consumer in a stronger position vis-à-vis merchants. All of these policies were attempts to strengthen the position of housewives because small retailers and artisans derived much of their authority from their specialized knowledge about products and their control over access to credit.

The industries that produced household goods (e.g., Siemens, for electronic appliances, or Schott, which manufactured Jena glassware) worked with the German Standards Committee and the urban and Catholic housewives' leagues to market their goods to German women. They lent or donated samples to housewives' exhibitions, agreed with new norming standards for the size and shape of products, and sought (and publicized) the seal of approval that their goods could get from housewives' testing centers. Overall, this was a loose partnership

---

[34] The testing center was publicized in almost all advice literature and housewives' magazines and often had a booth at the larger household exhibitions. See, e.g., Erna Meyer, *Der neue Haushalt. Ein Wegweiser zur wirtschaftlicher Hausführung*, 2nd ed. (Stuttgart: Franckh'sche Verlagshandlung, 1926), 152. For the background and operating procedures of the testing center, see Schlegel-Matthies, *"Im Haus und am Herd,"* 194–6. The center was modeled on the American Good Housekeeping Institute and was the first of its kind in Europe.

[35] *Heibaudi* stood for *Hauswirtschaftlicher Einkaufs-Beratungs-Auskunftsdienst*; see the article on it in the 1928 *Jahrbuch des Reichsverbandes Deutscher Hausfrauenvereine*.

between particular governmental agencies, bourgeois housewives' groups, and industries to promote new sorts of consumption: a bourgeois style of domesticity that was hygienic, orderly, rational, and modern.

Economic Nationalism and the Politics of Food

The consumer education of housewives' organizations included much more than just the promotion or evaluation of new technology and household rationalization. Much of their work in this area, perhaps even the bulk of it, was concerned with the more fundamental consumption issue of food. Housewives' associations had been originally created during the war to deal with issues relating to foodstuffs, and food politics were among these organizations' chief preoccupations. Leaders of housewives' groups acknowledged that not all households could afford durable goods, but all households had to purchase food: foodstuffs were therefore the area where they hoped to have the most impact on consumers' purchasing decisions. These organizations' exhibitions thus always devoted considerable space to cooking demonstrations and recipe distribution within the model kitchens; their advice centers included rotating exhibitions on nutrition and cooking; and their publications devoted as much space to food choices as they did to rationalized housework. But although they paid as much (or even more) attention to apples than they did to vacuum cleaners, their discussions of food still expressed the full range of anxieties and aspirations that the new consumer society evoked, and consistently urged a program of economic nationalism.

The most important fears and hopes in housewives' discussions about food centered on the promotion of "German" foods and the rejection of imported foodstuffs. This was part of the general support for protectionism predominant during the 1920s, and it reflected the anxiety that "unrestrained" consumption would undermine traditional social hierarchies. Buying German foods would help protect German farmers above all, but housewives' associations also linked German foodstuffs to more traditional diets, life-styles, and domesticity. Housewife leaders also associated buying foreign foods with the same lack of "social responsibility" that led many housewives to desert local businesses and artisans for department stores or chains. Housewives' economic nationalism also reflected their close alliance with the rural housewives' league, whose members demanded protective tariffs especially for "women's sphere of agriculture – milk products, poultry, eggs, fruit, and vegetables."[36] Throughout the 1920s, urban housewives' associations worked with German food producers to try to influence housewives' choices of products. In the process, they helped further develop categorizations of food begun during World War I, in which products were assigned ambivalent and conflicting attributes. They continued to promote rationalization, which stressed abundance in some areas (e.g., the acquisition of durable goods). Protectionism, however – usually conceptualized as "socially responsible" or patriotic consumption – was an even higher priority.

Some of the foodstuffs that housewives' organizations tried to promote were the same products they had stressed during World War I, because wartime autarky had relied on the same products that protectionism singled out in peacetime: potatoes and dark bread. Large sections of Germany's arable land supported rye or barley crops better than wheat. To be "self-sufficient" in grain, therefore, and support local farmers, German consumers would have to eat breads made with rye flour, and utilize the wheat that Germany had to the fullest by eating whole wheat bread. German consumers, however, shared the almost universal Western preference for lighter (or white) wheat breads, with their crisp crusts and connotations of luxury.[37] Housewives' organizations thus joined agrarian interests in promoting rye as the "patriotic" grain. They distributed booklets and presented slide shows to their members that explained how rye bread had more fiber, was more nutritious, and helped save German farmers. Wheat bread, especially the light rolls (*Brötchen*), ought to be seen as luxuries, and reserved for occasional use only. Housewives' associations promoted "rye days," and when a delegation from the housewives' National League met with President Hindenburg in 1928 (in conjunction with the opening of a large exhibition), the league's magazine later noted that President Hindenburg praised the league's promotion of rye. Hindenburg stressed

[36] Bridenthal, "Organized Rural Women," 401.
[37] The preference for white bread was widespread and widely bemoaned by social reformers, who simply could not understand why workers preferred the (less nutritious) white bread and rejected the cheaper foods associated with poverty.

that he ate only rye bread and proclaimed that "a patriot eats rye bread," a point that housewives' groups stressed repeatedly in their consumer education.[38]

Housewives' organizations went beyond the products promoted during World War I in their consumer education. Some of their most passionate rhetoric attacked the so-called southern fruits (*Südfrüchte*): imported tropical fruits, especially bananas and oranges. Housewives' publications repeatedly denounced mothers who bought oranges and bananas for their children, arguing that these imports hurt German farmers and Germany's balance of trade; tropical fruits were labeled unnecessary luxuries. Housewives' organizations recognized that Germany's climate did not supply local fruit year round, but argued that a conscientious housewife would buy German fruits in season and put them up or store them in her cellar over the winter. Magazines for housewives and advice literature published articles telling women about the various ways to store and preserve different sorts of local produce: putting them up in jars, storing them in bins, and layered among straw or sand. Hard work and thrift – mainstays of prewar discussions of proper German domesticity – were implicit in these discussions of household management and food choices.

Rural women kept and preserved some of what they produced, but many small town and urban women also went through annual routines of "putting up," drying, canning, or otherwise preserving jam, sauerkraut, beans, fruit, carrots, and so forth for their families' needs each winters. Often, the women grew the food in their own small garden plots, or even simply put up produce that they had bought in season at the market. One woman interviewed decades later recalled that she had filled five hundred glass jars each summer, and usually put up two hundred pounds of "spreads" (jams or other bread spreads) each year. "I think about this now that I am old," she added, "and I wonder: why did we work ourselves so hard? Why? We could have taken things a bit

---

[38] Promotion of rye bread was a regular theme in housewives' publications. For the meeting with Hindenburg, see *Die Deutsche Hausfrau* 13 (1928): 92–3. For an example of a "rye day," see *Die Deutsche Hausfrau* 15 (1930): 56. For correspondence with agricultural interests and examples of the protectionist propaganda distributed by housewives, see AKDFB, file 1–70–2. The promotion and government protection of rye had a long history, stretching back into the Wilhelmine period, when the Emperor had endorsed rye as the "patriotic" grain.

easier, and our families wouldn't have starved."[39] But homemade preserves were seen as healthier, better-tasting, and were also being touted
as more patriotic; many women simply accepted this as a normal part
of their work loads.

Housewives who avoided putting up or storing produce and who
chose instead to buy imported fruits during the winter were stigmatized
as being simply lazy and unpatriotic. Apples were particularly praised
as "the German fruit," and frequently juxtaposed against bananas or
oranges. One 1927 article in *Die Deutsche Hausfrau* criticized lazy
housewives who "shy away from the small efforts that are necessary
when apples are stored in the cellar": checking stored apples daily,
turning them regularly, and using up those that were going bad. "That
is why many housewives prefer oranges," the author concluded angrily,
"it is simply easier for them to buy as many as they need at the
moment."[40] Other writers combined the rejection of tropical fruits
with the recurrent distrust of advertising, blaming the promotion of
tropical fruits by the advertising industry. "'Eat bananas' scream hundreds of alluring advertisements at us," wrote one author in *Frauenland*, the Catholic Housewives' Union magazine, "is it any wonder,
then, when we fall victim to this unscrupulous advertising?"[41] The
most conservative members of the housewives' movement, such as the
DNVP activist Martha Voss-Zietz, even yearned for a more authoritarian solution to the insidious appeal of tropical fruits, praising the
Italian fascist leader Benito Mussolini for his restrictions on foreign
food imports and concluding "how can a responsible citizen today not
wish for a man like Mussolini, who ends with a stroke of the pen the
import of bananas and teaches Germans to eat German apples...?"[42]

---

[39] See this interview and other women's comments on the "norm" of extensive food
preservation each year in Bärbel Kuhn, *Haus-Frauen-Arbeit*, 82–4.

[40] "Hausfrauen, kellert Äpfel ein!," *Die Deutsche Hausfrau* 12 (1927): 168–9.

[41] "Eine Lücke in der Front! Betrachtungen zum Auslandskonsum," *Frauenland* 23
(1930): 188. Articles and other material that denounced purchasing imports, including
tropical fruits, were ubiquitous in housewives' publications. See, e.g., the articles
in *Die Deutsche Hausfrau* 11 (1926): 177; 12 (1927): 116; and 13 (1928): 179; in
Frauenland 23 (1930): 185 and 242 and 24 (1931): 130 and 194. For the discussions
within housewives' organizations about tropical fruits, see AKDFB 1-73-3 and NH
Hann 320 I no. 79, vol. 1.

[42] Martha Voß-Zietz, "Kauft deutsche Waren!" *Frauenkorrespondenz* 12, no. 3, January
16, 1930, quoted in Scheck, *Mothers of the Nation*, 118.

Maria Jecker (a leader in the urban housewives' league) also approvingly cited Mussolini's prohibition on imported bananas in Italy, and told her organization's members that "not a single banana or orange must appear on the table of a German housewife, so long as the beauty of German fruits beckons [in the marketplace]."[43]

Housewives' organizations also championed butter, although the politics of butter consumption were more complex and problematic than those of other foodstuffs. Butter had been heavily coveted during World War I, particularly among the bourgeoisie. The distribution of butter had been one of the most hotly debated issues during the war, while margarine had been one of the ersatz foodstuffs promoted in its place.[44] Butter, once again widely available, was thus a symbol of peacetime and normalcy. It was also produced in Germany and was seen as a "natural" product. By contrast, many housewife/consumers viewed margarine with suspicion, because of its "unnatural" and dubious ingredients. Its national provenance was also questionable because even if it was manufactured in Germany, it was made out of imported raw materials (including whale blubber and coconut oil). Some of the best-known brands, moreover, (such as *Sanella*) were owned by foreign corporations.[45] However, housewives' organizations could not simply promote the use of butter over margarine – as they did apples over oranges – because Germany imported a great deal of butter: Danish butter in particular was widely preferred. And leaders of housewives' associations were aware that many households could not afford butter, which cost about twice as much as margarine.

Housewives' groups could and did appeal to their members to buy German butter rather than Danish butter. To substitute for margarine and to aid German dairy farmers, housewives' organizations also began to promote a dairy product called *Quark*, a sour sort of curds made from the milk leftover from butter production. Unknown to many German consumers during the 1920s, and unavailable in many areas, *Quark* was used as a bread spread (in place of butter or margarine) or to make desserts. Both of the larger housewives' organizations, working

---

[43] See the reprint of a 1927 talk given by Jecker in BA R 8083 Bd. 8, Werbeschrift.
[44] For a discussion of the psychological significance of butter to German consumers, see Davis, *Home Fires Burning*, 97–102.
[45] See the correspondence of the Catholic Housewives' Union regarding margarine in AKDFB, file 1–74–5.

with the German Dairy Board, pushed it enthusiastically. Housewives' groups distributed samples of *Quark* to their members, to familiarize them with its taste, along with recipes that used *Quark*; they also lobbied local retailers to carry it.[46] These promotional campaigns, which the National Socialists carried forward after 1933, apparently established *Quark* as a product. It is a staple foodstuff in Germany today.

Finally, housewives' organizations worked with the fishing industry to promote the consumption of fish, especially herring. Fish was not promoted in competition to any foreign foodstuff, but rather advocated in order to protect the jobs of fishermen and the German fishing industry. Housewives' organizations distributed recipes and flyers promoting fish consumption, and sent some of their members to courses sponsored by the industry so that they would be trained in cooking unfamiliar varieties. Course graduates returned home to teach fellow housewives.[47]

Fish, *Quark*, rye bread, apples, and German butter were promoted specifically and vehemently, while white bread, oranges, and bananas were stigmatized. Above and beyond these particular foodstuffs, German housewives' organizations also argued in their publications and exhibits that housewives had a patriotic duty to buy German. Writers frequently criticized the German consumer for being partial to foreign goods, and asserted that other nations' consumers were far more loyal to native products. A typical 1928 article in *Die Deutsche Hausfrau* bemoaned the fact:

Doubtless the German consumer still has the belief that a foreign product is more interesting and elegant. . . . [S]he who buys perfume from the firm of Coty gives money into French hands. . . . [F]oreign carpets are also unnecessary, since the German carpet industry has been producing the most wonderful carpets

---

[46] For the Catholic Housewives' Union promotion of *Quark*, see the correspondence in AKDFB, file 1–70–2. For an example of one of the articles housewives' magazines ran to publicize its use, see *Frauenland* 24 (1931): 131. The correspondence in housewives' organization files indicates that many of their members were unfamiliar with *Quark*, hence the need to distribute *Kostproben* (samples for tasting). Complaints that it was not well known or widely carried in stores persisted into the 1930s; see Bundesarchiv Berlin-Zehlendorf NS 44/35, minutes of the schooling course for nutritional advisors, Sept. 20, 1937.

[47] See the correspondence regarding fish consumption in AKDFB, file 1–74–2. See also the articles promoting fish consumption as an act of solidarity with German fishermen in *Die Deutsche Hausfrau* 11 (1926):160; 14 (1929): 44; and 16 (1931): 51.

for decades; their patterns are easy for us to understand, while the figures on a Smyrna or Persian rug require a degree in philosophy to understand. . . . [Paris fashions] are also unneeded. In Germany there is also a fashion industry; its products may be somewhat different, but they perhaps are more suited to the essence of German womanhood.[48]

Housewives' leaders urged their organizations' members to be vigilant about the national origins of everything they purchased, even flowers for the dinner table. Martha Voss-Zietz circulated an open letter to members of the urban housewives' league, asking German housewives to stop purchasing foreign flowers for their homes during the winter because this undermined German flower growers and hurt Germany's balance of trade with other nations. Indeed, she called upon all German women to refuse floral tributes from admirers if they contained foreign, exotic plants. She appealed to actresses and singers to throw back foreign bouquets that were tossed to them on the stage, promising that "all men and women whose feelings are truly and deeply German will give you warm and lasting thanks for such a public display of sacrifice, which would awaken patriotism in the souls of hundreds, even in those who have only a remnant of such feeling left in them." At home, German table settings should remain pure because "the dignity of women in today's Germany is better suited to the simple, unpretentious German winter flower."[49]

Housewives' organizations and home economists consistently linked the individual woman's purchasing habits to the national economy, making explicit the link between personal consumption and the political. They argued that if the German housewife would only buy German, then unemployment would be reduced, Germany's balance of trade would be improved, and Germany would be better able to pay the "tribute" of reparations payments imposed upon her by the Treaty of Versailles. In her housekeeping manual, *The New Household*,

---

[48] From "Volkswirtschaftliche Verantwortung der Frau bei Einkäufen," *Die Deutsche Hausfrau* 13 (1928): 179–80.

[49] See the letter by Voss-Zietz (n.d., but probably early 1922) in the papers of the Reichsverband Deutscher Hausfrauenvereine, in the Bundesarchiv, Abteilung Reich und DDR (hereafter, BA) R8083 Bd. 22, S. 108. For yet another article urging housewives to "buy German," which was characterized as being "socially responsible," see Dr. Ellen Niemer, "Was wollen die Hausfrauenvereine," in the exhibition program "Die Hauswirtschaft," copy in BA 8083 Bd. 47.

Erna Meyer even blamed the hyperinflation of the early 1920s on Germans' purchases of unneeded foreign luxuries. During the early 1920s and after 1929, many writers indeed came close to arguing that German housewives could single-handedly rescue Germany's economy.[50]

After the onset of the Depression, the "buy German" campaigns mounted by both urban and rural housewives' associations became insistent and almost incessant, as housewives' groups (allied with German industrialists) hosted "German weeks" in most areas, with displays in store windows, public skits, musical performances and plays, or parades. Perhaps assuming that the Depression ruled out the purchase of foreign rugs and fashions for most consumers, the "German weeks" focused primarily on food products. One play, "Buy German Products!," produced by housewives' groups in many cities, was set in a marketplace. In the play, the farmwomen who sold German produce there banded together with female shoppers to drive out a woman who sold bananas and oranges.[51]

The American model of consumption and housework, along with rationalization in general, was thus attractive for German housewives' organizations, but not when it conflicted with protectionism. The argument that housewives should preserve apples rather than buying oranges year round was rooted in more than simple protectionism, however. It reflected specific notions regarding the trade-off between wasting labor and wasting resources when planning housework, notions that had become well-established during the nineteenth century. When it came to foreign fruits and mass-produced imports, housewives' associations fell back upon an older, more labor-intensive vision of housework and consumption, and demanded that housewives put up or recycle foodstuffs and clothing (which took more effort, but

---

[50] See Meyer, *Der neue Haushalt*, 135. For other examples of writers who linked the average household's consumption habits to the national economy, see Cilli van Aubel, "Bedeutung und Aufgabe der Frau als Verbraucherin in der Wirtschaft," in Katholischer Deutscher Frauenbund (Hg.), *Frau und Wirtschaft. Vorträge der 11. Generalversammlung des KDF in Breslau* (Cologne: privately printed, 1931); "Hausfrau-Einkauf-Volkswirtschaft," *Die Deutsche Hausfrau* 11 (1926): 177–9; "Was-wie-wo kauft die Hausfrau?" *Die Deutsche Hausfrau* 14 (1929): 163.

[51] See the copy of the play in NH Hann 320 I no. 50; material on "German weeks" in AKDFB, file 1–73–3. For the support and publicity given to the "German weeks" by women in the DNVP and DVP, see Scheck, *Mothers of Nation*, 116–18.

saved resources and cash) rather than buying cheap, mass-produced replacements (which was "wasteful" in terms of materials, but also labor saving). This strategy made sense within the budgets of lower income households, but housewives' organizations were clearly advocating this approach for all families, no matter how well-off because the approach was seen as virtuous per se. Even for the well-to-do, "socially responsible" consumption meant choosing more labor-intensive forms of housework in some areas in order to support economic nationalism.

In this respect, the American model – otherwise viewed in generally positive terms – made observers from German housewives' groups uneasy, as they perceived what they interpreted as the "wastefulness" of American households, which they linked to rationalization. The most extreme example of this critique was a 1928 article in *Die Deutsche Hausfrau* that argued that rationalization had taught American housewives to assign a market value to their own labor, which they then included in calculations as to whether tasks were "worth" doing. When it came to washing underwear, for example, American women concluded that it was cheaper to buy new underwear rather then washing it themselves or having it washed, which supposedly led to the custom of disposable underwear. The article concluded that in America "there are no homes in our sense of the word. People simply buy cheap underwear and throw it away after they have worn it. . . . Heaven preserve us from this Americanization of the household."[52] What would the writer have thought of Pampers?

"Americanized," rationalized housekeeping was associated not only with wastefulness, but laziness and self-centeredness because American housewives allegedly spent the time they saved playing bridge, sports, and going shopping.[53] Leaders of housewives' associations explicitly

[52] See "Erwerbstätigkeit und Hausfrauengeist," *Die Deutsche Hausfrau* 13 (1928): 50–2. One can imagine what the writer would have thought of disposable diapers.

[53] For stereotypes of American housewives as unconscientious housewives who spent most of their time pursuing interests outside the home, see a series of articles by Louise Diehl (who traveled to the United States during the 1920s and published her observations in a number of magazines and newspapers), including Diehl, "Die Berufsfrau in Amerika," *Hannoverscher Kurier* Dec. 29, 1927 (Nr. 606/07) Beilage *Die Frau*; Louise Diehl, "Amerikanischer Haushalt," *Der Bazar* (clipping, n.d., in clippings file of NH Hann 320 I, Nr. 47). Such articles appeared regularly in the bourgeois women's press during the Weimar period. Examples include Lissy Susemihl-Gliedemeister, "Über amerikanische Frauentätigkeit" in the 1929 *Jahrbuch des Reichsverbandes Deutscher*

rejected such "mindless Americanization," and assured their members
that rationalization was only being pursued in order to allow housewives to fill a vaguely described "cultural role." As a leader of the
Karlsruhe provincial league of urban housewives wrote in 1930, the
housewives' movement was not only an economic, but also a spiri-
tual movement, and if it promoted rationalization of housework "this
should be done not in order to make the household soulless, as happened in America, but free the housewife's energies for the great cultural tasks which are laid upon her as the 'priestess of the hearth' [a
characterization popular since the nineteenth century, which evoked
Germanic tribal imagery] and the carrier of German culture and tradition."[54] Other leaders within the housewives' movement agreed with
this use of free time (also using the "priestess of the hearth" image), but
added that women could also use the time gained through rationalization to have additional children, and thus increase Germany's lagging
birth rate.[55]

The preference for labor-intensive approaches to some areas of
housework was therefore a continuation of an older, prewar vision
of housewifery and domesticity, which competed with the American
model of scientific management during the Weimar period and ultimately eclipsed that model after 1933. Prewar notions of domesticity and household management resurfaced and indeed culminated in
an ideal figure, a new state certification proposed by Weimar housewives' organizations: the master housewife. Throughout the 1920s,
the Catholic Housewives' Union and the urban housewives' National
League promoted the concept of the master housewife, who was to
receive state certification after completing training, and passing a series
of examinations. They borrowed the language and hierarchy of German guilds and artisans to envision the ideal housewife.

Hausfrauenvereine, 141–55; "Hausfrau und Volkswirtschaft. Das Fiasko der Konsumfinanzierung in Amerika," in *Die Deutsche Hausfrau* 12 (1927): 74; Else Maria
Bud, "Shopping und andere Modern" *Hannoverscher Kurier* Dec. 22, 1927 (Nr.
596/7) Beilage *Die Frau*; Mrs. Emerson, "Amerikanische Ehen," *Hannoverscher Kurier*
Oct. 6, 1927 (Nr. 466/67) Beilage *Die Frau*; and Alice Salomon, "Frau und Politik in
Amerika," *Hannoverscher Kurier* July 24, 1924 (Nr. 342/43) Beilage *Die Frau*. See
also Schmidt, *Reisen in die Moderne*; Nolan, *Visions of Modernity*, 109 and 206–34.
[54] See Niemer, "Was wollen die Hausfrauenvereine," 8.
[55] For the argument that rationalization would lead to larger families, see Reagin, *A
German Women's Movement*, 230–1.

The master housewife was a woman who had taken special training courses and passed tests (as did artisans), which certified her as
knowledgeable and skilled in every aspect of homemaking. Once she
had achieved this certification, she could take on "apprentices," girls
who had finished their schooling and would now be trained for careers
as servants: ultimately, the servants would rise (marry) and become
housewives.[56] As depicted in Weimar discussions, the proposed master
housewife was an expert at saving resources (and wasting labor): she
could "make new things out of worn-out objects." She put up, canned,
or stored foods of every kind when they were in season; sewed clothes
for all family members; repaired and cut down worn clothes; ensured
thriftiness through meticulous bookkeeping; and wasted not. She was
a rationalized, state-certified version of the ideal bourgeois housewife
of the prewar period.

The proposal for the certified master housewife was closely linked
to demands for a mandatory apprenticeship in domestic service for
all young women. In practice, housewives' organizations argued that
young bourgeois women could continue the prewar practice of a year
at a domestic science school, or training in a relative's home. But many
leaders of housewives' organizations argued that young working-class
women should serve out their "apprenticeships" (sometimes called
the "home economics year of mandatory service") in the homes of
bourgeois housewives, in effect working as servants for little or no
pay. Other supporters of the "home economics year" conceded that a
year of additional domestic science training in a school might suffice.
Either sort of training would teach working-class girls about "rational"
housekeeping, the thrifty use of resources, and how to reach modern
levels of hygiene (a continuation of the prewar bourgeois suspicion
that working-class housewives did not maintain extremely high levels of cleanliness). Only through such training, as the members of a
housewives' organization pointed out to their local city council, "can

---

[56] See Bridenthal, "Professional Housewives," and "Organized Rural Women," 395–6;
Schlegel-Matthies, "*Im Haus und am Herd*," 222. The "apprenticeship" proposal –
which some supporters wanted to make mandatory for all female *Volksschule* graduates – was in part an attempt to obtain domestic servants without pay. The "master
housewife" proposal was a real bid for professional status and state certification,
based on prewar traditions of housekeeping. For petitions that described and justified the *Pflichtjahr*, see BA R 8083, vol. 14, 233.

our women reach competence in domestic science and the role of the *Hausmutter*, which will lead to the economic, physical, and moral healing of family life, and counteract the serious problems and dangers that threaten the entire life of our *Volk*."[57] Only a prewar standard of German domesticity could restore family life and, thus, save the nation.

These proposals served two purposes. First, they helped the housewives' leagues to refashion housework as a profession, and one that required training by a state-certified "master" housewife, akin to other professions or artisanal trades. The introduction of a mandatory service year would also have helped ease the shortage of servants among the bourgeoisie. Working-class women moved increasingly into service-sector jobs during the Weimar period, while the economic security of many in the middle classes had been undermined by the hyperinflation of the early 1920s. As a result, it was more and more difficult for bourgeois housewives to find or even afford domestic servants. Although the percentage of the German workforce that was female stayed broadly constant during the Weimar period (about one-third of the total), the percentage of female employees who were employed as servants fell about one-third during the period, from 16.1 percent of the total to 11.4 percent.[58] At the same time, servants were freed from the semifeudal regulations that they had worked under, and the effect of this, combined with the reduced supply of domestic servants, meant an upswing in employer-employee tensions and complaints in this sector.

An "apprenticeship" that compelled (nonunionized) young working women to be "trained" by housewives for low or no wages would have solved the bourgeois "servant problem," reinforced class distinctions, and shored up the status of bourgeois housewives. Housewives' organizations publicized and lobbied for the mandatory home economics year in localities across Germany. They apparently succeeded in some

---

[57] See NH Hann 320 I, no. 23, petition to the city of Hanover from the Arbeitsgemeinschaft für hauswirtschaftliche-hausmütterliche Erziehung, dated Nov. 24, 1925. For reports on similar initiatives launched by housewives' organizations in other cities, dating back to the prewar period, see BA NS 5/VI, vol. 6863. For the tendency of bourgeois women's organizations to use rationalization as a new vehicle to critique working-class housekeeping, see also Nolan, *Visions of Modernity*, 222.

[58] Detlev Peukert, *The Weimar Republic* (New York: Hill and Wang, 1989), 95.

cities, including Bremen and Halle, and laid the basis for a more sustained and successful campaign after 1933.[59]

Housewives and the End of Weimar

Even during the middle years of the decade, after the German currency stabilized and Germany's economy was growing, the Weimar parliamentary system had never worked smoothly or easily. From the start, a block of the electorate (25 percent in the beginning, and this share had increased by the late 1920s) voted for parties such as the Communists or DNVP and later the Nazi Party (NSDAP), which were all bitterly opposed to the Weimar regime and generally voted against the ruling coalition. Germans distributed their votes among a broad array of parties ranging across the political spectrum, which meant that it could be difficult to piece together a coalition with a majority of the Reichstag seats, with that majority still able to agree on common policies and legislation. After the beginning of the Depression, it gradually became impossible to piece together any working majority and the parliamentary system became paralyzed by September 1930.

In every election after 1928, mass unemployment and political turmoil led voters to increasingly desert moderate or centrist parties for small interest group parties or for parties on the far right or left of the political spectrum. The National Socialists were able to increase their share of the national vote from 2.6 percent in 1928 to18.3 percent in 1930, reaching a peak of 37.3 percent in the last free national election of July 1932.[60] Indeed, after the July 1932 elections, the Communists and Nazis held a majority of the Reichstag seats between them, which brought the work of the Reichstag to a stop. Street violence between supporters of different parties became common. The final series of Weimar cabinets and increasingly authoritarian chancellors ruled without Reichstag majorities, surviving only because of emergency decrees issued by the Republic's President von Hindenburg.

---

[59] See the newspaper reports on agitation by housewives' organizations across Germany and their success at forcing the introduction of a "duty year" in Bremen and Halle in NH Hann 320 I, no. 22.

[60] Hajo Holborn, *A History of Modern Germany* (Princeton: Princeton University Press, 1982), 687–8.

The DVP was unable to position itself as a viable alternative to the Nazis and far right during this period, and declined sharply in elections after 1930. The DNVP, on the other hand, ended its participation in ruling coalitions (the party had been an uneasy and critical member of some ruling coalitions during the late 1920s) and went into opposition, radicalized by its authoritarian leader, Albert Hugenburg. Hugenburg led the DNVP into an electoral alliance with the National Socialists. DNVP and Nazi representatives walked out of the Reichstag together in February 1931, and the two parties (allied with other right-wing splinter groups) formed a radical right coalition, the Harzburg Front, in late 1931.[61]

Although women in both the DVP and DNVP opposed the Nazis' approach to religion and their plans to restrict the role of women in public life (and the Nazis' refusal to nominate any women for elective office), both parties – particularly the DNVP – shared many of the National Socialists' goals. At any rate, the DVP's decline after 1930 meant that all but one of its female representatives disappeared from the Reichstag, and its voters drifted to other parties (mostly to the right). The women of the DNVP, on the other hand, generally strongly approved of the Nazis' anti-Semitism, opposition to parliamentary democracy, and their vision of a racialized *Volksgemeinschaft* (a term used to describe the imagined German "racial community"). Similar to Nazi voters and activists, most of the women active in the DNVP were ecstatic at the destruction of the Weimar Republic in March 1933.[62] As the most important study of women in the DNVP notes, "the DNVP women in this period never forgot what united them with the Nazis, namely their racialized vision of the *Volksgemeinschaft*.

---

[61] For the decline of centrist parties and the growth of parties on either end of the political spectrum, see Michael Kater, *The Nazi Party: A Social Profile of Members and Leaders, 1919–1945* (Cambridge, MA: Harvard University Press, 1983); Thomas Childers, *The Nazi Voter: The Social Foundations of Fascism in Germany, 1919–1933* (Chapel Hill: University of North Carolina Press, 1983); and Peter Fritzsche, *Germans into Nazis* (Cambridge, MA: Harvard University Press, 1998).

[62] For an account of the substantial overlap between the ideology of the DNVP and its women and that of the Nazis, and of the DNVP's support for the Nazi take-over, see Scheck, *Mothers of the Nation*, 240–7. See also Süchtig-Hänger, *Gewissen der Nation*, who argues that the women's groups within the DNVP were among the most vehement in rejecting parliamentary democracy, and that they were strong supporters of Hugenberg's radical course.

The racist message of the leading DNVP women permeated their articles, speeches, and programmatic writings. The *Deutschnationale Frau*
[the main newsletter for women in the DNVP] poured out a mass
of untranslatable *völkisch* jargon to encourage women to become the
breeders and educators of a racially conscious people."[63]

Housewives' organizations, many of whose leaders and members
belonged to the DNVP or other right-wing parties, also endorsed much
of the Nazi's program. Many leaders of local housewives' chapters were
also active within the DNVP, and thus worked enthusiastically for their
party's alliance with the National Socialists, sometimes in conjunction
with local chapters of Nazi women's organizations.[64] It is clear that
many members of the housewives' leagues must have switched their
votes from the DVP and even the DNVP to the National Socialists
after 1930 when the Nazi Party closed its gender gap, began to win as
many votes among women as men, and attracted the bulk of the votes
cast by the German bourgeoisie.

Because many leaders within the urban and rural housewives'
leagues were now part of the radical right opposition to the Weimar
government, they lost patience with the national bourgeois women's
movement, which was increasingly polarized. Still officially constrained to partisan "neutrality," the more liberal organizations and
women within the national women's movement made their distaste for the Nazis clear, and urged women voters to vote for parties that respected women's rights (clearly a veiled rejection of the
National Socialists). The two largest housewives' organizations no
longer wanted to be part of an umbrella group for all women, and chose
to affirm their loyalty to the Harzburg Front by resigning from the
League of German Women's Associations in 1932. Bertha Hindenberg-
Delbrück defended the decision to leave the women's movement and
predicted that

[i]n the near future we will see which group of women leaders possessed more
insight and foresight . . . [the housewives' organizations left the umbrella organization for the women's movement, the BDF] not because the goals of the

---

[63] Scheck, *Mothers of the Nation*, 247.
[64] For a detailed examination of the steady drift of houswives' organizations to the right
in one city, and their support for the Harzburg Front alliance, see Reagin, *A German
Women's Movement*, 242–7.

housewives' movement are too narrow, but rather because they are broader and aim higher than those of the BDF.... The BDF concentrates on *women*, on their importance, their rights.... The housewives' movement has concentrated from the very beginning on the *family*, the *Volk*, and the *nation*, within which the housewife takes her place as an achiever, a producer, and a servant.... On the one side [the BDF, the goals are determined by] the individual, gender and freedom (in the sense of liberalism) – on our side, organic incorporation into a natural, higher community life.[65]

There was now little that divided the rhetoric of the main housewives' leagues from that of the National Socialist women's organizations.

After the Nazis gained control of the national government in early 1933, many women who had belonged to the DVP, DNVP, and the housewives' leagues rushed to join the Nazi Party. Some were accepted as members, while others were rejected because of critical statements about the National Socialists that they had made while active for the other right-wing parties. In any case, they were not persecuted by the new regime, and most continued their work in some form after 1933. The work of the Catholic housewives' league was suspended, but both the urban and rural housewives' organizations were absorbed into their Nazi counterparts (instead of being dissolved outright, as was the fate of most of the bourgeois women's movement) and some of their leaders found new careers within Nazi organizations after 1933.[66] This was very gentle treatment compared to what was happening to organizations and individuals to the left of the political center.

There was thus a great deal of overlap between Weimar housewives' organizations and their Nazi successors, both in terms of membership and organization. And there would be substantial continuities in policy, rhetoric, and goals. In the new government, Weimar housewives' leaders finally got a regime that supported many of their goals: the restriction of tropical fruits and the continuation of autarkic consumer policies; the imposition of a mandatory year of service for young women; the certification of "master housewives"; and much more. The National Socialists picked up and carried forward much of the agenda of the Weimar right, taking forward the vision of domesticity

---

[65] Bertha Hindenberg-Delbrück, "Geistige Ziele der Hausfrauenbewegung," *Mitteilung-en des HausFrauenvereins Hannover* 7 (August 1932): 74–6 (italics in original).

[66] For the subsequent careers of many DNVP and DVP female activists after 1933, see Scheck, *Mothers of the Nation*, and Süchtig-Hänger, *Gewissen der Nation*, 362–84.

and housewifery promoted by housewives before 1933. Nazi organizations that dealt with women and family policy would have new and varied sorts of compulsion and persuasion at their disposal, however, as they racialized and expanded the scope of Weimar domestic science programs and policies. The result was that an older vision of German domesticity (now further racialized and often compulsory) was implemented on a broader scale than its creators could have ever imagined.

4

Domesticity and *Volksgemeinschaft*

The master housewife's training... will enable her to manage a household that will be a model for others, and that will be an example of how to fulfill [a housewife's] obligations to the *Volk* and State, which are a great responsibility.

From the 1939 curriculum of a course for state-certified master housewives

The educational settlement currently houses about 60 families, who have been corrupted though drunkenness, laziness, uncleanliness, or other vices.... [The wives'] household management, particularly how clean they keep their homes, will be strictly supervised.

From a 1937 newspaper report on the Hashude settlement for "asocial" families, in Bremen

In early 1937, Frederike N.'s household was referred for incarceration in the Hashude Educational Settlement for "asocial" families by the Bremen public housing office and by the social workers who dealt regularly with the family. Like some other families who received various forms of social welfare assistance, the N. family had fallen behind on its rental payments to the public housing office, and local social workers argued that the entire family would benefit from a year-long mandatory relocation to the Hashude settlement, where Frau N.'s housekeeping and child care skills would be overseen (and forced to improve), and her husband compelled to find regular employment. Frau N. filed an appeal against the referral, but her protests were dismissed curtly by a social worker sent by the housing office to inspect the household who remarked that "order and cleanliness are unknown concepts to N. For these reasons alone, severe educational measures are warranted." The family was compelled to move to Hashude shortly thereafter.[1]

At the settlement (discussed in greater detail in this chapter) poor families were assigned to small homes built within an area enclosed within a barbed-wire fence, and their domestic life was subject to daily inspection and intervention by women from a variety of Nazi organizations. The family would not be allowed to move until the husband found gainful employment and the wife's housekeeping was considered satisfactory. Between 1934 and its closure in 1940, hundreds of poor Bremen families passed through the settlement's domestic "educational process." The women in these unwilling households were settlement officials' particular concern because, as one settlement social worker argued, "among them, there are many cases where the woman was largely responsible for the family's referral [to the settlement], whether through her disputes with neighbors, or extravagance, or her failures in character, laziness, or simply indifference [to her domestic duties]."[2]

The Hashude Educational Settlement was unique: social welfare officials in Nazi Germany did not establish a chain of such domestic reeducation camps. But the coercive impulse that the settlement represented was present in several Nazi social policies vis-à-vis housewives (and other social groups). At the same time, the 1930s witnessed enormously increased exhortatory propaganda campaigns that attempted to "improve" German women's housekeeping, as the scale and scope of Weimar housewives' organizations' efforts were broadened and expanded. The next two chapters explore the substantial continuities between Weimar and Nazi groups' goals, along with new techniques that the regime used to reach those goals. Nazi organizations cherry picked, for their own purposes, the notions of housewifery and domesticity that had been popular among conservative housewives' groups before 1933 and incorporated many of the Weimar housewives groups'

---

[1] Staatsarchiv Bremen (hereafter, STAB) 3-W.11 no. 467.6, "Beschwerde der Ehefrau Frederike Nolte gegen die Einweisung," May 1937. See also the discussion of the Hashude Colony in Pine, *Nazi Family Policy*, 132–46.

[2] From "Fürsorge für gefährdete, unsoziale, und asoziale Familien," in *Wohlfahrtsblatt Der freien Hansestadt Bremen. Amtliches Organ der bremischen Wohlfahrtsbehörde* 7 (1936): 2.

goals and programs into Nazi social policies toward women and the family. But the scale of Nazi programs were much more ambitious and alongside the pedagogical, interventionist approaches of the Weimar period, some Nazi social polices (e.g., the Hashude settlement) incorporated coercion and intimidation.

Like all the other policy initiatives discussed in this chapter, the Hashude settlement was guided by the bourgeois standards regarding cleanliness, order, and rational housekeeping that Weimar housewives' groups, and social workers, had assiduously promoted. Bourgeois models of housekeeping had been implicit in public policies long before 1933. But in Nazi discourse and practice, the bourgeois model of the good housewife was not only impressed upon women from all backgrounds (as had been the case for decades) but also further nationalized and fused with a now-racialized notion of "Aryan" German identity. Nazi programs and policies toward housewives represented the skewed, racialized, and sometimes coercive apotheosis of the domestic practices that had originally emerged among bourgeois families in the nineteenth century. In Nazi Germany, older bourgeois notions of domesticity were now refashioned and incorporated into the National Socialist (NS) vision of the *Volksgemeinschaft*, or the racial community of all "Aryan" Germans.

The Nazi vision of German domesticity also notoriously and vigorously pursued prenatal policies vis-à-vis "Aryan" women whom the regime deemed to be "hereditarily sound" (*Erbtüchtig*). As is well known, such women were to be compelled or cajoled into bearing as many children as possible, a policy that led some Germans to cynically refer to the Mother Cross (a medal awarded to prolific "Aryan" mothers) as the "rabbit medal."[3] But the ideal German woman (as

---

[3] See Giesla Bock, *Zwangssterilisation im Nationalsozialismus: Studien zur Rassenpolitik und Frauenpolitik* (Opladen: Westdeutscher Verlag, 1986); Michael Burleigh and Wolfgang Wippermann, *The Racial State: Germany, 1933–1945* (New York: Cambridge University Press, 1991); for the pressures put on Jewish women *not* to reproduce, see Marion Kaplan, *Between Dignity and Despair: Jewish Life in Nazi Germany* (New York: Oxford University Press, 1998); Gabrielle Czarnowski, "'Der Wert der Ehe für die Volksgemeinschaft': Frauen und Männer in der nationalsozialistischen Ehepolitik" in Kirsten Heinsohn, Barbara Vogel, and Ulrike Weckel, eds., *Zwischen Karriere und Verfolgung. Handlungsräume von Frauen in nationalsozialistischen Deutschland* (Frankfurt: Campus Verlag, 1997), 78–95. For a comparison of the status and reproductive experiences of married and unmarried women in both the Nazi and postwar periods, see Elizabeth Heineman, *What Difference Does a Husband Make? Women*

Nazi organizations envisioned her) was not only fertile: she was a model housewife. Nazi-era family policies attempted to ensure that German women would run orderly, properly "German" homes. The Mother Cross embodied this combination of efforts to promote both fertility and a certain model of heterosexual domesticity: to be awarded the Mother Cross, a woman not only had to have borne at least four "hereditarily sound, German-blooded" children within wedlock, but she also had to prove herself to be "Mother Cross worthy," by being a clean, orderly, and thrifty housekeeper.[4] Beyond such propaganda, Nazi women's organizations took the domestic science training proposals and trial programs launched by conservative Weimar housewives' organizations and expanded them enormously. Thus, while the content of Nazi home economics courses was not always new, the size and scale of such courses – supported by both the Nazi Party and state – far exceeded previous efforts to train women in domestic science.

Nazi organizations also built upon earlier domestic practices in their celebration of Christmas, which further nationalized and racialized a key aspect of Christian domestic life. Like Frederika N., those who resisted or failed to maintain the norms of orderly domesticity also came under increased pressure during this period, as Nazi policy sought to punish those who were "asocial" housekeepers. And finally, Nazi women's organizations began to export all these domestic practices to ethnic German minorities abroad, as their outreach programs to *Volksdeutsche* women and girls (women in ethnic German minority groups who were citizens of Eastern European nations) promoted the same models of domesticity that were being inculcated in home economics courses inside of Germany. "German"-style housekeeping evidently entailed the same domestic practices and norms across the entire *Volksgemeinschaft*, whether inside Germany or abroad.

Training for Domesticity: Nazi Women's Organizations and Home Economics Programs

The various branches of the Nazi Party and its affiliate organizations tended to be polycratic, with overlapping, sometimes competing

---

and Marital Status in Nazi and Postwar Germany (Berkeley: University of California Press, 1999).

[4] See the discussion of criteria for awarding the Mother Cross in the following text.

agencies and bureaucracies that struggled to stake out and defend their turfs. As in other areas of social policy, therefore, a variety of NS women's agencies handled questions related to family life and housekeeping. Some of these bureaucracies absorbed the Weimar women's organizations that had preceded them if these groups had formerly been to the right of center politically (centrist and liberal Weimar women's organizations were forced to dissolve themselves soon after the Nazis came to power). The rural housewives' league was absorbed by 1935 into the Nazi agricultural mass organization, the *Reichsnährstand*, while the urban housewives' organizations were taken over by the German Women's Bureau (the *Deutsches Frauenwerk*), which was subordinate to the Nazi Women's League (*NS-Frauenschaft*).

The Nazi Women's League was intended to be the "elite" Nazi women's umbrella organization. Its leadership overlapped heavily with that of the Women's Bureau, which was to be the less selective, "mass" organization for German women. Getrud Scholtz-Klink, whom Hitler appointed *Reichsfrauenführerin* in 1934, led both organizations, which were sometimes more separate on paper than in practice at the local level. By absorbing conservative Weimar women's organizations and adding to their numbers through aggressive recruitment efforts, the combined membership of the NS Women's League and Women's Bureau grew steadily during the 1930s. By 1939, about 3.3 million women in Germany and Austria (or about 11 percent of the total female population over the age of eighteen) belonged to either the Women's Bureau or Women's League. Still, most members of Women's Bureau chapters at the local level were "passive" members, who only turned up for lectures or entertainments. But over one million of the total were fairly active members, volunteering as "block wardens" (who oversaw or mobilized women in a neighborhood), as leaders of local chapter organizations, or as volunteers who helped to run particular programs or courses.[5] After the beginning of World War II, the memberships

---

[5] For membership figures for the NS Women's League and Women's Bureau, see BA NS 44 (Reichsfrauenführung)/56, Reichsfrauenführung Jahresbericht for 1938, 11; see also Susanne Dammer, "Kinder, Küche, Kriegsarbeit – die Schulung der Frauen durch die NS-Frauenschaft" in Frauengruppe Faschismusforschung, *Mutterkreuz und Arbeitsbuch. Zur Geschichte der Frauen in der Weimarer Republik und im Nationalsozialismus* (Frankfurt: Fischer Verlag, 1981), 224; and for an overview of the NS women's bureaucracies, see Jill Stephenson, *The Nazi Organisation of Women* (London: Croom

of the various subdivisions of the Nazi Women's League continued to grow steadily.

The work of the combined leadership of the NS Women's League and Women's Bureau was divided into a number of sections, or *Abteilungen*. These were separate agencies that between them offered thousands of domestic science courses, programs, lectures, radio broadcasts, and cooking demonstrations each year, and distributed millions of pamphlets and other educational materials. The Section for the National Economy and Home Economics (*Abteilung Volkswirtschaft-Hauswirtschaft*) had absorbed the largest Weimar urban housewives' league and focused much of its efforts on consumer education, attempting to persuade German housewives to alter their cooking and shopping choices to support the regime's goals.[6] But this section also did extensive work in broader home economics training efforts, offering thousands of home economics courses in different areas and running a chain of 148 advice centers by 1938, which focused both on consumer issues and general housekeeping questions.[7]

Another division of the German Women's Bureau, the National Mothers' Service (*Reichsmütterdienst*) also ran thousands of domestic science courses each year in its Mothers' Schools. In 1938 alone, over half a million women attended classes on cooking, child care, and general housekeeping offered in the Mothers' Schools.[8] The Women's Bureau Section for [ethnic] German Women Abroad (the *Abteilung für Grenz- und Auslandsdeutschen*) cultivated contacts with ethnic German women throughout Eastern Europe (and particularly in regions that had belonged to Germany before 1918) and throughout

Helm, 1980). Gertrud Scholtz-Klink, in her tendentious apologia *Die Frau im Dritten Reich. Eine Dokumentation* (Tübingen: Grabert Verlag, 1978), 79, claimed that the combined membership of these organizations even reached six million by 1941. I am not sure that this figure is reliable.

[6] The work of this section in the area of consumer education – which mobilized housewives to support the goals of the Nazi Four-Year Plan – will be examined in Chapter 5.

[7] Pine, *Nazi Family Policy*, 82–4. Almost two million women had attended this section's cooking courses alone by 1938.

[8] BA NS 44/56, Reichsfrauenführung Jahresbericht for 1938, 40. Pine, *Nazi Family Policy*, 82–4, comments that the cooking courses offered by the Home Economics Section seemed to be more popular with working-class women because they were helpful to those on small incomes, while the Mothers' School courses were apparently more attractive to bourgeois women.

the world. Mothers and housewives also received advice and training from Nazi Party bureaucracies outside of the Nazi Women's
League. For example, the Nazi People's Welfare Organization (the NS
Volkswohlfahrt, which was responsible for most social welfare programs) maintained an Assistance Bureau for Mother and Child, which
ran a chain of almost twenty-nine thousand advice centers across Germany by 1941. In 1937, over three million people visited these advice
centers for help with infant and child care questions, household management, and all types of domestic problems.[9] A variety of other Nazi
Party and state organizations and agencies also worked in conjunction
with (and sometimes in competition with) the various sections of the
Nazi Women's League to promote a "German" model of household
management.

Mothers' Schools

The Mothers' Schools' courses were one of the largest domestic science training initiatives launched by the Women's Bureau. The shorter,
most popular version of the courses lasted twenty-four hours total
(not including assignments to be completed at home), and consisted
of two-hour sessions that were spread over six to twelve weeks. The
cost was low (between 2–5 Reichsmarks) and could even be waived for
unemployed young women. By 1939, three hundred and fifty permanent Mothers' Schools in cities across Germany offered such courses.
Rural populations were served by "mobile mothers' schools," which
exposed young women in the countryside to the sorts of "modern"
appliances and life-styles more common among the urban bourgeoisie.
The mobile schools were housed in trailers, which contained demonstration kitchens and sewing rooms, outfitted with electric and coal
stoves, hot water heaters, sinks and iceboxes, and sewing machines.[10]
For better-off women, *Internat* mother schools offered longer-term,
more intensive training in four- to six-week courses. These schools,
which were reminiscent of the pension training popular among upper-
middle-class young women in earlier periods, tried to attract the fiancés
of SS (*Schutzstaffel*, the NS quasi-military elite), SA (*Sturmabteilung* or

---

[9] Ibid., 34.
[10] See report on mobile Mothers' Schools in BA NS 44/46, "Rundfunk Anregungen für
den Monat Juni 1939."

NS storm troopers), and Army officers. They cost much more and were apparently much less popular; by 1941, only about eighteen hundred young women had taken such courses.[11]

But the shorter courses attracted a mass audience. The number of participants in such courses given in the annual internal reports of the Women's Bureau between 1935 and 1941 ranged between four hundred and fifty thousand and five hundred and fifty thousand young women per year. Thus, the total number of young women reached by the mother schools by 1943 was probably over two million.[12] By 1938, The Mothers' Service Section claimed that 20 percent of the female population in Germany over the age of eighteen had taken at least one of its courses in domestic science, infant care, first aid, or "womanly duties."[13] The courses included ideological units on "racial hygiene," along with cooking and consumer education that was in line with the consumption policies of the Nazi Four-Year Plan.

Mothers' Schools became the preferred form of outreach to women in communities where the Nazi Party had relatively few supporters before 1933: "red" working-class districts (which were heavily Socialist or Communist) and areas where the Catholic Church was very influential. Mothers' Schools offered domestic science courses within factories to working women (which were often partially financed by employers, a carry-forward of Weimar and even prewar arrangements) or compelled women who received unemployment insurance or other

[11] See BA NS 44/49, "Mitteilungen aus der Frauenarbeit," (June 1940), which includes a report on the *Internat*-style Mothers' Schools (*Reichsbräuteschulen*).

[12] Estimates regarding how many women took courses at the Mothers' Schools vary somewhat according to the source, although the total figure was certainly in the millions. Dammer, "Kinder, Küche, Kriegsarbeit," 237, concluded that about 1,140,000 women took these courses during the first four years they were offered (1934–8), while Scholz-Klink, *Die Frau im Dritten Reich*, 176, claims that 1.7 million young women were enrolled in such courses during the same period; BA NS 44/56, Reichsfrauenführung Jahresbericht for 1938, 40, says that approximately 511,000 women took Mothers' School courses in 1938, while BA NS 44/49, "Mitteilungen aus der Frauenarbeit," (June 1940), says that about 450,000 women had taken Mothers' School courses between Sept. 1939 and May 1940. Matthew Stibbe, *Women in the Third Reich* (London: Oxford University Press, 2003), 37, concluded that 1.7 million women took Mothers' Service courses by March 1939, while Pine, *Nazi Family Policy*, 76–9, says that a total of about five million young women had attended some sort of course offered by the Mother Service Section by 1941.

[13] See Dorothee Klinksiek, *Die Frau im NS-Staat* (Stuttgart: Deutsche Verlags-Anstalt, 1982), 89–90.

sorts of public aid to enroll in the Mothers' Schools. In many regions, chapters of the Mothers' Service Section were able to persuade local authorities to make the awarding of a "marriage loan" (a state incentive that rewarded young women who quit their jobs upon marriage) to young women dependent on the woman's completion of a mothers' school course. In one industrial area in Westphalia, for example, a local Women's Bureau activist was able to persuade the authorities to agree to such a requirement, arguing that district was "a Communist stronghold ... the population here is very immoral, and in need of domestic science training."[14] In the minds of Nazi Party activists, poor housekeeping was often linked to criminality, immorality, and Communism, which was inherently un-German and outside the "national community." Here, as in the criteria used to award the Mother Cross and in other policies, there was a strong linkage between domestic and sexual order and between cleanliness in the home and sexual propriety.

The curriculum of such courses incorporated the same housekeeping norms and practices that Weimar housewives' organizations had promoted: bourgeois approaches to holiday celebrations, table settings, interior décor, cleaning schedules, thrift (buttressed through detailed bookkeeping), and menu planning. Mothers' Schools offered courses in cooking; both basic and advanced sewing techniques; infant and child care; proper approaches to washing and ironing; crafts (e.g., how to make children's toys at home); and what one Mothers' Service pamphlet described as courses in "the popular practices of our *Volk* [e.g., folk songs], which will guide and encourage a woman's care for her family's daily life, for the arrangement of the home, and to a rebirth of enthusiasm for the cultural treasures of the German *Volk*."[15] In practice, courses in cooking, sewing, and washing appear to have been overwhelmingly more popular than courses on "*Volk* culture," which were few in number. The minimum goals of the Mothers' Schools planners were that a young woman who completed the curriculum "should understand how to complete the simplest chores, above all cleaning and

---

[14] See the Nordrhein-Westfälisches Staatsarchiv Münster (hereafter, NWSM), Bestand NS-Frauenschaft Westfalen Nord no. 106, Activity Reports from the Leaders of Mothers' Schools, 1935, report by Josefine Stein (dated July 13, 1935). See also Pine, *Nazi Family Policy*, 78.

[15] From BA NS 44/45, pamphlet on "Was hat das Deutsches Frauenwerk Reichsmütterdienst unseren Frauen und Müttern zu sagen?"

washing, that she should be able to keep a simple household accounts book . . . and that she knows what do to with the most important food-stuffs available on the market."[16] The supply of foods "available on the market," however, were strongly influenced by the import and export policies of the Nazi Four-Year Plan, and young women were thus being implicitly trained in menus that supported German agricultural autarky.

In the workplace, the Women's Bureau of the German Labor Front also asserted oversight over the many varied private housekeeping courses for female workers that had been a staple in many German factories since the late nineteenth century. In Berlin, for example, the Siemens Corporation had offered a small set of infant care and domestic science courses for young female employees since 1914. After 1933, these were expanded to include instruction by a Nazi Women's League teacher on the "need for genetically healthy offspring," while the cooking course was revamped to focus on the menus required to support the Nazi Four-Year Plan. As Carole Sachse notes, Siemens was "quite adaptable, in a culinary sense. From the standpoint of its management, it was all the same whether the menus used electrical appliances to prepare a 'finer' cuisine or instead relied on the meals using local ingredients, required by an autarkic nation: the main thing was that [the Siemens' appliances such as] Protos were included."[17] Between two hundred and four hundred Siemens employees took the courses each year.

But in the long term, the leaders of the Women's Bureau wanted to persuade or compel most young German women to devote much more than twelve weeks to domestic science training. Ultimately, they sought to realize their Weimar predecessors' proposal of a mandatory home economics year for all German women. Nazi pedagogical reformers argued that a year's "training" as an unpaid servant in a rural or urban household would "equip a girl for the homemaking and caretaking duties of the woman, whose job it is to look after others and to raise [children]. . . . [T]he training should focus on practical ways to serve

---

[16] From the Nachrichtendienst der Reichsfrauenführung, May 1935, quoted in Dammer, "Kinder, Küche, Kriegsarbeit," 235.

[17] Carole Sachse, *Siemens, der Nationalsozialismus und die moderne Familie. Eine Untersuchung zur sozialen Rationalisierung in Deutschland im 20. Jahrhundert* (Hamburg: Rasch und Röhring Verlag, 1990), 224–5.

other people, so that the girl progressively becomes more ready and able to call on her essential maternal qualities in order to live for others."[18]

The Women's Bureau Section for National Economy and Home Economics expanded the voluntary program created by its Weimar predecessors after 1934 by recruiting fourteen year olds who had finished the *Volksschule*, but who had not yet found employment, for placement as apprentice servants (*Anlernmädel*, or "girls in training") in rural and urban households. Initially, some districts also hoped to resocialize poor girls from "red" urban neighborhoods – and simultaneously alleviate the shortage of farm maids – by placing such girls on rural farms, which Nazi ideology insisted had a more authentically German (and conservative) domestic culture. Some of these placements appear to have terminated prematurely, when parents reclaimed their homesick daughters or slipped them money for the fare home. But the government offered tax incentives for households that took in such girls, and these pilot programs persisted and grew slowly. In the district of Northern Westphalia, for example, about fifteen hundred girls were placed in private households through this program in 1935. If a young woman stayed in her "training household" a second year, she could then take an examination (which tested her basic cooking, mending, cleaning, washing, and ironing skills) and become a "state certified household aide," which would presumably facilitate a career in domestic service. [19] Initially, the programs did not target girls from better-off families. Repeating the proposals of Weimar housewives' groups, Women's Bureau activists argued that young bourgeois women could be trained in the household of a friend or relative, as better-off housewives traded daughters and trained them in what was called a "daughter exchange program" (*Töchteraustausch*).

---

[18] Magda Tiling, ed., *Grundfragen pädagogischen Handelns. Beiträge zur neuen Erziehung* (Arbeitsbund für wissenschaftliche Pädagogik auf reformatorischer Grundlage: Stuttgart, 1934), 101–2, quoted in Dammer, "Kinder, Küche, Kriegsarbeit," 39.

[19] See NWSM, Bestand NS-Frauenschaft Westfalen Nord no. 313 (Rundschreiben der Gau, 1934–35), report on Gau activities for 1935. For reports from chapters on their efforts to place such girls in different districts, see NWSM, Bestand NS-Frauenschaft Westfalen Nord no. 340 (Monatliche Tätigkeitsberichte der Abteilung Volks- und Hauswirtschaft bei den NSF-Kreisleitungen, 1936) and no. 309; no. 340 in this Bestand contains a May 1936 report on the tests administered for "state certified household aides" in Münster.

During the first few years after the Nazis came to power, the unemployment rate among young women remained high, and in many districts there were enough unemployed young women to keep these voluntary programs going. The economy had substantially recovered by 1936, however, and labor shortages began to appear. The Women's Bureau might have faced increasing difficulties in recruiting teenagers for unpaid domestic service had the program remained voluntary. But at the same time, federal authorities began to issue decrees that sought to compel more and more young women to complete a mandatory home economics year (or at least show proof of competence in domestic science) before they pursued other educational or vocational training. In 1935, the Ministry of Education decreed that girls in secondary education had to pass a domestic science test before they could finish their schooling. A second decree from the Labor Ministry mandated that young women could not begin apprenticeships as seamstresses, laundresses, and so forth until they could show that they had been employed in a household (in some sort of domestic service position, but not for pay) for at least one year. [20]

Finally, in late 1938, the authorities in charge of implementing the Nazi Four-Year Plan issued the more comprehensive decree that the Women's Bureau had been pushing for several years: a mandatory year of service (a *Pflichtjahr*) for all young women under the age of twenty-five became compulsory in January 1939. In theory, a young unmarried woman now could not take any other job until she had served for at least one year in a rural or urban household. In practice, some were able to escape this service if they took a job in certain industries that carried an "exemption," a way to channel female labor toward industries favored by the regime such as armaments, which were crucial to the Nazi Four-Year Plan. [21] After this, the number of women in "service year" programs rose dramatically. In the *Gau* of Northern Westphalia, the number of young women in the program rose from about fifteen hundred to over twelve thousand during the first year after the decree was issued. By 1943, about 1.5 million young

[20] Ingrid Wittmann, "'Echte Weiblichkeit ist ein Dienen' – Die Hausgehilfin in der Weimarer Republik und im Nationalsozialismus" in Frauengruppe Faschismusforschung, *Mutterkreuz und Arbeitsbuch*, 44–6.

[21] See Richard Grunberger, *A Social History of the Third Reich* (London: Weidenfeld and Nicolson, 1971), 255; see also Wittman, "Echte Weiblichkeit," 45–6.

German women were completing their "service years."[22] At the same time, the needs of a wartime economy led to the breakdown of the program's original purpose: rather than being solely employed (and presumably trained) in private homes, the young women were drafted for the most varied sorts of jobs. They worked gathering wild fruits and herbs; collected household detritus for recycling; distributed ration cards; took care of the sick, wounded, elderly, and very young in a variety of institutional settings; and did household and garden work for rural housewives (who were now needed to work in the fields because their husbands had been drafted).[23]

Besides, the mandatory "apprenticeship" year, the NS women's bureaucracies also picked up and carried forward another program that had been dear to the hearts of Weimar housewife activists: training programs to produce "Master Housewives" (*Meisterinnen der Hauswirtschaft*). Indeed, the NS women's organizations went one step further, and ultimately achieved state certification for such housewives, a form of official recognition that Weimar housewives' groups had never come near to winning. Weimar organizations had often promoted the notion of the master housewife in their rhetoric and petitions, but, lacking state support, their training programs had produced relatively few graduates: by mid-1932, about 542 women had passed the private tests held by housewives' groups for "master housewives."[24] NS women's groups were able to expand the scope of such programs and to standardize their training programs nationwide, just as they had standardized other sorts of home economics courses.

The prospective master housewife was a woman who had run her own household (or worked as a housekeeper) for at least five years, and had done so in an orderly, satisfactory fashion. Preferably, she had completed some sort of secondary education (i.e., she was implicitly bourgeois or at least lower middle class), although the guidelines for NS programs stipulated that a *Volksschule* graduate could also attend

---

[22] See BA NS 5/VI DAF Zeitungs-Ausschnittsammlung vol. 6883, Hauswirtschaftliches Pflichtjahr, Statistik 1938–1943, especially the report from *Der Angriff*, dated Dec. 12, 1943.

[23] Renate Wiggershaus, *Frauen unterm Nationalsozialismus* (Wuppertal: Hammer Verlag, 1984), 45.

[24] See BA R8083, Reichsverband Deutscher Hausfrauenvereine Bestand, vol. 46, "Lehrlingswesen dargestellt auf 5 Tabellen," dated Apr. 1, 1932. The same file contains a variety of newspaper clippings from 1930–2 about the origins of the "master housewife" initiative in a number of German cities.

training courses, if she proved that she could speak and write clearly, and keep a detailed account book. Women who met these requirements could enroll in a two-year course that took five hours per week: four hundred hours of advanced training in home economics, plus additional special sessions on air raid protection measures and infant care, and assignments that had to be completed at home.[25]

The curriculum for master housewives' training was heavily based on the practices and values that had been prevalent in bourgeois households for many years, combined with Weimar approaches to the rationalization of housework and introduction of labor-saving appliances, and some additional material that reflected NS ideology and the imperatives of the Nazi Four-Year Plan. More than half of the course time was thus devoted to topics that would have been found on the curricula of courses in domestic science even before 1914: how to wash, iron, and rehang fancy pleated curtains; remove spots and stains of every description; cut down, resew, and recycle used clothing; care for silver, glass, and porcelain; clean and maintain various sorts of floor coverings and furniture; and prepare sophisticated table settings and flower arrangements (given under the rubric of "table culture"). But the courses also incorporated Weimar attempts to "modernize" housework. Housewives were taught "rational" approaches to cleaning and home décor, and were trained in how to use a variety of electronic domestic appliances.

Although much of the curriculum carried forward Weimar domestic science content, some of it was undoubtedly new and more ideologically driven. In cooking classes, time was given to Nazi Women's League guidelines on "correct" approaches to shopping and menu planning, and the ways in which housewife/consumers could support the needs and importation restrictions of the Nazi Four-Year Plan. About twenty hours were given to Nazi "racial studies" and "hereditary conditions," and ten hours were devoted to "national political schooling" (including an overview of the history of the Nazi Party, and the party's view of the Versailles Treaty and Germany's territorial claims). The "racial studies" sessions reflected the regime's focus on racist and eugenics-driven pronatalism, and stressed the need for

---

[25] See the guidelines distributed by the Berlin headquarters for the Section for National Economics and Home Economics in NWSM Bestand NS-Frauenschaft Westfalen Nord no. 309.

"racially fit" women to reproduce prolifically. Finally, pupils were given a quick introduction to large-scale food preparation ("feeding large groups," or *Massenverspeisung*), which might be useful in wartime volunteer efforts.[26]

After completing the courses, housewife-pupils had to pass a test, which led to state certification as "masters of home economics." The term *Meisterin* made the new certification seem equivalent to the guild status of a master craftsman. If housewives did not have the time to complete courses and tests, they could still achieve the secondary sort of title of the "Diploma Housewife" (*Diplom-Hausfrau*), if they had trained two "apprentices" (*Anlernmädel*) who had passed their own "household aide" certification tests.[27] Both the *Meisterin* title (with its guild associations) and the *Diplom-Hausfrau* title (which sounded like a professional certification) offered their holders a claim to status and rank; but status and prestige (to whatever degree they were thus conferred) were the courses' only benefit for housewives. Once finished and certified, these women returned to their households, and no material benefits would ensue. But like Gretel B., who took the certification course during the war, many no doubt were interested in advanced courses in cooking and tailoring, which polished their skills in these areas.[28] With the lure of state-sponsored training and certification, Nazi women's groups were able to expand the "master housewife" program somewhat before the needs of the war led to the program's contraction after 1943, but even so, nationwide the number of "state certified master housewives" probably never exceeded a few thousand.[29]

---

[26] See BA NS 44/59, Rahmen-Lehrplan für die Ausbildung von Meisterinnen der Hauswirtschaft (n.d., 1939).

[27] For the *Diplom-Hausfrau* variation, see the announcement in BA NS 5/VI DAF Zeitungs-Ausschnittsammlung, vol. 6924, NSDAP und Hauswirtschaft, article from Deutsche Allgemeine Zeitung, dated Feb. 4, 1938.

[28] See the account by Gretel B. (who seems to have taken the course simply out of an interest in cooking and sewing) in Gerda Szepansky, *Blitzmädel, Heldenmutter Kriegerwitwe. Frauenleben im Zweiten Weltkrieg* (Frankfurt: Fischer Verlag, 1986), 87–91.

[29] I was not able to locate any reliable totals for how many women completed the courses and certification tests before 1945. One 1937 press release (written by a master housewife) claimed that there were now 800 *Meisterinnen*, nationwide. Within the first two years of state certification being introduced, about 100 Berlin housewives had completed the training and tests, and by late 1941, almost 1,800 women were enrolled in the two-year training program, nationwide. The number of women who finished the

Nazi women's organizations carried forward, expanded, and further politicized all of the core domestic science programs that had been first developed by Weimar (or even prewar) housewives' associations: extensive home economics courses, advice centers, mandatory "apprenticeship" programs for teenagers, and state-certified master housewife training. The ideal of domesticity promoted by these bureaucracies – grounded in extreme cleanliness, thrift, order, and careful household planning – had changed little, although Nazi programs also wove anti-Semitism, pronatalism, support for the Nazi Four-Year Plan, and other ideological goals into the fabric of such programs. The Nazi Women's League and other Nazi bureaucracies also devised a host of other smaller initiatives that served to draw the private household into support of the war effort, or which simply served to connect daily domestic life to the broader *Volksgemeinschaft*.

Domestic Practices and the Nation

Of the smaller domestic programs that connected the household to the nation, one of the best-remembered was the so-called *Eintopfsonntag* ("One Dish" or Goulash Sunday), which received enormous publicity. One Sunday per month, German housewives were supposed to prepare a single dish (which combined meat or legumes with vegetables and starches) instead of a roast or fancier multicourse meal for Sunday dinner. The money saved by each household was later collected by Nazi groups for poorer members of the *Volksgemeinschaft*. The "One Dish Sunday" campaign was depicted in Nazi rhetoric as a unifying moment during which all members of the German nation were unified in a single *Tischgemeinschaft* or group that ate together. As one Nazi housewife enthused, on One Dish Sundays

for me, it is as if a fine, happy, strong song floated through this day, a song about the solidarity of one [German] for the other... for me, it is as if all members of the German *Volk* sat around the same table on this day.[30]

certification process before the war's end therefore probably did not exceed 5,000, and might have been lower. See NS 5/VI DAF Zeitungs-Ausschittsammlung, vol. 6929, Elfriede Gruhn, "Hauswirtschaft und Volksernährung," May 5, 1937; NS/VI vol. 6930, report in the *Berliner Bürsen-Zeitung*, Dec. 13, 1940, and article in *Völkischer Beobachter*, Nov. 26, 1941.

[30] Anna Katterfeld, *Vom Ich zu Wir. Eine Großstadtpfarrfrau erlebt den Umbruch der Zeit* (Bad Blankenberg: Harfe Verlag, 1936), 194.

The symbolic collective meal of the "One Dish," taken always on Sundays, indeed almost suggested a sort of nationalist Eucharist, a communion of Nazi Party believers.

Similarly, the "pound donation" program required each child to bring a pound of some foodstuff to his or her school at regular intervals: again, the food was distributed to poorer "Aryans." The nation also called upon women's needlework skills: the "knitting sacrifice" program pushed housewives to each knit a pair of mittens, socks, or a cap to donate to the poor. The "mending bag action" organized housewives who volunteered to do the mending for working mothers (after the beginning of World War II) who had several children. Bags of mending were collected from working mothers by Nazi block wardens or women activists and distributed among volunteers for processing. [31] Such programs helped the Nazis to gain popular credit for succoring poorer "racial comrades," and generated a variety of rhetorical depictions of housewives who worked or sacrificed for the nation in the course of their daily rounds. School books during the 1930s, for example, not only valorized hard-working housewives, but incorporated the *Eintopfsonntag* into assigned readings or, for example, depicted housewives and their daughters fetching bags of potatoes from their families' cellars for the NS Winter Help Bureau collectors. [32]

The Winter Help Bureau (*Winterhilfswerk*, or WHW) exhorted or coerced both individuals and families to donate money or goods for the poor (recipients had to be both impoverished and "German blooded") at Christmastime each year. It was one of the most important programs to promote a Nazified version of Christmas, but not the only such initiative. As we have seen, Christmas was already seen as the essential German holiday even before 1914, and had become a vehicle for the domestic articulation of national identity during the Imperial period. After 1933, the National Socialists worked to reshape Christmas celebrations for their own purposes, further politicizing its celebration. [33] The regime's efforts to Nazify Christmas were two-tiered. First,

---

[31] NS bureaucracies were endlessly inventive in creating ways to compel individuals and private households to "donate" resources to NS charitable organizations. See Wiggershaus, *Frauen unterm Nationalsozialismus*, 77.

[32] Pine, *Nazi Family Policy*, 60–72.

[33] This brief overview of "Nazi Christmas" is largely taken from Perry, "Private Life of the Nation," which offers a fascinating account of the Nazification of the holiday.

the Nazi Party promoted its own addition to the religious holiday: a "Germanic" winter solstice celebration. Beyond this, however, Nazi organizations also politicized Christmas in more pervasive and subtle ways.

The extensive winter solstice celebrations mounted in the 1930s built on prewar popular and scholarly notions of the "Yule" celebrations of pre-Christian German tribes. Long before 1914, novels, magazines, and academic publications had helped create a widely shared belief that bourgeois Christmas practices (especially the tree and its candles) continued and reflected "ancient" Teutonic tribal holiday celebrations. This popular understanding of the historical "roots" of the holiday meshed well with the Nazi emphasis on a nation grounded in "blood and soil."

The Nazis were thus able to present their solstice celebrations (an invented tradition) as a "revival" of old Germanic customs, while also echoing some Christian aspects of the holiday. NS women's and youth organizations distributed textbooks to their members, giving directions on how to stage solstice festivities (which were based on the use of fire and nature imagery) or on how to blend these practices into broader Christmas celebrations (which never mentioned the religious roots of the holiday). In some localities, the solstice was celebrated by Nazi organizations as a sort of pre-Christmas ceremony, entitled "Light in the Night." Nazi affiliate groups also commissioned the writing of new songs and carols for the solstice holiday. One song, "High Night of the Clear Stars," apparently achieved some popularity.[34]

Solstice celebrations were public festivities staged in schools by Nazi Party affiliate organizations and depicted in Nazi media productions: there is no evidence that the Nazi solstice was widely observed in private homes. But NS organizations also mounted extensive (nonreligious) Christmas programs commemorating the holiday and linking its domestic celebration to the *Volksgemeinschaft*. The WHW Christmas drive, which mobilized more than a million volunteers each year to collect and distribute holiday "gifts" to poorer "racial comrades," simply dwarfed the Weimar Christmas charity collections. Members

---

[34] For examples of texts and handouts distributed to NS women's groups, directing how to stage solstice celebrations, see BA NS 44/52, Rundschreiben 1936–9. See also Perry, "Private Life of the Nation," 225–33.

of Nazi women's and youth groups went door to door or set up what amounted to "roadblocks" in public places, partially coercing donations. The WHW drive collected over 358 million Reichsmarks alone over the first Christmas holiday after the Nazis came to power, and collections increased in scope steadily thereafter. The WHW distributed decorative badges (styled after the small *Erzgebirge* wooden tree ornaments that had become popular before World War I) to those who had already donated; wearing the badge thus protected the wearer from further importuning. The WHW badges became popular, even collectible – 169 million were distributed during the Christmas season of 1938 – and were often hung on trees along with more traditional ornaments. The WHW not only supplied decorations, but even the trees to some who could not afford one. About seven hundred thousand Christmas trees were distributed each year during the mid-1930s along with other gifts. WHW Christmas "gifts" appear to have been popular and well received, and even came to be seen as a sort of entitlement in many poor neighborhoods.[35]

Nazi women's groups staged politicized Christmas celebrations in a variety of venues that reached all classes: they performed plays in kindergartens, created public Christmas exhibitions, and organized Nazi Christmas markets in many cities. For private festivities, the Nazi Women's League distributed millions of texts that suggested ways to celebrate the holiday, including songs and plays for domestic performance; "Germanic" holiday decorations for the home; instructions for decorating and wrapping presents; and recipes for "German Christmas dishes," which made allowances for the shortages of cooking fats and eggs caused by the Nazi Four-Year Plan.[36]

The consumer industries that profited from the holiday also incorporated NS symbols into some of their products, selling tree decorations with Nazi Party insignia and swastikas, chocolate SA men for children, Christmas cards with swastikas, and Advent calendars with pictures of SS and SA men. The Nazi Party issued decrees to ban some of these products in order to control the use of their own symbols, so that these could not be appropriated by private businesses.[37]

---

[35] Perry, "Private Life of the Nation," 259–61.
[36] Ibid., 268–71.
[37] Ibid., 272–3.

But domestic Christmas practices could still be nationalized in subtle, even unintentional ways. The trees that were hung with WHW badges were often joined by a new *Volksempfänger* radio (a popular Christmas gift during the 1930s) that often sat under the tree. As families gathered in the evening to listen to the popular Christmas radio programs, the regime's broadcast featured a combination of solstice and Christmas carols, Rudolf Hess's address to the nation, and the live broadcast of ringing Christmas bells from famous cathedrals across Germany. Joseph Perry persuasively argues in his history of the holiday that "the rituals and symbols of Nazi Christmas had real resonance in numerous German households," but this politicization of the holiday was, in many respects, a continuation of the prewar notions of a German Christmas.[38] As they had before 1933, Christmas celebrations continued to articulate national identity through domestic rituals, using new media and formats and a more explicitly politicized rhetoric. But during the Nazi period, the Nazi Party's promotion of a "German" Christmas yoked Germanness together more firmly with both Christianity and "race."

"Asocial" Housewives and Nazi Public Policy

Nazi programs for housewives carried forward many aspects of Weimar housewives' groups' promotion of a specific style of household management, and Nazi Party affiliate organizations furthered the incorporation of the domestic practices of the "good housewife" into definitions of national identity. But some of their policies escalated the exhortatory tactics of Weimar home economists to compulsion. Before 1933, housewives' organizations and domestic science experts had largely relied on pedagogical methods. Social planners had used what might be termed interventionist approaches to alter behaviors, such as the separation of rooms by functions and the abolition of the older *Wohnküche* in Weimar residential architecture. But Nazi programs attempted to reach German women on a scale unknown in previous periods, through mass organizations and decrees that ultimately applied to almost all young "Aryan" women, forcing them to periods of mandatory service to the nation. And Nazi policies on the

[38] Ibid., 278.

family occasionally went even further, embracing degrees of coercion and intimidation that far surpassed those employed by Weimar social welfare organizations. The Hashude Settlement in Bremen was only one of the more extreme examples of this tendency.

The most coercive family policies were applied to "asocial" house-wives and their families. Such women were allegedly the opposite of the "good German housewife"; their poor (and "un-German") house-keeping helped to define German domesticity through implicit contrast. Housewives whose homes were not well scrubbed and orderly, whose children were not dressed in clean, well-mended clothes, and who were seen by social workers as spendthrift and lazy (and possibly immoral) had certainly always existed in Germany (as elsewhere). For decades, such housewives (if they were poor) had come under scrutiny and pressure from social workers, philanthropists, and their own neighbors to clean up their acts (and homes). But they were not explicitly placed outside the national community before 1933.

After 1933, social workers continued to scrutinize and intervene in the households of women who were "poor" housekeepers (in both senses). As the example of the selection of Mother Cross recipients (discussed in the following text) makes clear, such families were often already well "known" to authorities even before the Nazi period. Like the family of Frederike N., they had often come to the attention of local public housing offices, school authorities, social workers, district nurses, or police, because they might have been receiving some sort of social assistance or might have had minor brushes with school or police authorities. Such families often already had a file in the housing office or municipal *Fürsorge* office. Their poverty, and need for public support, had already opened their homes to local social workers' scrutiny long before 1933.

But Nazi social policy went further and began to define the national community in ways that excluded such homemakers and applied new sorts of compulsion against them. For example, Nazi officials decreed that incompetent housewives, no matter how many children they might have produced, were "unworthy" to receive the Mother Cross, whose recipients embodied Nazi notions of German womanhood. Women thus labeled as unworthy could lose their entitlement to *Kinderbei-hilfe*, the monetary supplements given to large families. In extreme cases, if their homes were truly untidy and dirty, housewives could find themselves labeled "asocial." In Bremen, such housewives were forcibly interned in the Hashude Educational Settlement. And German Jewish (and Sinti) housewives were placed outside of the *Volksgemein-schaft* by definition, no matter how clean their homes might be.

The Mother Cross program was one of the best-known (indeed, emblematic) propaganda initiatives launched by the Nazi state and one that targeted millions of German women. Conceived as a prona-tal propaganda device, the Cross – which resembled and echoed the most important military decoration for German men, the Iron Cross – could be awarded to any "German-blooded and hereditarily sound" woman who had given birth to four or more living children. The first Mother Crosses were awarded in mass ceremonies staged on the birth-day of Hitler's mother in August 1939. More than three million were distributed in 1939, and millions more were awarded before the end of the war.[39]

The process of identifying and selecting the first batch of Mother Cross recipients was an enormous task because millions of applicants had to be processed in a short period of time in order to meet the first set of deadlines set by the regime. The women who served as Nazi Party block wardens were required to identify neighbors who had borne four or more children and to help them fill out the application for a Mother Cross, although some women clearly applied on their own. But it took more than simple proof of having given birth to four children to receive the Mother Cross. The applicants' life-styles and home lives had to be investigated. For this job, authorities fell back upon the "local knowledge" of households contained in municipal authorities' files.

Each application file was circulated among a variety of municipal and local Nazi Party offices, including the police, the Health Office, and other local social welfare authorities, before being given to the Nazi

---

[39] The Mother Cross program is mentioned in almost every social history of the period and was such a notorious propaganda measure that it forms the title of some of the earliest work in German women's history (e.g., *Mutterkreuz und Arbeitsbuch*). I have drawn from a number of monographs and articles in this discussion of the Mother Cross, but am most indebted to Irmgard Weyrather's, *Muttertag und Mutterkreuz. Der Kult um die 'deutsche Mutter' im Nationalsozialismus* (Frankfurt: Fischer Ver-lag, 1993), which analyzes large numbers of individual applications for the cross. Weyrather, *Muttertag und Mutterkreuz*, 75, estimates that 4.7 million crosses were awarded by 1941.

Party chapter for final approval. Each of these bureaucratic instances could enter objections or information into an applicant's file, and sometimes did in cases where the family was already "known" to social workers or local police. These objections might then lead to a more extensive investigation or denial of the application. For some women, it would have been better if they had never been compelled by the block warden to apply because this brought them to the attention of the public health authorities who were responsible for forcible sterilizations of the "hereditarily unfit." Denial of the Mother Cross could also lead to the loss of the financial subsidies that parents of large families received (e.g., the *Kinderbeihilfe*) because "unworthy" families were ineligible for state aid.[40]

The selection criteria for the Mother Cross specified that the mothers of "asocial" families could not be given the Mother Cross, no matter how many children they had raised. Mothers could be classified as "asocial" if they were "profligate and [financially] unrestrained," as demonstrated, for example, through the "use of the *Kinderbeihilfe* to buy unreasonable luxury goods." Because expenditures would only be seen as "unreasonable" if they were made by poor families (bourgeois families could afford luxury goods without raising eyebrows), this definition assured that "asocial" families would be drawn from among the ranks of the poor. Such mothers, moreover, "are not capable of maintaining an orderly household without oversight [by social workers] because they lack a sense of responsibility, and cannot raise their children to become useful members of the *Volk*." It was "impossible" to give a Mother Cross to such women.[41]

Because millions of applications were being processed in a relatively short period of time, thousands of somewhat profligate, disorganized low-income housekeepers undoubtedly slipped past these guidelines and were awarded the Mother Cross anyway. In Hamburg, the Health Office estimated in May 1939 that its workers had to process twelve thousand applications per month, and complained that it simply could

---

[40] Ibid., 90.

[41] From the "Merkblatt für die Auslese der Mütter, die für die Verleihung des Ehrenkreuzes der Deutschen Mutter vorgeschlagen werden sollten, Anordnung des Parteikanzlei 37/39 vom 15.2.1939," in *Verfügungen, Anordnungen, Bekanntgaben, hrsg. Von der NSDAP-Parteikanzlei*, vol. 1 (Munich, 1942), quoted in Weyrather, *Muttertag und Mutterkreuz*, 59.

not keep up with the pace. Fifty-three additional clerical workers had
to be hired to process the Mother Cross files.[42] But if a family was
already "known" to social workers or other local authorities, an applicant's household management, her family members' health, and their
domestic arrangements might well come under scrutiny. The Health
Office might reject an application if the applicant or any member of
her family had a "hereditary condition," such as alcoholism, feeble-
mindedness, or mental illness. One study of women who applied for
the Mother Cross estimated that about 5 percent of all applicants were
denied, and that of these about 30 percent were turned down because
they or a family member had a "hereditary condition." But a far more
common ground for being denied was being categorized as having an
"asocial family" (which, in this context, referred to the woman's thriftiness, housekeeping, and domestic arrangements); 61 percent of those
rejected were turned down for this reason.[43]

Social workers often vetoed giving the Mother Cross to particular
mothers because they were poor housekeepers, and included lengthy
and critical appraisals of a woman's cleaning, laundry, and children in
her application file. Social workers wrote of one mother from Detmold,
who applied for the Mother Cross in 1941, that "Frau P. is one of
the dirtiest women, whom I have ever met. . . . She attempted to sell
the baby clothes that the Assistance Bureau for Mother and Child
gave to her." Another applicant was denied because "the family is an
asocial family, whose house is dirty and untidy. . . . [B]oth [parents] are
not careful with money and lack any sense of responsibility."[44] Such
housewives were not representatives of German womanhood, but were
considered to be "Mother Cross unworthy."

Not only the applicant but her entire family was examined before
the Mother Cross was awarded because the woman was seen as a representative of her "family line" (*Sippe*): if any member of the "line"
had an "undesirable trait," then the woman was possibly "unworthy."
Like other hereditary conditions, being "asocial" and a poor housekeeper could also be labeled a "hereditary condition." One applicant
from Detmold was apparently unobjectionable herself, but was denied

42 Ibid., 75.
43 Ibid., 88.
44 Ibid., 105.

the Mother Cross because some of her relatives were undesirable. One of the local officials who entered an objection in this applicant's file recommended that she be denied the Mother Cross because, among other reasons, "her sister is not a good housekeeper."[45]

The pattern of decisions regarding Mother Cross applicants made it clear who was a "worthy" German mother: a worthy German mother was a married housewife (implicitly heterosexual) who observed bourgeois domestic norms and practices. As one survey of Mother Cross applicants concluded, the successful applicant "had a thoroughly cleaned, orderly, and tidy dwelling; she wore clean, feminine clothing, was faithful to her husband, and had borne her children within wedlock." She had never had an abortion, "didn't smoke, and drank very little alcohol. Her husband might smoke, but he did not drink too much.... Both of them paid their bills and their rent on time.... If the children were grown, they too had these qualities, and the grown daughters were also good housewives."[46] Women who lacked these domestic qualities were not worthy to represent the nation and were to be excluded from the *Volksgemeinschaft*. Their husbands, although they did not have to pass such stringent tests, were also expected to be productive citizens, having avoided overt alcoholism or chronic unemployment.

If a family fell far short of this domestic ideal, more drastic measures could be taken against it than the denial of a Mother Cross. Most Nazi writers and social policy experts considered "asocial" families to be beyond reform because such personal qualities were seen as hereditary and implicitly genetic. The favored official approach in such cases became the curtailment of social welfare benefits and, for thousands of unfortunates, even forcible sterilization in order to prevent future transmission of "hereditary conditions." But during the 1930s, a minority faction among Nazi Party ideologues argued that such "asocial" families could perhaps be reformed, using surveillance and well-planned, thorough, and coercive domestic interventions. In Bremen, members of this school were able to put their ideas into practice for a few years in a special "reeducation camp" for disorderly families, which particularly targeted "asocial" housewives. Established in 1936, the camp was

---

[45] Ibid., 107.
[46] Ibid., 123–4.

named the "Hashude Educational Settlement"; local officials tended to refer to it in correspondence simply as the "asocial colony."

Nazi authorities had already established work camps in many cities for "work shy" men and others who were undesirable from their standpoint. But the problem with work camps for men, social workers in Bremen argued, was that women could not be included in such "reeducation efforts." And yet, as a local newspaper report on the settlement argued, "The entire family can only be reformed by reaching the mother and children; special emphasis must be put on their *re-education*. The mothers must be taught and trained in their duties to the family and within the household."[47] A new sort of camp, which would include entire households, and particularly target mothers and children, was needed for disorderly families. The original proposal for the Hashude Settlement promised that the housewives interned in the camp would be instructed in housekeeping by a social worker who was assisted by volunteers from the local Nazi Women's League. These instructors would not be from the upper middle class, but rather "simple, clean, thrifty women ... if one can influence these women's household budgets and show them how to keep an orderly and clean home, this would be a great step forwards [for these families]."[48]

Eighty families were compelled to move into the Hashude Settlement in October 1936. Some were sent to the camp because they had repeatedly fallen behind on their rent payments to the public housing authorities; others were apparently referred simply because they were "well known" to local social welfare agencies and their social workers thought they might benefit from the experience. The Bremen Welfare Office, the *Jugendamt*, the public housing office, and local police could all submit recommendations for a family's referral and placement in the Hashude Settlement.

In the camp, families were placed in small row houses, which were built radiating outward from a central administration building, so that the entrance to each house could be kept under surveillance. The camp was surrounded by a barbed-wire fence, and all visitors had to check in and out through a central gate. Families usually stayed at the camp

[47] "Bremens Wohnungsfürsorgeanstalt" in the *Bremer Nachrichten*, June 13, 1937, no. 159. Italics are in the original.
[48] From a report dated July 11, 1935, in STAB 4. 124/1. F. 3. b. 10 no. 3.

for about a year; they were released only if the father went to work regularly and if the mother kept an orderly and clean house. Adults who repeatedly violated the camp's rules, or refused to improve themselves, were referred to concentration camps. Local social workers soon noted that the mere existence of the camp gave them a new and effective tool to use as leverage when dealing with all the area's local poor families: they could threaten to throw defiant recipients of poor relief into the Hashude Settlement.[49]

Camp regulations attempted to counteract the parents' influence over their children, by mandating that children had to spend their free time in the camp's Children's Center, where they were cared for by volunteers from the Hitler Youth and League of German Girls (BDM). Thus freed up from caring for their children, mothers were to spend the time cleaning their homes. Doors had to be kept unlocked and social workers or volunteers from Nazi women's groups could enter any home unannounced in order to inspect each woman's housekeeping. Further:

Each dwelling must be tidied and clean each morning by 11 a.m. at the latest. Every Friday, or two days before important holidays, the house must be cleaned from top to bottom. All garbage must be placed in a pail in front of the door by 7 a.m. each day. . . . [All visitors must leave, and everyone must be in his/her home] by 10 p.m. in the summer, and by 9 p.m. in the winter. All children under the age of 15 must be in bed by that time, and all lights must be turned off by one hour after curfew begins. . . . [F]amilies cannot buy anything on credit, but rather must pay cash for all purchases.[50]

The Hashude Settlement was based on a premise that ran contrary to the received wisdom among most "racial studies" experts, because it was operated under the assumption that "asocial" families could be salvaged or improved if they were placed in controlled environment. And indeed, the housewives interned there were given the strongest of incentives to reform their household management practices and conform to bourgeois domestic norms in order to be released from the colony. Most appear to have "improved" their housekeeping, at least while they were there. A 1940 report on the "asocial colony" by the

---

[49] STAB 3-W.11 no. 467.9, "Einweisung der Familie Oppermann," Nov. 1939.
[50] "Haus- und Wohnordnung" for the colony, in STAB 4.13/1 W.3 no. 20, records for Senator für die innere Verwaltung, Akte betreffend die Wohnungsfürsorgeanstalt Hashude.

head of the Bremen Welfare Office – who was urging that the settlement be closed down after six years of operation – did acknowledge grudgingly that "in most cases, the attempt to improve the housekeeping of the inmates was successful in this institution."[51]

But he still argued that most of these families were basically "incurable" because their "asocial" traits were hereditary. By this time, the received wisdom regarding allegedly hereditary traits now permeated social policy, and the Bremen camp was now seen as out of step with larger trends. Quoting a "racial studies" expert, the Welfare Office official argued that the only proper approach to such families was to sterilize most of them, and concluded that the camp should be closed down and the housing stock given to "healthy" families. Ultimately, his recommendation was accepted. The colony was closed down in late 1940, and the homes were given to families that were both "child rich" and orderly.[52] "Asocial" housewives and their families stood outside of the *Volksgemeinschaft* and had no claim to public support.

These families were ultimately judged to be "hopeless" by racial studies experts. But the judgment was based not on their physical appearance (the eye or hair color tests commonly associated with Nazi racial studies) but rather with life-style and behavior. The Hashude Settlement would thus appear to support the argument advanced by Chad Bryant, who has argued that when "racial experts" assessed applicants for German citizenship during the war (in Bohemia and Moravia), "clean houses, . . . class, . . . sexual morality, and social behavior" could become key criteria for judging "race," as much as physiognomy or ancestry. Bryant concludes from this that "race was above all a political concept used to transform society" in the sense of social engineering, which sought to reward those who exhibited "worthy" behavior in their private lives, while punishing or excluding the less orderly.[53]

"Asocial" housewives were thus excluded from the national community in Nazi social policy. But race, in the narrower sense of ancestry,

---

[51] From a report on the colony written by the head of the Welfare Office, dated Aug. 14, 1940, in STAB 4.13/1 W.3 no. 20, records for Senator für die innere Verwaltung, Akte betreffend die Wohnungsfürsorgeanstalt Hashude.

[52] Ibid., and also Pine, *Nazi Family Policy*, 145–6.

[53] Chad Carl Bryant, "Making Czechs German: German Nationality and Nazi Rule in the Protectorate of Bohemia and Moravia, 1939–1945" (Ph.D. diss, University of California, Berkeley, 2002), 223 and 257.

was also grounds for exclusion. German Jewish housewives had never been part of the *Volksgemeinschaft* to begin with, according to Nazi ideologues, and their un-German identity was allegedly reflected in their poor housekeeping. It had long been a cliché in German literature and popular culture that Jewish homes (especially those of less assimilated Jews) were dirty, even though most German Jewish housewives had thoroughly internalized bourgeois practices of domestic cleanliness and order. Some Jewish housewives perhaps even "overconformed" to these norms in order to ward off anti-Semitic criticisms from their gentile neighbors.[54] Nazi propaganda picked up and expanded stereotypes about dirty and disorderly Jews and their homes, which reached virulent extremes in notorious anti-Semitic productions such as the film *The Eternal Jew*, and in discussions of the homes and life-styles of Eastern European Jews. The reality of German Jewish homes was irrelevant in such discussions; Jewish women were still "othered" as allegedly poor housekeepers.

But although German Jews stood outside of the *Volksgemeinschaft* as defined by the Nazi Party, the household goods of German Jewish families could apparently still be cleansed and repatriated into the homes of "real" Germans. In 1941 and 1942, as Jewish families in Germany were being rounded up and deported to concentration camps in the east, municipal tax offices in every locality were assigned the job of seizing and auctioning the household possessions of the deported Jews; the proceeds swelled government coffers. A flood of personal property thus came suddenly on to the market in many towns, sometimes faster than the tax office could dispose of it. Public auctions were often quickly organized in front of the homes of the deported Jews, a horrid parody of windfall yard sales. Neighbors and sometimes even cleaning ladies showed up, hoping to scoop up objects that they had previously admired when they had visited Jews' homes. Some Germans

---

[54] The conviction that Jews were unclean in their persons and their homes had formed a core part of anti-Semitic mythologies for centuries. For the trope of "dirty" Jewish homes in popular culture before World War I, see Brent O. Peterson, "The Fatherland's Kiss of Death. Gender and Germany in Nineteenth-Century Historical Fiction," in Patricia Herminghouse and Magda Mueller, eds., *Gender and Germanness. Cultural Productions of Nation* (Oxford: Berghahn Press, 1997), 90–3. For German Jewish women's often fervent embrace of bourgeois housekeeping practices, see Kaplan, *The Making of the Jewish Middle Class*.

refused to touch or participate in this wholesale expropriation, but others lined up to purchase household linens, dishes, and furniture, as one witness later recalled:

They [the Jews] had to leave everything behind. For weeks, the goods of the Jews were being auctioned. Jewish auctions, ohhh!... And one woman would say, "oh, she had such a pretty satin coat. If that is auctioned, then I'll buy it." But that didn't come on the market. The best things were taken [beforehand] by the Nazis... but some nice things were sold. Mostly beautiful linens and similar items. They had such nice household linens, and they couldn't take it all with them.[55]

Why Jewish families could not take their belongings with them, and where they were sent, was always elided in these recollections. Many Germans found it acceptable to acquire the most private goods – including body linens and bed sheets – in this fashion because the property had been "laundered" and its sale officially sanctioned by the tax office and therefore by the state. Household objects that were severed from their personal histories, and thus normalized, graced the homes of some gentile Germans for decades to come. The goods – although not their former owners – belonged in German homes, a pattern that was also repeated in occupied Poland after 1939.

"German" Domesticity outside the Reich

The Nazi Women's League launched a number of outreach programs that targeted *Volksdeutsche* (ethnic German) women and families in Central and Eastern Europe. In some respects, such ethnic German women were diametrically opposed to German Jewish housewives in Nazi rhetoric. German Jewish women were citizens of the Reich, whose ancestors in many cases had lived in Germany for hundreds of years, and who tended to observe widely shared German domestic norms. But Nazi authorities argued that such women did not keep German homes, were not members of the *Volksgemeinschaft*,

---

[55] From an interview with a woman who witnessed such street auctions in Franziska Becker, *Gewalt und Gedächtnis: Erinnerungen an die nationalsozialistischen Verfolgung einer jüdischen Landgemeinde* (Göttingen: V. Schmerse, 1994), 83. When a few of the survivors or their children returned to this locality after the war, seeking their families' property, local officials told them that no one who had bought property in these auctions could be located.

and were not entitled to full German citizenship (which they lost under the Nuremberg Laws of 1935). *Volksdeutsche* women in Eastern Europe, on the other hand, were women who were citizens of other nation, whose ancestors had *left* German-speaking Europe sometimes centuries ago, and who in many cases did not even speak passable German. Nevertheless, in keeping with Nazi racial ideology, *Volksdeutsche* women from Eastern Europe were claimed for the *Volksgemeinschaft* by Nazi authorities, at the same that time that German Jewish women were being expelled from the body politic. Nazi policy makers often followed earlier scholars' work on the *Volksdeutschen* of Central and Eastern Europe, and assumed that such ethnic Germans possessed a timeless and intrinsic Germanness. The family lives of such *Volksdeutschen* were therefore presumed to reflect an essentially German domesticity. Once the war began, Nazi agencies would extend German citizenship to millions of *Volksdeutschen* from throughout Eastern Europe.

The Nazi Women's League Section for [ethnic] German Women Abroad was the agency most active before 1939 in locating and cultivating contacts with ethnic German women who lived outside of Germany, particularly in Eastern Europe. In 1937 and 1938, this section organized gatherings of women from ethnic German communities all over the world in order to strengthen their ties to Germany and to Nazi women's groups. The Nazi Women's League also hosted meetings for about three thousand *Volksdeutsche* women who attended the seventh annual congress of ethnic Germans from all over the world (the *Reichstagung der Auslandsdeutschen*), held in Stuttgart in 1938. Leaders of ethnic German women's groups were invited to special receptions with Getrud Scholtz-Klink and other NS dignitaries.[56]

Within Germany, the Nazi Women's League attempted to familiarize ordinary housewives with the lives of ethnic German women abroad through an extensive series of radio shows on ethnic German housewives in other nations. Some of these broadcasts were reportage, while others were dramatic plays. In November 1936 alone, for example,

---

[56] See the report on the women's meetings within the congress in a report dated October 1938 in BA NS 44/50, Reichsfrauenführung, Anordnungen, 1936–9; see also the report on a camp held for leaders of ethnic German women from around the world in BA NS 44/60, memo by Arbeitsgemeinschaft der deutschen Frau im Ausland.

broadcasts directed at women in various regions included shows on "a German woman pioneer in Brazil," "the German housewife in Turkey," and "from the life of an *Auslandsdeutsche* mother in Russia."[57] As in the Imperial period, the community of imagined German housewives clearly still included women who did not hold German citizenship. The Nazi Women's League organized collections among its listeners for these "German" sisters abroad, gathering donations of clothing and toys to send to ethnic German communities at Christmas time. Ethnic German mothers of large families were also brought back to Germany to rest in the special "recuperation homes" run by the Nazi Women's League for "child rich" mothers.[58]

Among the most substantial efforts to bring *Volksdeutsche* girls and women into the national community were the schools run by the Nazi Women's League for young ethnic German women from Eastern Europe. There seem to have been at least two that operated for a number of years, in Stuttgart and Berlin. Each school offered a one-year training program for pupils who were sixteen or older. The main focus of these schools – which were founded in order to strengthen the "German" identity of their pupils – was home economics. As the graduates of one school reported, "the duties of the adult woman, who is the carrier of German ethnic identity, formed the core of our instruction. . . . [W]e became familiar with the duties of a housewife through practical work in the household, kitchen, and laundry [of the school]." Their courses covered not only cooking, mending, knitting, ironing, gardening, bookkeeping, child care, and first aid, but also German folksongs and dances, arts and crafts, how to celebrate a German-style Christmas, and "racial studies."[59]

---

[57] Shows on *Volksdeutsche* mothers and housewives abroad showed up frequently on the lists of women's radio programs during the late 1930s. These examples were taken from BA NS 44/44, Program of Women's Broadcasts for Nov. 1936.

[58] Clifford Kirkpatrick, *Nazi Germany. Its Women and Family Life* (New York: Bobbs-Merrill, 1938), 81–3 and 275.

[59] See the scrapbook allegedly compiled by the graduates from one year's course, "Auslandsdeutsche Mädel geben Bericht von ihrer Arbeit" (which appears to have been produced by the Verein für das Deutschtum im Auslande staff) in the U.S. Library of Congress Prints and Photographs Division, Third Reich Collection, LOT 11422F. This collection also contains photo albums and scrapbooks of other domestic science courses for *Volksdeutsche* pupils. See also BA NS 5/VI vol. 6869, Nachrichtendienst der Reichsfrauenführung, report on Stuttgart school dated April 1938.

Conclusion

In the end, the specific practices promoted by housewives' associations in Imperial and Weimar Germany had become so central to German identity that Nazi programs and organizations picked up and expanded those that served their own purposes. They cherry picked those that served their own goals and expanded those programs, which then touched the lives of millions of women and girls. The bourgeois approach to "proper" domestic thrift, cleanliness, order, decoration, and holiday celebrations formed the foundation for a broad panoply of home economics programs. It became an important yardstick for determining who was to be included or excluded from the *Volksgemeinschaft* as a "worthy" German mother or an "asocial" housewife. And when Nazi women leaders decided to reach out and attempt to solidify the "German" identity of young ethnic German women abroad, the tool that apparently came first and most naturally to mind was this same approach to household management. Domesticity and *Volksgemeinschaft* were intimately and inextricably intertwined in Nazi social policy.

It is difficult to determine exactly what percentage of the female population was influenced by Nazi organizations' domestic science educational programs. Certainly, the percentage was highest among the cohorts of girls and younger women who were exposed to home economics within the BDM or compelled to do a year's service in a job that required domestic skills. But even among older cohorts, millions of German women were exposed to the domestic educational and propaganda efforts of Nazi women's organizations: through the Mothers' Schools; the enormous variety of cooking and housekeeping courses offered by the Home Economics Section; the "master housewife" courses; the advice centers run by competing sections of the Women's Bureau; the millions of recipe booklets, pamphlets, and other materials distributed by the Women's Bureau; and the many smaller efforts that targeted the private household, such as the "One Dish Sunday." Women from groups that stood on the margins of the *Volksgemeinschaft* – such as poor and disorderly families or the *Volksdeutschen* – were the targets of programs that tried to "Germanize" their housekeeping, either through compulsion or persuasion. What these policies all shared were common roots in a bourgeois model of household management – a *habitus* that emphasized thrift, order, and extreme cleanliness – that was seen as a core part of German identity. But this template for household management was now used in service of the expansion and domestic "purification" of the *Volksgemeinschaft.*

As we have seen, Weimar housewives' groups had linked the bourgeois approach to housekeeping with both economic nationalism and with German identity in a broader sense, long before 1933. Nazi social policy was thus carrying forward a legacy of politicized home economics. At the same time, however, Nazi policies had added new elements of compulsion and coercion in some areas, even as they expanded the scope and scale of earlier domestic science education to new levels. By 1939 the coercive aspects of Nazi family policy included a mandatory "year of service" for almost all young Germans, and could even reach such extremes as the "asocial" colony of Bremen, which was surely a dismal environment for the families involved.

But Nazi women's programs not only increased, but also racialized the promotion of domesticity; even beyond the degree of racialized domesticity deployed in German colonial rhetoric. Nazi propaganda used the symbols and practices of domesticity to support Nazi notions of racial hierarchy and to reshape women's housekeeping to meet the needs of the Nazi Four-Year Plan. The regime's efforts to enlist housewives' support for its policies would become especially insistent in the area of consumer "education." NS policy makers established some of the clearest and most direct linkages between family life, daily housework, and the goals of the Nazi state.

5

The Autarkic Household and the Nazi Four-Year Plan

[In the Third Reich] we attempted [to guide housewives] to return to the healthier foods of our ancestors, and above all to reduce the excessive demand, common in all highly civilized societies, for meat [and fats, like butter].... [W]e especially advocated the use of whole grains... and whole grain bread.

From the memoir of Else Vorwerck, leader of the Home Economics Section of the NS Women's Bureau

Guns will make us strong, but butter will only make us fat.
Hermann Goering

The leader of the Women's Bureau chapter in Gelsenkirchen, a town in Westphalia, complained regularly during the mid- and late 1930s to her superiors about the difficulties of persuading women in her town to change their housekeeping routines and family menus. Under the Nazi Four-Year Plan, some cuts of meat, butter, and cooking fats of all sorts were occasionally in short supply, as the regime diverted resources away from consumer goods production. The Gelsenkirchen Women's Bureau offered cooking courses to teach housewives how to cook with alternative ingredients and to persuade them to try new menus. But no matter how many substitutes were offered, many women still wanted to buy butter (or if they could not afford that, margarine) and pork cutlets for Sunday dinner.

The head of the local bureau chapter admitted that permanent changes in women's housekeeping were very difficult to effect. "My impression," she reported to the provincial central office in late 1935, "is that when one speaks to housewives about housekeeping matters – it doesn't matter, what the exact topic is – then they are all interested, even enthusiastic; they ask questions, and participate [in the program]. But once they get back home, then the majority of women show themselves to be *very conservative* and simply cannot change how they do things."[1] She also blamed Gelsenkirchen shopkeepers for making housewives anxious about what these shortages might portend, reporting angrily that "unfortunately our local retailers make difficulties about distributing fats, no matter what type of fat it is. It reminds consumers of the old 'getting things through the back door' of the war period."[2]

Shortages of consumer goods and particular foodstuffs during the late 1930s did remind many housewives of the privations of World War I. Their sense of déjà vu may have been heightened by the regime's propaganda, which persistently linked women's frugal use of available foods to the national interest. For example, there was one writer in a leading home economics journal who praised women's thrift for making reductions in overall domestic consumption possible, which meant that "resources...[can then be used] to build western fortifications, which gives the Führer greater freedom in diplomatic negotiations."[3]

His comment about the need for western fortifications reflected the fact that the National Socialists had not come to power simply to promote orderly housekeeping. Hitler and his party intended to establish German hegemony by force across most of Europe and to reorganize society in ways that reflected their vicious racism. In pursuit of these goals, the regime launched a campaign of militarization after the mid-1930s, which directed resources away from private German households and toward war industries. As part of this campaign, Nazi organizations worked to reshape housewives' consumption patterns

[1] See the records of the Westphalian Gau Nazi Women's League in the Nordrhein-Westfälisches Staatsarchiv Münster (hereafter, NWSM), Bestand NS-Frauenschaft Westfalen-Nord no. 60, Monatsbericht for Sept. 1935 from Kreis Gelsenkirchen.

[2] NWSM NS-Frauenschaft Westfalen-Nord, no. 60, Oct. 1935 report from Kreis Gelsenkirchen and no. 340, Feb. 29 report from Gau Dortmund.

[3] See Walther Herbert, "Die Hausfrau spart!" *Hauswirtschaftliche Jahrbücher* 11 (1940), 97–100.

and shopping habits in order to persuade them to manage their house-holds in ways that supported German rearmament. Nazi organizations picked up and made use of many aspects of German domesticity, partic-ularly widely shared practices of thriftiness. But now, domestic thrift, hard work, and order were to serve the regime's goals.

Consumers and the Nazi Four-Year Plan

Nazi consumption policies reflected several goals that were often in conflict and were therefore carefully balanced against one another throughout the 1930s. Some of these goals were crucial to ensuring the Nazis' political legitimacy and support from the bulk of the Ger-man population: the pursuit of rapid economic recovery; ending the widespread hunger and misery of the Depression; ensuring modest gains in consumption; and, above all, the reduction of unemployment levels. The "conquest" of high levels of unemployment (which led to the end of widespread hunger) was the one achievement that ensured popular support for the new regime.

Guaranteeing a "decent" standard of living for the bulk of the population was necessary not only to maintain legitimacy, but also was seen as crucial to ensuring military success. Nazi leaders were erroneously convinced that Germany had lost World War I because resource-starved, hungry civilians were "seduced" by Jewish revolu-tionaries, and had been led to "stab the army in the back," leading to popular uprisings and subsequent military defeat. To avoid any future repetitions, Nazi Party leaders were insistent throughout the 1930s that ordinary Germans should not be asked to sacrifice too much, although they might be asked to postpone some sorts of consumption in order to support rearmament.[4] Received wisdom within the nationalist right about the causes of Germany's defeat in the last war thus strongly influenced how Nazi leaders approached the preparation for the next one. Parallel to this, popular memories of consumer deprivation during

---

[4] See Timothy Mason, *Sozialpolitik im Dritten Reich* (Opladen: Westdeutscher Verlag, 1977); Hartmut Berghoff, ed., "Enticement and Deprivation: The Regulation of Con-sumption in Pre-war Nazi Germany," in Martin Daunton and Matthew Hilton, eds., *The Politics of Consumption. Material Culture and Citizenship in Europe and America* (New York: Berg, 2001), 165–84; see also R. J. Overy, *The Nazi Economic Recovery, 1932–1938*, 2nd ed. (Cambridge: Cambridge University Press, 1996).

World War I often formed the backdrop for housewives' reactions to the policies of the Nazi Four-Year Plan.

As during World War I, the drive to prepare for the Second World War necessarily led to economic policies that worked against civilian consumers' interests, a trade-off that did not escape some civilians. Germany's economic planners carried forward the protectionism of the Weimar period and worked toward an autarkic, or self-sufficient, German economy, so that Germany's reliance on imported raw materials and foodstuffs would never again become the weakness that it had proven in World War I. Imports were therefore discouraged or often restricted (in the case of some luxury goods), and war-related industries usually had first call on those raw materials that were imported. At the same time, policy makers encouraged the production of synthetic products that would replace imports (such as synthetic fuels and fabrics).

In order to restrain "excessive" consumer demand and thus reduce the need of consumer industries for raw materials, the regime adopted a policy of *Lohnstopp* (wage freezes) in many industries, and simultaneously increased the tax burden on ordinary Germans, so that consumers would have less discretionary income. Government polices that slowed the growth of consumer demand were largely successful, even as Germany's economy recovered rapidly after 1933. Although the German gross national product (GNP) grew dramatically during the mid- to late 1930s, the increase in private consumption did not keep pace, and thus declined from 71 percent of the nation's GNP in 1928 to 59 percent by 1938.[5]

But by 1935, the conflict between rising consumer demand and the drive to prepare for war was becoming more difficult to manage. The German economy was now essentially at a state of full employment, and although the growth of consumers' discretionary incomes was slowed by wage freezes and tax increases, the end of unemployment meant that pent-up consumer demand was now increasingly felt. At the same time, war-preparedness measures (e.g., the refurbishment of the railroad system) and growth in heavy industries meant that Germany was running out of raw materials, and Germany's gold and foreign

---

[5] Ibid., 261–4. See also Berghoff, "Enticement and Deprivation," 183–4. The policy of wage freezes was not uniformly successful because shortages of skilled labor in some industries did lead to pay increases in the form of bonuses or overtime pay.

currency reserves were depleted. In order to continue to rearm while not restricting consumption too much, Hitler announced the implementation of a Nazi Four-Year Plan in 1936.[6]

After the Nazi Four-Year Plan was introduced, armaments production (which had played only a subordinate role before 1936) now became the chief determinant of economic policy. The plan emphasized rapid rearmament, an increase in the production of militarily important raw materials, the creation of new synthetic products (where sufficient raw materials were not easily obtainable), and general war preparation. Eventually the plan "encroached on all the major areas of economic policy-making...by 1938 [Hermann] Goering was 'economic dictator' in all but name," with control over agriculture, labor, trade, and prices.[7]

But Nazi Germany during the 1930s was not isolated from the trends of popular consumption prevalent elsewhere in the West, nor could consumer industries be drastically shortchanged, as happened in the contemporary Soviet Union. Germany's leaders still felt the need to secure popular support by allowing some growth in consumption, along with many of the features of a modern consumer culture, such as broad selection of American imports (Coca-Cola established its first bottling plants in Germany during the 1930s), a flourishing film industry, and the broad dissemination of key consumer goods, such as the radio.[8]

The demand for the products of American popular culture, electrical appliances, and other such goods was hardly new because these products had begun to penetrate the German market during the Weimar period. But the Depression had suppressed demand for nonessentials. With the resumption of full employment, this hiatus ended and Nazi policy makers were well aware that they could not ignore consumers' desires entirely. One historian has astutely described the cumulative

---

[6] The problem of competition between consumer and war-related industries for raw materials was also eased by the acquisition first of the Saar province, and later Austria, the Sudentenland, Bohemia, and Moravia. See ibid.; and R. J. Overy, *War and Economy in the Third Reich* (Cambridge: Cambridge University Press, 1994), 185–6.

[7] Overy, *War and Economy in the Third Reich*, 185–6.

[8] See Hans-Ulrich Thamer, *Verführung und Gewalt. Deutschland 1933–1945* (Berlin: Siedler Verlag, 1986), 511–10; and Paul Betts, "The Nierentisch Nemesis: Organic Design in West German Pop Culture," *German History* 19 (2001): 196–7; and Eric Rentschler, *The Ministry of Illusion. Nazi Cinema and Its Afterlife* (Cambridge, MA: Harvard University Press, 1996).

effect of the regime's consumer policies as leading to the "enticement and deprivation" of consumers, as government economic policies combined the suppression of consumption in some areas with widespread distribution of key goods in selected high-profile areas and the promise of future consumption in others (e.g., the Volkswagen, promised but never mass-produced before 1945).[9]

With the exception of the coupons for household goods given to marriage loan recipients, most of the "enticement" dangled before consumers came in the form of "status" products formerly associated with the upper middle class, or through the entertainment and leisure industries: the Nazi state promoted key aspects of consumption that were closely associated with modernity. Thus, the regime allowed real increases in the production of goods and performances for popular culture, such as hit-parade radio shows, movies, fan magazines, and the cheaper, more widely available domestic vacations or entertainments promoted by *Kraft durch Freude* (KdF, the state-subsidized mass tourist agency). The NS hoped that these consumer goods would integrate and unify the population behind its leadership. Widespread ownership of goods such as the *Volksempfänger* (the cheaper, widely distributed radio of the 1930s) would promote shared experiences and homogenized collective identities among German consumers.[10] To further entice consumers, the Nazi state held out the promise of cars and more prestigious sorts of holidays (e.g., the KdF cruise ships, which relatively few Germans actually experienced during the 1930s) in the future.[11]

But although the regime allowed an increase in consumption in some areas (and promised more in the future), the demands of rapid

---

[9] Berghoff, "Enticement and Deprivation," 173. See also, *Konsumpolitik. Die Regulierung des privaten Verbrauchs im 20. Jahrhundert* (Göttingen: Vandenhoeck and Ruprecht, 1999) and "Konsumgüterindustrie im Nationalsozialismus. Marketing im Spannungsfeld von Profit- und Regimeinteressen," *Archiv für Sozialgeschichte* 36 (1996): 293–322.

[10] Victoria de Grazia notes that this goal was shared by other governments of the period. See her "Nationalizing Women. The Competition between Fascist and Commercial Cultural Models in Mussolini's Italy," in Victoria de Grazia and Ellen Furlough, eds., *The Sex of Things. Gender and Consumption in Historical Perspective* (Berkeley: University of California Press, 1996), 337–58.

[11] Berghoff, "Enticement and Deprivation," 173–8. For KdF, see Shelley Baranowski, "Strength through Joy: Tourism and National Integration in the Third Reich," in Shelley Baranowski and Ellen Furlough, eds., *Being Elsewhere: Tourism, Consumer Culture, and Identity in Modern Europe and North America* (Ann Arbor: University of Michigan Press, 2001).

militarization unavoidably entailed the restraint or redirection of consumption in many other sectors, particularly in foodstuffs, textiles, and other household goods. It was in the household – in the erratic shortages of meats, fats, imported foods, fabrics, toys, and through the introduction of inferior *ersatz* products – that ordinary Germans first felt the pinch of the Nazi Four-Year Plan. And housewives, who managed their families' budgets and purchased most consumer goods, were among the first to see the impact of Germany's rearmament. Because their job was to mediate between their families' desires and the reality of what was on local store shelves, housewives also became the targets of intensive Nazi propaganda.

Nazi Party and state agencies sought to "spin" the ordinary housewife's experience of the marketplace, redirect her purchasing choices, and increase her work load. Ultimately, the regime's goal was to adjust demand to fit supply, within the framework of a partially autarkic economy, in which the armed forces had first call on resources. Nazi consumer "education" efforts built on, exploited, and manipulated the ways in which domesticity previously had been used to define German identity and continued earlier programs (e.g., the promotion of rye bread) that had linked housewives' private consumption patterns to patriotism and the national interest.

In effect, Nazi women bureaucrats were attempting to overcome the heterogeneity created by differences in regional background, class, and custom, and were advocating unified, autarkic patterns of consumption and household management. But in trying to reach and change housewives' attitudes and workloads, Nazi women's organizations ultimately confronted the fact that mass consumption contained both centralizing and centrifugal impulses. Their leaders could not completely overcome the segmentation inherent in mass markets and consumption patterns, which were divided along fault lines of class, gender, region, and even locality.

The Section for Home Economics and the Autarkic Diet

The Nazi Women's Bureau Section for Home Economics was the chief organization responsible for reaching female consumers, although (as in every area of Nazi policy) there were other Nazi Party and state agencies involved. The Home Economics Section also worked closely with the women's division of the *Reichsnährstand,* which was responsible for reaching rural housewives. After 1936, the work of all of these agencies was coordinated and their propaganda overseen by the *Reichsausschuss für Volkswirtschaftliche Aufklärung* (the National Committee for Popular Economic Enlightenment) a subdivision of the *Werberat der deutschen Wirtschaft* (the German Business Advertising Consultancy) a private, state-sponsored agency charged with responsibility for Germany's national economic propaganda.[12]

The broader audience of German housewives was a constituency that was more difficult to reach and mobilize than were German men, however, because women spent more time within the household and in more free-floating sociable activities.[13] In order to reach every German housewife, Nazi organizations embraced a variety of vehicles and techniques. Propaganda and housekeeping tips supporting the Nazi Four-Year Plan were featured in the Women's Bureau's own house organ, *Deutsche Hauswirtschaft* and in the *NS Frauenwarte.* Recipes and weekly menu plans were distributed in the form of millions of flyers and brochures, tucked into female workers' paycheck envelopes, featured on the *Schwarzes Brett* (a common bulletin board) in factories and workplaces, and published in local newspapers. Nazi women's organizations mounted hundreds of public exhibitions and cooking demonstrations, large and small, in every *Gau,* and produced slideshows, cinema newsreels, and radio programs to advocate particular patterns of consumption and housekeeping. The Section for Home Economics set up its own chain of 148 advice centers for housewives (separate from those of the Mother's Service), which focused largely on advising women on consumer issues: recycling; the proper use of *ersatz* products, preserving foods, promoting dark breads and *Quark,* and so forth.

Their publications were generously funded by the *Reichsausschuss für Volkswirtschaftliche Aufklärung,* and Nazi women's groups often claimed that staggering numbers of flyers and other publications were produced. Between 1936 and 1940, for example, the *Reichsnährstand*

---

[12] Kate Lacey, *Feminine Frequencies. Gender, German Radio, and the Public Sphere, 1923–1945* (Ann Arbor: University of Michigan Press 1996), 180.

[13] Victoria de Grazia notes that in Fascist Italy women were much more difficult for the regime to organize than were men. See de Grazia, "Nationalizing Women," 342.

distributed almost nine million copies of pamphlets that touted *Quark*, a featured Nazi Four-Year Plan product. This agency also passed out eight million brochures on how to make preserves or jams, and five million copies of recipes designed to make the humble potato more attractive. The 1936 campaign launched against waste or spoilage, *Kampf dem Verderb* ("fight waste/spoilage") included the distribution of 3.6 million copies of a pamphlet featuring the campaign's catchy slogan, "*weg mit dem Groschengrab*" ("end [waste], the penny grave!"). The Women's Bureau even produced a board game for girls as part of this campaign, *Wettlauf mit dem Verderb* ("compete against waste"), while the *Reichsnährstand* gave away eighteen million *Kampf dem Verderb* postcards for women to use in their private correspondence.[14]

Some of these efforts (e.g., the promotion of *Quark*, rye bread, and putting up produce) were building upon programs first developed by Weimar home economists and housewives' organizations. Such propaganda expanded upon widespread attitudes toward housekeeping already present among the German bourgeoisie, and attempted to popularize and manipulate these established patterns of housekeeping and consumption. But in other areas (e.g., the promotion of new *ersatz* products, or the "One Dish Sunday"), Nazi women's leaders were attempting to change or disrupt deeply entrenched customs and attitudes in private households in order to support the rearmament efforts that were the core of the Nazi Four-Year Plan. Their efforts to "reform" German women's housekeeping and consumption were also shaped by the larger political and cultural meanings assigned within Nazi Germany to housewives' private choices regarding shopping and household management. In effect, Nazi women's leaders selected themes that had long been present in German discussions of consumption and housekeeping (e.g., the value of thrift, or the virtues of "natural" foods) and incorporated them into a vision of autarkic housekeeping, which served the needs of the plan.

Nazi women's organizations were attempting to use these values and assumptions – which underlay the mentality of German domesticity – as leverage in order to influence the most ordinary sorts of household decisions. The housewife's management of the household entailed a

---

[14] Margarete Adelung, *Der "Kampf dem Verderb" im Haushalt mit sparsamen Mittlen* (Ph.D. diss., Munich, 1940), 26.

constant series of smaller or larger choices regarding the allocation of her time and labor: what she should do and what she would not do herself. Such decisions, in turn, shaped the housewife's shopping list. Should she purchase canned fruits and vegetables or put them up herself in season? Should she sew her family's clothing herself or purchase ready-made clothes? Should she serve a "cold" evening dinner of *belegtes* bread (topped with spreads, meat, or cheese), or cook the second "warm" meal of the day? Should she participate in Nazi programs to recycle scarce resources, which (like almost all attempts to be thrifty) entail additional labor? Should she draw up a weekly *Küchenzettel* (menu plan) and keep household account books, which might enable her to track expenditures more closely and stay within a budget, but that also entailed more work? As in other sectors of production under the Nazi Four-Year Plan, the regime's approach to housework stressed an intensification of labor, rather than an increase in productivity.

Much of the propaganda message was old, although the scale of these attempts to influence ordinary domestic choices was new. Housewives' educational materials had stressed for years that Germany could not be self-sufficient in foodstuffs unless German housewives followed specific consumption patterns and practiced thrift. Housewives' organizations had admonished their members throughout the Weimar period, for example, to rely on locally grown produce, rather than imports. This reflected these organizations' economic protectionism, and also served the interests of rural housewives (who were producers of produce and dairy products) in particular.

The "homegrown" diet touted by economic protectionists during the 1920s thus overlapped heavily with the foods stressed by the Nazi Party promoters of autarky during the 1930s: whole-grain, dark bread; potatoes; lowered consumption of meat and fats (because Germany lacked enough fodder to be self-sufficient in meat and butter production); and indigenous fruits and vegetables (cabbages and apples, in place of oranges and bananas). Some aspects of the "homegrown" diet – particularly the reduced consumption of meat and fats – were reminiscent of the shortages of World War I. Many of the basic outlines of the autarkic diet were thus already well established in older women's minds even before 1933. The associations thus raised in consumers' minds might be mixed as this diet could be associated with either patriotic protectionism or with the deprivations of wartime.[15]

The Nazi Party was able to pick up and absorb these preexisting housewives' groups, and dramatically expand the scale and budgets of their programs. Many women who had been active in home economics or housewives' associations before 1933 were now given enhanced status and assignments within the Women's Bureau or other Nazi women's agencies, particularly after the Nazi Four-Year Plan was introduced. But although their careers were dramatically improved under the Nazi Four-Year Plan, such home economists were not empowered; rather, they served as mouthpieces for the regime, trying to best implement a set of policies over which they had little control. Still, like the *Reichsfrauenführerin* Gertrud Scholz-Klink, many of them were able to make rather successful professional careers by telling other women that their highest calling was to be full-time housewives and mothers.

After 1933, housewives' groups no longer had to admonish women to avoid seductive "Southern" foreign fruits: all such imports were brought under government controls by the end of that year. Now, "buy German" campaigns no longer referred to foreign goods as much as they did to products manufactured or retailed by Jewish-owned firms. Like the other boycotts mounted by the regime during the 1930s, these efforts seem to have been largely unsuccessful because local chapters of the Women's Bureau had to repeatedly remind members not to shop in Jewish-owned stores.[16]

Nazi women's organizations picked up and drastically expanded the attempts of Weimar housewives' groups to promote such products as *Quark* and fish. *Quark* was a favored product (apparently the subject of more flyers and brochures than any other single foodstuff) for several reasons. It was made from the sour milk left over in the process of butter production, something that had previously often gone to animals.

---

[15] See Belinda Davis, *Home Fires Burning*; Reagin, "Comparing Apples and Oranges"; and Anne Roerkohl, *Hungerblockade und Heimatfront*.

[16] See the articles urging housewives to boycott Jewish firms in the NS *Frauenwarte* 1 (1932/33): 471 and 2 (1933/34): 90. For an article that touted a new label for clothing made only by "Aryan" producers, see *Die Deutsche Hausfrau* 20 (1935): 103. The local NSF attempted to organize boycotts by members of NS organizations in every *Gau*; see, e.g., NWSM, NS Frauenschaft Westfalen-Nord no. 326, "Boykottanordnungen." But the reports from the various Kreise also note that it was repeatedly necessary to admonish female party members to refrain from buying from Jewish merchants, which makes one skeptical about the success of these efforts.

Learning to use up this milk fit perfectly with the overall theme of *Kampf dem Verderb*. More importantly, it could be used as a spread for bread, in place of butter, margarine, or *Schmalz* (which were all in occasionally short supply by the late 1930s), and it contained protein. Nazi women's organizations mounted much more extensive efforts to promote this produce than those of their Weimar predecessors: passing out *Kostproben* (samples); offering public cooking demonstrations and special cooking courses centered on *Quark*; trying to persuade local merchants to stock the product; and distributing millions of *Quark* recipes. The shortage of butter and margarine no doubt aided their attempts to persuade housewives. Women's Bureau internal reports, and correspondence from provincial chapters, consistently claimed that German consumption of *Quark* rose dramatically in the 1930s.[17]

The Women's Bureau and the *Reichsnährstand* also picked up and expanded Weimar housewives' efforts to promote the consumption of fish. Before 1933, housewives' groups had promoted fish as part of their larger campaigns of economic protectionism in order to aid the German fishing industry. Under the Nazi Four-Year Plan, however, fish was suggested as a substitute for the sometimes scarce pork cutlet or sausage (by the late 1930s, a lack of fodder resulted in periodic shortages of pork and beef). Herring in particular was promoted as it could be more easily preserved.

The Home Economics Section offered tens of thousands of public cooking demonstrations of fish cookery and short-term fish cooking courses under the Nazi Four-Year Plan: almost 7,800 such courses (lasting a few hours or days each, usually with eighteen to twenty participants) in 1938. Reports sent to the section from provincial chapters consistently claimed that fish cooking courses (along with other cookery courses) were among their most popular offerings, while other

---

[17] For the Catholic Housewives' Union promotion of Quark during the Weimar period, see the correspondence in the Archive of the Catholic German Women's League (hereafter, AKDFB), file 1–70–2. For an example of one of the articles housewives' magazines ran to publicize its use see *Frauenland* 24 (1931): 131. The correspondence in housewives' organization files indicates that many of their members were unfamiliar with Quark, hence the need to distribute *Kostproben* (samples for tasting). Complaints that it was not well known nor widely carried in stores persisted into the 1930s; see BA NS 44/35, minutes of the schooling course for nutritional advisors, Sept. 20, 1937. The DFW claimed that Quark consumption rose 60 percent due to its efforts, a figure that could not be confirmed independently; see Adelung, "Kampf dem Verderb," 48.

campaigns apparently met with little response. Like the *Quark* campaign, the promotion of fish was undoubtedly made easier because pork was sporadically in short supply in many areas. After such courses, leaders of local chapters of Nazi women's groups asserted that fish sales usually rose. Nationally, fish consumption rose almost 50 percent between 1934 and 1938.[18]

But Nazi women's organizations not only carried forward the protectionism of Weimar housewives' groups. They also attempted to alter housewives' attitudes and shopping lists in other respects, urging housewives to work harder in order to conserve resources. Bourgeois housewives' groups and home economists before 1933 had always preached a message of thrift and economic self-discipline to housewife consumers. The housewife had been told for decades that the responsibility for her family's health and diet lay in her hands, that through proper budgeting and expenditure, she could single-handedly raise her family's standard of living.[19] Now, housewives were told that the success of the Nazi Four-Year Plan depended on their shopping patterns and household management. Toleration for even the slightest wastage, or any labor-saving shortcuts – which German home economics had never been noted for – now dropped to zero.

A "letter from a reader" published in the NS *Frauenwarte* at the beginning of the *Kampf dem Verderb* campaign nostalgically invoked

---

[18] For the national consumption levels of fish, see Walther Hoffmann, *Das Wachstum der deutschen Wirtschaft seit der Mitte des 19. Jahrhunderts* (Berlin: Springer-Verlag, 1965), 624 and 632. However, Hans J. Teuteberg, "Der Verzehr von Nahrungsmitteln in Deutschland pro Kopf und Jahr seit Beginn der Industrialisierung (1850–1975)," *Archiv für Sozialgeschichte* 19 (1979): 346–7, concludes that fish consumption rose only about one-third during roughly the same period. For the Women's Bureau's national figures regarding cooking courses, see BA NS 44/56, NSF and DFW 1938 *Jahresbericht*, 43–6. For local reports on the success of cookery courses, see NWSM, NS-Frauenschaft Westfalen-Nord, no. 340, Monatliche Tätigkeitsberichte des DFWs. Local chapters' reports are a source that must be treated with the greatest caution. Their claims regarding the popularity of cooking courses are substantiated by the relative popularity of cooking courses nationwide and also are lent credence by the fact that the same local writers often bemoaned the apathy of housewives regarding other programs and their failure to change women's behavior or housekeeping in other respects, which will be discussed in the following text.

[19] See the discussion on thrift in Chapter 1; see also Kaplan, *The Making of the Jewish Middle Class* and Ute Frevert, "Fürsorgliche Belagerung." Thrift as a *leitmotif* throughout the socialization and actual practice of bourgeois housewives is also abundantly documented in Kuhn, *Haus-Frauen-Arbeit*.

her childhood in a large civil servant's family as a model for a happy, thrifty family life. "In a well-managed household, absolutely nothing must be wasted," she admonished, recalling her own mother's impressive, tedious, and labor-intensive efforts at economizing. Every bit of worn or shabby clothing was cut down and resewn to create new clothes for smaller children; not a scrap of fabric could be wasted. Water that had been used for boiling vegetables was never thrown out, but recycled and used as stock for cooking other dishes the next day. The author's mother raised small animals and kept a garden, which supplied most of her family's diet; and she put up or canned enormous quantities of produce in season in order to provide food throughout the winter.[20]

This sort of idealized bourgeois household economy could have been taken directly from the nineteenth-century advice manuals published by Henriette Davidis, although the message was now being distributed to an even broader audience. But the larger context of such thrift was now quite different. In Imperial and Weimar Germany, women had often been encouraged or praised for their self-sacrifice on behalf of their families. Working harder, scrimping, and saving had been a way for the entire family to "get ahead" in life. Small savings might help to pay for a son's school fees; build a daughter's dowry; maintain an "appropriate" (*standesgemäss*) household among the bourgeoisie; or simply ensure an adequate domestic standard of living among poorer families. But in this context, a housewife was making a martyr of herself for her own loved ones, who were not to feel the pinch. Thus, a mother might insist on always taking the "worst" piece of the Sunday roast, so that her husband and children could eat better portions. She might cut down and resew an old dress for herself in order to save money for a son's schoolbooks. And when housewives' associations promoted such "thrift" among their members before 1933, they were, after all, organizing their own sort: the message was designed and controlled by housewives, for housewives.

But under the Nazi Four-Year Plan, the Women's Bureau's proposed thrift served an entirely different purpose. Now, housewives were being organized "from above," for the benefit of the Nazi state. They were now supposed to serve as agents of the state within the household,

---

[20] See the letter from a "reader" in *NS Frauenwarte* 5 (1936/37): 130.

disciplining their families' eating habits and consumption patterns to meet the shifting needs of the plan. Women were asked to sacrifice not in order to meet their own families' needs and strategies, but to meet the state's goals. And the entire family would feel the pinch: housewives were being asked to "sell" their families on the Nazi Sunday "One Dish" dinner instead of a roast, and to persuade their husbands to accept herring in place of a pork cutlet.

The Home Economics Section often went much further than its Weimar forerunners, moreover, in its recommendations to housewife/consumers, attempting to influence the smallest daily habits and increase women's work loads. Women were repeatedly told that they must use metal spoons and not wooden ones when cooking any dish that contained fat: when dipped into the pot, a wooden spoon might soak up a miniscule bit of fat. They should teach their children never to put butter or jam on a plate, but always to spread it directly onto a slice of bread, so that none was "wasted" on the plate.[21] Radio programs for housewives bemoaned the fact that "a great fortune could be saved for our economy, if only all households would take the trouble to be more careful [about waste]. Every day, dishtowels have small holes poked in them by the tips of forks [when silverware is dried]."[22] Provincial chapters of the Women's Bureau organized traveling exhibitions that reached the smaller towns, which included displays on "A Full Garbage Can: How It Should and Should Not Be," demonstrating how the housewife should separate out empty cans, tubes, cigarette cartons, old nails, bits of wood, newspapers, glass, and rubber for recycling. Another exhibit to promote the "German apple" featured a recipe for making a cheap drink out of leftover apple peels (which were generated in the process of baking but must not be thrown out).[23]

There was little need to convince consumers to eat potatoes. But the Women's Bureau was terribly concerned about how those potatoes were peeled. Sloppy peeling (where some of the inner, white part of

---

[21] See NWSM NS-Frauenschaft Westfalen-Nord no. 133, Presse, "Praktische Winke für die Hausfrau, Oct. 20, 1936.

[22] BA NS 44/58, script for radio programs from winter, 1938, "ohne Geld ein Vermögen gespart."

[23] From descriptions of traveling exhibitions in Kreis Bielefeld in NWSM NS-Frauenschaft Westfalen-Nord no. 60, Monatliche Tätigkeitsberichte der Abteilung Volkswirtschaft/Hauswirtschaft, 1935.

the potato was cut off with the peel) was allegedly responsible for the wastage of tons of potatoes every year. To avoid this, Nazi women's groups repeatedly urged consumers to eat *Pellkartoffeln*, because peeling cooked potatoes meant that the peel came off easily (although they admitted that peeling hot potatoes stung one's fingers). Cold, unappetizing, leftover bits of potatoes were another recurring problem for the Home Economics Section: not a scrap should go to waste. Nazi Party women's agencies generated hundreds of recipe tips, offering housewives recipes (often entailing much more work than the original menu that had created the leftovers) to enable them to recycle and use up those cold remnants.[24] For special occasions, housewives were urged to consider fancier potato dishes in place of traditional favorites that called for meat or butter. There was one set of radio shows and pamphlets featuring festive potato recipes entitled "The Potato in Holiday Dress."[25]

"German" Fashions and Furniture

In emphasizing extreme thrift, Nazi women's groups were building on a hallowed tradition in German home economics. But the Nazi Four-Year Plan also required them to break new ground in some areas to persuade housewives not only to recycle clothing scraps, but also to "aryanize" their clothing or furniture, which sometimes involved accepting *ersatz* products. The push to "aryanize" clothing and furniture predated the Nazi Four-Year Plan. Soon after the Nazis came to power in 1933, the Women's Bureau also began a campaign against the manufacturers of ready-made clothing, who were often Jewish. These campaigns (like the nationwide boycott of Jewish-owned businesses of April 1933) were largely a failure, as even members of the NS Women's League were fruitlessly and repeatedly admonished not to shop in Jewish-owned shops.

The "aryanization" of German fashion and interior design – as in other industries – was ultimately accomplished not through consumer boycotts, but through expropriation. The steady and relentless policy

[24] *Pellkartoffeln* were endlessly promoted; see, e.g., *Deutsche Hauswirtschaft* 20 (1935): 123.
[25] See BA NS 44/58, Anregungen für das Rundfunkprogram in den Wintermonaten 1938/39.

of "aryanization" of the clothing and textile industries resulted in the liquidation of essentially all Jewish-owned firms in these sectors by 1939. In Frankfurt, Jewish-owned businesses had dominated the textile and retail clothing trades: 253 of the 364 textile firms that existed in the region in 1933 were owned by Jews. By 1939 all of these had been forcibly sold or confiscated, thus reflecting a policy that was carried out across Germany.[26] The liquidation of Jewish firms was accompanied by the creation of special clothing labels placed on clothes manufactured by "Aryan" firms. Associations of such firms such as the League of German-Aryan Clothing Manufacturers mounted campaigns that urged German housewives to buy only clothes with the "Aryan" label, arguing that only "Aryan" firms knew "what really reflects German tastes; only [such clothes] are free from the influence of Jewish tastes."[27] Clothing manufacturers and Nazi women's groups also urged consumers to free themselves from the influence of French clothing design. The regime hoped to end the demand among elite groups, who regularly purchased clothing from France or Italy, along with perfume and jewelry.

But although it was often clear what sorts of consumption the regime opposed (clothes and design that came from Jewish-owned or French manufacturers, or even that somehow indefinably reflected a Jewish or French spirit), it was often much less clear what should replace these designs. In fashion and décor, just as in other areas of the arts and media, Nazi cultural policies were often undercut by the polycratic nature of the Nazi system of government, which led to constant low-level fights over jurisdiction, influence, and implementation of policies. Individual manufacturers or designers could easily find patrons among competing Nazi Party or state agencies, and thus exploit loopholes

[26] For the "aryanization" of the Frankfurt textile industry, see Almut Junker, "Das Frankfurter Modeamt" in Almut Junker, ed., *Frankfurt Macht Mode, 1933–1945* (Frankfurt: Jonas Verlag, 1994), 17; for the same process in Berlin and elsewhere see Sigrid Jacobeit, "Clothing in Nazi Germany," in Georg Iggers, ed., *Marxist Historiography in Transformation* (New York: Berg, 1991), 227–45; and Kenneth McDonald, "Fascist Fashion: Dress, the State, and the Clothing Industry in the Third Reich," (Ph.D. diss., University of California, Riverside, 1998), 184–6.

[27] See, e.g., the promotion of this label in "Deutsche Menschen – deutsche Kleidung," in *Deutsche Hausfrau* 20 (1935): 103; for the work of national "Aryan" clothing and leather goods manufacturers' leagues, see McDonald, "Fascist Fashion," 184.

or inconsistencies in how policies were articulated or implemented. As a result, no single line or vision as to what constituted German design was or could be pursued by the regime, and the relationship between industries and the regime was characterized by a great deal of cooperation and accommodation, but also by uneven oversight by the government.[28]

German fashion and home décor was allegedly characterized by the use of German-made raw materials and produced by "Aryan-owned" firms. Housewives were repeatedly told by the Women's Bureau's exhibitions, magazines, and home economic courses, for example, that the most "appropriate" German furniture was made from the tree most closely associated with Germany in symbolism, the German oak. But what distinguished it beyond these features was unclear. Women were admonished in one educational campaign that "the housewife wants her home decorated according to her own tastes," which were generally characterized as "solid," "simple," "German" styles of décor, ideally produced by a local artisan, rather than being purchased in a department store.

Chapters of the Women's Bureau division on home economics held evening gatherings nationwide in the mid- and late-1930s that allowed artisans and craftsmen to present displays of their furniture and other housewares to groups of local housewives.[29] Shoppers were admonished not to buy mass-produced goods (*Dutzendwaren*) for their homes, as these were cheap and would not last long, leading housewives to fall for the trap of what would later be called "planned obsolescence" because such styles changed regularly, necessitating a fresh redecoration of the home. Instead, press releases and exhibitions urged women to stay with the older bourgeois pattern of buying at the time of marriage one "solid" set of furniture and decorations that would

---

[28] For examples of how individual firms could make use of conflicts or inconsistencies in Nazi policies and agencies, see Berghoff, "Konsumgüterindustrie im Nationalsozialismus," and McDonald, "Fascist Fashion," 191. See also Irene Guenther, "Nazi 'Chic'? German Politics and Womens' Fashions, 1915–1945," *Fashion Theory* 1 (1997): 29–58.

[29] See the monthly Women's Bureau chapter reports in NWSM NS-Fruaenschaft Westfalen-Nord no. 90; see material on the slide shows and suggested programs distributed nationally in BA NS 44/47, Reichsfrauenführung: Rundschreiben FW 1939.

last a lifetime.[30] A slide show and brochure entitled "Our Home" and distributed to Women's Bureau chapters nationwide argued that

[o]nly simple furniture, with a good, refined shape and executed at a high level of quality has lasting work. . . . [T]he housewife can help to bring prices under control if she does not fall for the trap of "fashions" promoted by the furniture industry and instead consciously chooses pieces that will not be out of style only a few years later, but which will instead remain serviceable and attractive for years.[31]

Going into department stores (instead of patronizing the local artisans) should be avoided. It could only lead to impulse purchases of cheap products, as one press release pointed out:

[A housewife goes] to a department store, where all sorts of products lie side by side, and where she believes that she can purchase things more cheaply. But then when she later comes out of the department store, she is laden with things that she never would have bought at a local merchant's. Like many others, she has fallen victim to the way in which department stores stimulate the urge to purchase [in consumers]. . . . German consumers must learn to buy quality products because in the long run, they are a better value.[32]

But to suppress frequent purchases and the turnover of style was to help cut back on consumer demand, as Nazi women leaders were well aware. The campaign against a style-driven turnover in home décor thus fit well within the framework of the Nazi Four-Year Plan. The promotion of a simple, more traditionalGerman style of furniture was popular during the 1930s; such styles would sell well during the 1950s as well.[33]

Propaganda on the subject of home décor was thus usually vague, and aimed mainly at promoting domestic materials, with as little

---

[30] See the monthly reports on activities of Women's Bureau chapters in NWSM NS-Frauenschaft Westfalen-Nord no. 313; see also Else Vorwerck, "Hauswirtschaft in Selbstverwaltung. Ein erster grosser Versuch, 1934–1945," unpublished ms., 1948, 53–4.

[31] Federal Archive in Berlin, NS 44/47, n.d. (1938/1939).

[32] See the press release "Richtiger Einkauf," Nov. 24, 1936 in NWSM, no. 373; similar press releases are also in NWSM, no. 133.

[33] One of the most popular of such furniture styles was the Gelsenkirchener Baroque (named after the town where it was produced), which remained popular throughout the mid-1950s. See Paul Betts, "The Nierentisch Nemesis: Organic Design in West German Pop Culture".

turnover in style as possible in order to suppress demand. Clothing was the subject of some propaganda that was similarly vague. But clothes were also the topic of often much more specific and even contradictory guidelines. As in the case of furniture, women were urged to purchase or sew styles that "suited the German spirit" and that perhaps even incorporated the traits of older "Germanic" clothing. None of this had much effect, however. German fashions (especially those produced for better-off women) continued to ape French haute couture well past the start of World War II, although fashion magazines rarely acknowledged this fact.[34]

But although the style and cut might still follow French fashions, the textiles used for clothing were increasingly *ersatz*. Synthetic fabrics were a hallmark of the Nazi Four-Year Plan; they were used to eke out Germany's inadequate supplies of wool and linen, while saving foreign currency reserves for the armaments industries. Synthetic silk had become popular during the 1920s for some articles in women's clothing, but the newer synthetics were intended to largely replace the textile staples of wool and cotton, which the regime no longer wished to import in such quantities. Moreover, the military had first call on domestic stocks of these natural fibers. During the 1930s newer synthetics were created out of a base of chemically treated beech wood, which was broken down into a pulpy mass that could be spun and dyed. Cellulose was initially used for hats, accessories, and clothing trim. By the late 1930s, shortages of wool and cotton, and the cheaper prices for cellulose, pushed German consumers to use these fabrics for many sorts of clothes. Indeed, after 1934, the regime issued decrees on the compulsory addition of synthetic fibers to textiles, and (officially, at least), the production of pure cotton or wool fabrics ceased.[35]

Pure synthetic fabrics were developed as substitutes for natural fiber fabrics: they were *ersatz* silk, cotton, and woolens. But to label these

---

[34] See Junker, "Das Frankfurter Modeamt" and Guenther, "Nazi 'Chic'."

[35] The popularity of synthetic silk during the 1920s was symbolized in Imgard Keun's best-selling Weimar novel about a "new woman" character who wore this fabric, *Das kunstseidene Mädchen*. For the technical advances that made a variety of new cellulose fabrics possible during the 1930s, see Heidi Blöcher, "Zellwolle und Kunstseide, die neuen Spinnstoffe" in Junker, *Frankfurt Macht Mode*, 73–82. For the ban on pure wool or cotton fabrics, see Berghoff, "Enticement and Deprivation," 181.

fabrics *ersatz* would invoke the shortages of the war years and produce consumer resistance. The terms *Zellwolle* (which literally means "cellular wool") and "the new fabrics" were used instead. The Women's Bureau publications tried to convince consumers that these synthetics were modern, yet at the same time natural, German products because they came from the German soil (wood). Women's magazines argued that cellular wool was even superior to wool and linen. One article in *Deutsche Hauswirtschaft* claimed that the label "pure wool" "is no longer a sign of good quality, but rather only a sign that the producer is behind the times."[36] Another article reminded readers that the airplane and automobile had originally been skeptically received by ordinary people, and predicted similar future popularity for cellulose.[37] In America, where people certainly had no shortage of wool or cotton (German housewives were told) educated American consumers had even come to *prefer* cellulose fabrics.[38]

These claims were undermined, however, by the simultaneous mass distribution of instructions on how to wash these new fabrics, which implicitly admitted that they were not as durable as wool, cotton, or linen. Consumers were warned that they must never wash these fabrics at any temperatures higher than seventy degrees Celsius, or they would be damaged; indeed, they were best washed at thirty degrees. This contradicted many housewives' preference for washing linens at one hundred degrees – boiling temperature, which Germans call *Kochwäsche* or "boiling washing" – which even today is held in order to get fabrics really clean.

Ordinary consumers quickly discovered how inferior early synthetic fabrics really were. An American living in Berlin during this period noted with amusement that prewar uniforms for the police and army were quickly discovered to "bleed" dye and not to repel water as well as wool did. "Experimenting with the uniform cloth went on continuously in beer halls and cafes, as scientifically-minded Germans tested it against water, beer, and even fire... [dye leakage occurred to such

---

[36] "Neue Stoffe, Neues Denken," *Deutsche Hauswirtschaft* 22 (1937): 120.
[37] "Kunstseide und Zellwolle, die Spinnstoffe der Neuzeit," *Deutsche Hauswirtschaft* 23 (1938): 53.
[38] Propaganda promoting synthetic fabrics as simultaneously modern *and* natural was ubiquitous in 1930s German media; for typical examples, see *Die Deutsche Hausfrau* 20 (1935): 69 and 147; 22 (1937): 53.

an extent that] privates became known in jokes as 'men from Mars,' because they all took on a greenish hue."[39]

German wardrobes were also constrained by the lack of leather that the Nazi Four-Year Plan mandated. Under the guidance of the German Fashion Institute and the Women's Bureau, consumers were offered shoes with cork or even Plexiglas soles (the Plexiglas came from munitions production scraps) and hats made out of straw or cellophane. Synthetic leather, Mipolam, was also offered for belts and gloves. As with cellulose, consumers were assured that the synthetic was superior to its traditional counterpart because Mipolam "in many respects is much better than the older material, 'leather', which was formerly used for men's belts."[40] An even more commonly used substitute for shoes, belts, and purses was fish skin, which women's organizations referred to as "fish leather." Consumers, especially those who could afford better and who were accustomed to more luxurious materials, remained unconvinced, which led the Director of the Frankfurt Fashion Institute, Margarete Klimt, to assure haute couture customers in 1937 that

[these] materials are the answer to the assignment that economic circumstances have imposed on us. But we should not meet this shortage with the resignation that was called for when we were given the old "ersatz materials" [in the last war] because: Vistra, cellulose, cellulose fabrics, artificial silk…straw soles, etc. are all new creations of the German economy and therefore are just like fashionable materials of other nations, which spring from the soil of the native economy.[41]

Here again, patently "artificial" materials were presented as being intrinsically "German," springing from the German "soil," and thus somehow also "natural."

After the war began, leather shortages became even more acute, which led to tension over the distribution of shoes. The military and Nazi Party organizations had first call, moreover, on the leather that was available, which led to civilian complaints that "workers were angered when they could not get ration cards for shoes while civilian

---

[39] See William Bayles, *Postmarked Berlin* (London: Jarrolds Limited, 1942), 106.

[40] From an article on Mipolam in *Textilwoche*, quoted in Junker, "Frankfurter Modeamt," 33.

[41] Quoted in Junker, "Frankfurter Modeamt," 27–8.

uniform-wearers [e.g., Nazi Party members] got to wear brand new boots of the finest leather."[42]

Recycling, Self-Sufficiency, and Adjusting to the Market Order

But the propaganda for *ersatz* products, which was aimed primarily at getting the bourgeoisie and upper classes to accept substandard materials, was matched and far exceeded by the push to get German housewives to cut down, resew, and recycle clothing, a campaign that was aimed at women of all classes. The goal was to avoid the purchase of new clothes (whether made of natural or synthetic fibers) as far as possible. The propaganda and courses on how to make "new out of old" proliferated, and reached high levels of specialization and detail. A course offered throughout Westphalia in the late 1930s and early 1940s, for example, trained housewives to make house slippers out of old straw or felt hats.[43] Brochures, magazine articles, and courses taught housewives how to use and reuse every scrap of fabric.

Housewives were therefore endlessly admonished (and offered patterns and courses) to recycle and resew every scrap of fabric: this was presented as a kind of domestic magic, where mother made "old things new again." Sheets that were worn too thin could be made into serviceable dresses and aprons; housewives were cautioned to dye the fabric to a dark shade first so that the dresses would not be transparent. Men's suits could be retailored into skirts and vests and (like Scarlett O'Hara) women could take down old curtains and make them into new formal gowns and suits.[44] Men's shirts could be turned into undershirts and handkerchiefs; a baby's baptism dress could be recycled into a summer jacket; old handbags could form the upper section of wooden clogs; or a men's silk scarf could be retailored into a women's slip.[45] Nothing was to be wasted; every scrap should be reused. If clothing shreds were

---

[42] From a 1940 letter from the Reichswirtschaftsministerium to all other ministries, quoted in McDonald, "Fascist Fashion," 168.

[43] See the report on the Gau's educational activities from the early 1940s in NWSM, Bestand NS-Frauenschaft Westfalen-Nord, no. 122.

[44] Patterns and instructions for "cutting down" and recycling fabric were widely distributed. These examples are taken from BA NS 44/49, "Merkzettel: Mutter findet in der Flickenkiste."

[45] See the instructions for such transformations in the brochure "Mother Finds in the Mending Basket" in the Federal Archive, Berlin, Bestand NS 44/49 (n.d., probably

good for nothing else, a housewife could recycle a heap of them by making a hooked or braided rug (which had been a staple in preindustrial households, e.g., in colonial America). Local chapters of the Women's Bureau offered classes on how to make such rugs.[46]

The Women's Bureau waged a long-running campaign against the representatives of the ready-made clothing industry, arguing that a larger amount of cloth ought to be allocated to fabric stores in order to encourage home sewing. Even after 1941, when many women were now mobilized to work outside the home (or had other war-related responsibilities), the Women's Bureau was still arguing against allocating fabric to ready-made clothing.[47]

Consumers were thus presented with obvious contradictions (as elsewhere in Nazi society). They were told on the one hand that *ersatz* materials were not *ersatz*, even as platoons from the Hitler Youth were sent door-to-door to collect bones, buttons, old fabric, and metal scraps to be used for the war preparation that allegedly was no such thing. The Hitler Youth's feminine counterpart, the BDM, was similarly employed to gather fallen fruits, wild herbs, and old LP records. Plants such as rose hips, dandelions, nettles, and wild mustard – which both housewives and girls' groups were urged to collect in forests or meadows and put up – were referred to as "wild vegetables." Starting in 1938, girls were also asked to clean the combed-out hair from their families' hairbrushes and combs and deliver the hair to local hairdressers, where it was collected and passed on for the production of military goods that required felt.[48] The similarities between the materials and recycling strategies used in World War I inevitably awakened consumers' fears and mistrust.

1939). For examples of magazine articles with instructions (which were ubiquitous in late 1930s women's publications) see *Die Deutsche Hausfrau* 22 (1937): 98 and 226.

[46] For courses on how to make braided rugs (which had been supplanted in most of the West in the nineteenth century by machine-woven rugs), see the report by the local chapters of the NS in Kreis Detmold from late 1935 in NWSM, Bestand NS-Frauenschaft Westfalen-Nord, no. 60.

[47] See Vorwerck's memoir, "Hauswirtschaft in Selbstverwaltung," regarding the wartime allocation of fabric production to fabric stores versus its delegation to manufacturers of ready-made clothing.

[48] Dagmar Reese,"Bund Deutscher Mädel – Zur Geschichte der weiblichen deutschen Jugend im Dritten Reich," in Frauengruppe Faschismusforschung, *Mutterkreuz und Arbeitsbuch. Zur Geschichte der Frauen in der Weimarer Republik und im Nationalsozialismus* (Frankfurt: Fischer Verlag, 1981), 177–9.

What the Women's Bureau and other Nazi women's groups were urging housewives to do was not merely to accept products at more than face value, but also to get by on as little as possible in order to suppress consumer demand. Their goal was to extract the private household, as much as possible, from the cash nexus in order to encourage economic self-sufficiency and household autarky. Thus, a prime focus of the propaganda and cooking courses was instructions on how to can, put up, and preserve foods and jams. Food preservation was already the norm in rural areas and small towns where consumers had their own plots and gardens to supply produce: because it was their "own" food they would not want to waste any that they did not eat in season. But NS women's groups wanted to persuade *all* housewives, even those in big cities (who might not have sufficient storage space or already possess the equipment required for canning) to invest a great deal of labor every summer and fall in putting up produce that was seasonally available in urban markets.

The stress on household self-sufficiency and autarky in the private sphere was thus often carried to extremes that were irrational. Harvest surpluses of leeks and potatoes, for example, could probably have been more easily "saved" by industry, which (unlike many urban housewives) already possessed the necessary equipment for canning and preserving foods. Instead, the Women's Bureau tried to mobilize housewives on a month-to-month basis (depending of which foods were currently in "surplus"), train them to can or preserve the foods, and try to make sufficient canning supplies available in stores. Ready-made clothing also offered economies of scale and efficiency. And yet this too was associated with mass, standardized, industrialized living (before the war it was associated with Jewish-owned firms). Household autarky, self-sufficiency, traditional thrifty practices, and domesticity were inextricably intertwined in this vision of housekeeping and consumption.

And yet, the autarkic household was not merely to make as few demands on the broader economy as a whole; it was also engaged in an intricate, ever-changing minuet with agriculture and industrial production. The regime was trying to persuade German housewives to make ongoing adjustments to their *Küchenzettel*, or weekly menu, and to constantly fine-tune their shopping lists and menus to reflect products that were available that month. In magazines, newspapers, and on the *Schwarzes Brett* in many workplaces, women were given lists each month of products that were currently abundant and those that were in shorter supply, and urged to adjust their purchasing patterns and diets accordingly. If the grain crop had been better one year, they were to eat more *Vollkorn* (whole grain) bread; if the potato crop was larger the next, they were to switch to potato recipes. One season there might be an abundance of leeks (which must be purchased and correctly preserved); the next season there might be an excess of apples, which housewives were urged to put up. Thus, the regime was trying to adjust demand instead of supply in order to keep prices constant and to steer around shortages of more popular goods.

Housewives were not only expected to bridge the gap between supply and demand by adjusting and disciplining their households' consumption so that demand "met" supply. By making their households as self-sufficient as possible and by extracting their families (in part) from the cash nexus, housewives were also expected to facilitate the regime's policy of wage freezes. The Women's Bureau's hope was that if housewives were as thrifty and efficient as possible, their families and husbands would not feel the pinch of wage freezes and increased taxes, and could live more comfortably on modest salaries. The capital saved on wage increases could then be invested elsewhere, for example, in rearmament.

This approach required that housewives and their families sometimes give up favorite family or regional dishes, and to regularly experiment with new foods and products. Nazi women's groups were thus struggling (with mixed success) against deeply entrenched tastes and habits, and a note of exasperation often crept into their admonitions, as in a *Deutsche Hauswirtschaft* article that exclaimed that "it would be very desirable, if housewives would not always fall back upon the old favorites, but would rather also learn how to make tasty dishes out of other cuts of meat. When the asparagus crop comes in, people want to eat cutlets and *Schnitzel* [with asparagus], and prices immediately rise for these cuts."[49] Instead, housewives were urged to substitute the Sunday "One Dish" meal for their roast; told to use *Quark*, instead of butter or margarine; and exhorted to try dishes that might be common in some regions, but not others: the "flour dishes," barley, or

---

[49] "Das 'Ich' und 'Wir' der Hausfrauen," *Deutsche Hausfrau* 19 (1934): 51.

milk soups. They should use synthetic silk instead of linen (and wash it carefully, using soap that had been "adjusted" to lower levels of fat).

In a broader sense, housewives were also being urged to adapt their work patterns to the needs of an autarkic economy. In both large and small ways, they were exhorted to alter daily habits and work methods, as domesticity became the chief expression of women's involvement in the national effort. They were to sort their garbage into five separate categories for recycling and make a special note of packages (e.g., toothpaste tubes) with the "red dot," which marked items that had to be recycled. They were told that there was one (and only one) right way to do every household task: from hanging socks to dry, to measuring sugar for cooking.[50] They were urged to keep detailed records in their household account books, drawing a daily, weekly, and quarterly balance. They were also supposed to draw up weekly "work plans" (which made time for labor-intensive home production of foodstuffs and clothing) and *Küchenzettel* that adjusted to monthly market fluctuations.

For decades, German home economists and leaders of housewives groups had urged German women (especially working-class women) to pursue more rational, self-disciplined styles of housekeeping. But under the Nazi Four-Year Plan they were being asked to become almost surreally efficient and self-sufficient, renouncing both free time and any weakness for butter. And now, they were to make "martyrs" of themselves not for their families but rather for the state. In some ways, these sacrifices resembled those that were asked of American or British women during the two World Wars (e.g., the "meatless" or "wheatless" days in the United States in 1917–18), but German housewives were being asked to retool their menus and households during peacetime.

The Women's Bureau heads, along with other Nazi Party leaders, recognized that the desire to consume could not always be restrained. In the case of new households (especially those that had received marriage loans from the regime), larger purchases of children's goods, furniture,

---

[50] The "one right way" of consumption and housekeeping was illustrated each month, e.g., in a *Deutsche Hausfrau* column entitled "Was stimmt hier nicht?" The "red dot" on packaging material that should be recycled was mentioned in a few *Deutsche Hausfrau* articles, but it is unclear whether this program was ever widely implemented.

and appliances were expected. In oral histories of the period, women's recollections often focus on these sorts of "approved" acquisitions: complete kitchens purchased with the marriage loan or goods for new babies that came *gratis* from the regime.[51] The official goal was to educate housewives to avoid cheap *Dutzendwaren* (e.g., ready-made clothes and mass-produced, standardized housewares) but buy "German styles" from local artisans, which helped lengthen the life of purchases.

Another household purchase that (similar to the Volkswagen car) was dangled in front of housewives but never actually mass-produced was the so-called Volk's refrigerator. Like KdF cruises and automobiles, the Volk's refrigerator was a form of enticement that represented modernity and luxury, a product associated with the upper middle class. But only a few models designed for private households were ever built. Housewives were thus being asked to work harder, suppress or redirect their families' consumption patterns, and go back to older methods of self-provisioning to obtain goods (gathering wild herbs, putting up their own produce, making their own rugs), at the same time that they were being promised high-status, modern appliances.[52]

The language and imagery used to describe the ideal autarkic household were drawn from many sources. One root was the language of traditional bourgeois domestic thrift. Thus, some writers called for housewives to return to keeping the traditional German *Fettopf* (a container, in which women stored fat that had run off from cooking, blended with beef lard, kidney fat, or other lards) to use as a source of fats in place of margarine or *Palmin* (shortening). "We have let many such German [housekeeping] customs fall by the wayside," one concluded, "and adopted American [labor-saving] styles of work; away with these!"[53] More often, Women's Bureau writers used a language

---

[51] See the interviews done with women who married during this period (and who used marriage loan coupons to acquire new kitchen furniture and utensils, or who received baby clothes, etc., from Nazi Party organizations) in Anne-Katrin Einfeldt, "Auskommen – Durchkommen – Weiterkommen. Weibliche Arbeitserfahrungen in der Bergarbeiterkolonie," in Lutz Niethammer, ed., *Die Jahre weiss man nicht, wo man die heute hinsetzen soll. Faschismus-Erfahrungen im Ruhrgebiet* (Berlin: Dietz, 1983), 267–98.

[52] Berghoff, "Enticement and Deprivation," 176–7.

[53] Flyer by Martha Voss-Zietz; copy in NWSM NS-Frauenschaft Westfalen-Nord, no. 231.

of efficiency and order to describe their approach to housekeeping and consumption. Germany was engaged in a "production battle" in order to achieve "nutritional liberty." To reach this goal, the regime was practicing "the guidance of consumer demand," which was to take place within the framework of a new, regulated *Marktordnung* (market order). Housewives might well come up against "temporary shortages" of favorite products, but "a clever housewife will adjust her menu plan according to the surpluses and shortages of the current market, ... [S]he knows that rational use of leftovers" helped her budget, her family's health, and the Four-Year Plan.[54]

A good *Küchenzettel* was not only adapted to the new *Marktordnung*, it was also "closer to nature." Nazi women's groups argued that consumers not only needed to adapt to the plan's ongoing surpluses and shortages, but that they needed to go back to "natural, seasonal" rhythms of consumption. For example, city women had to learn that they could no longer demand fresh eggs at Christmastime (when hens did not naturally lay them). As the 1936 annual report for the Westphalian Home Economics Section claimed:

The boundless imports of the postwar period seduced our housewives into making demands on the German market no longer connected to the soil, as in earlier times. City women had actually come to ignore the growth and cycles of the natural environment that surrounded them. Fresh strawberries in winter were now simply seen as a delicacy.... [We must] bring the city woman back to a way of thinking that is bound to German soil and nature.[55]

To eat "naturally" was also healthier, as Nazi Party publications constantly reminded housewives. The excessive consumption of meat and fats was a distressing symptom of modern civilization; a diet based on whole grains and vegetables would be much better. It was sometimes asserted that it was even more "Aryan." Staff members who worked in regional advice centers for housewives were taught that "all [ancient] Aryans, possessing the surer instincts of primitive man, chose whole grains as the main source of nutrition dictated to us by Nature.... [Mass production] led us onto a false [dietary] path. But now modern nutrition again recognizes the vitamin content and value

---

[54] "Hausfrauen helfen den Vierjahresplan erfüllen," *Deutsche Hauswirtschaft* 23 (1938): 195.
[55] NWSM NS-Frauenschaft Westfalen-Nord, no. 378, 1936 Jahresbericht.

of *Vollkornbrot.*"[56] The emphasis on health and nature accorded well with other aspects of Nazi public health policy.[57] But although the diet being promoted by the Women's Bureau was indeed healthier (in some respects, in ways that the Nazis could not have known), the food choices discussed were primarily promoted not to improve consumers' health, but to meet the needs of an autarkic economy.[58]

The Limits of Persuasion

But this appetizing blend of nature, rationality, and tradition could not always tempt housewives who did not always want to work harder, who could not stretch their budgets even further, or who simply wanted to eat their favorite foods. Sources offer many glimpses of consumers who – although they might be compelled to follow some of the Women's Bureau's suggestions because they could afford or obtain nothing better – often voiced reluctance, resistance, and fear about what these consumption patterns portended (because they were reminded of World War I), or exhibited a stubborn insistence on doing things as they had always done. Reports from many regional divisions offered evidence that the cooking courses and public demonstrations were often oversubscribed (such courses offered by housewives' organizations before 1933 had been as well) and often claimed success in enlisting women in recycling efforts.[59] But other attempts to change

---

[56] BA NS 44/7, minutes of an Apr. 1939 schooling course for nutritional advisors; for similar arguments, see also Vorwerck, "Hauswirtschaft in Selbstverwaltung," 30; BA NS 44/58, scripts for radio broadcasts for housewives from 1938, "Gesunde Volksernährung"; and "Über die deutsche Volksernährung," *Deutsche Hauswirtschaft* 21 (1936): 129, which concluded that "the digestive process and biochemistry is different for each race."

[57] See Robert Proctor, *The Nazi War on Cancer* (Princeton: Princeton University Press, 1999), esp. 120–72.

[58] As Proctor notes, German medical experts strongly suspected that a diet richer in fresh produce would help to reduce rates of stomach cancer. The links between meat consumption and heart disease, or between whole grain fiber and colon cancer, however, were not yet understood during the 1930s. Thus, in some respects, the Four-Year Plan diet was fortuitously "healthy."

[59] For examples of *Kreis* reports that emphasize the consistant popularity of cooking courses (while admitting that other programs usually were not well received) see NWSM, NS Frauenschaft Westfalen-Nord, nos. 60 and 340. See also Jill Stephenson, "Propaganda, Autarky, and the German Housewife," in David Welch, ed., *Nazi Propaganda. The Power and the Limitations* (London: Croom Helm 1983), 132.

women's habits (to get them to keep account books, do more canning or putting up, or get by without margarine) seem to have met with resistance. As the minutes from a 1936 meeting of Westphalian *Gau* Home Economics Section advisors noted:

We must still do a great deal of economic educational work with many women, who have still not made the transition from thinking about "me" to "us." Many housewives still insist that it is their own business how they do their work, and whether they make mistakes [in housekeeping and consumption]. . . . [T]he most important goal must be to create understanding and acceptance of the new *Marktordnung.* . . . [W]e must learn to do without that, which is currently not available in the market, and take that, which the market currently delivers. Here, it is urgent that we educate women quickly and persuasively. There is enough food available for all; there are simply a few temporary shortages of pork and butter. Unfortunately, during the last few months, more and more hoarding has been going on, which is making matters worse.[60]

The monthly reports from Women's Bureau workers in a variety of localities regularly passed on the complaints from housewives about rising prices for food, and shortages of pork and fats. Many women did not want to switch to a diet of herring and *Pellkartoffeln*, which were traditionally the diet of the working poor. Although working-class or poor families might not have any choice about following a regime of thrift and self-denial, eating potatoes and herring, bourgeois housewives certainly did have a choice and often resisted. The relative degree of "deprivation" being imposed on consumers thus varied according to their previous life-style and options: the Women's Bureau was asking greater sacrifices from the middle and upper middle classes. Home Economics Section leaders sometimes recognized this fact and often attempted to persuade bourgeois housewives to alter their choices *within* the category of "luxury" foods, for example, switching from imported (or unobtainable) pork cuts to locally grown chicken for Sunday dinners,. But bourgeois husbands were probably the demographic group most accustomed to enjoying their "favorites." And in some instances, there was no luxury substitute for a product that was a staple on upper-middle-class tables, such as butter.

[60] NWSM NS-Frauenschaft Westfalen-Nord, no. 88, Protokolle of 1936 meeting of Gau Abteilungs-Leiterinnen.

Other women, from both the working class and bourgeoisie, resisted the idea of cooking the "warm" evening dinner that most of the proposed menus were pushing. The more common pattern (in many regions, but not all) was a warm midday meal and then bread with some sort of spread or sausage for dinner; a custom that the Women's Bureau repeatedly criticized with little success. The shortages of such *Belege* meant that housewives would have to do additional work for dinner, cooking "warm" evening meals of potato or noodle dishes.[61]

In addition, the Women's Bureau was encountering stubborn regional differences in its promotion of a pan-German diet. The national headquarters of the Home Economics Section regularly collected and evaluated the household account books of about one hundred and forty households from the lower income groups across a variety of regions; the average monthly income of these households was about 150 Reichsmarks. This somewhat small sample was the basis for a detailed longitudinal study and gives some idea as to the actual patterns of consumption and expenditures among Germans of modest means during the late 1930s. The results of these evaluations were regularly forwarded to the Ministries of Health and Nutrition and apparently used to help calculate the government's cost-of-living index.

The account books confirmed the regular complaints from Women's Bureau volunteers about the strong regional variations in diet and consumption, which made doing propaganda about the plan's needs more difficult. Fat consumption (butter or *Schmalz*) was relatively high in Northern Germany, while Bavarians ate almost twice as much meat per capita as the national average. Milk soups and noodles were popular in the west and the south, while East Prussian housewives apparently stubbornly rejected all attempts to alter their regional cuisine.

East Prussian and Bavarian housewives were heavily rural, which put them in a different position vis-à-vis the market. Unlike urban housewives, who generally had to rely on what the local markets offered, rural housewives had more control over the ingredients available for their menus and thus more control over their diets. Finally, the

---

[61] In internal correspondence, DFW advisors repeatedly complained that in many regions, housewives just wanted to place *Wurst* or cold meats on the dinner table. See, e.g., the analysis of actual household account books in BA NS 44/45, Rundschreiben FW 96/37 (Oct. 1937).

Berlin office switched to the approach of simply forwarding to each region the list of each month's "desirable" (i.e., currently available) ingredients to be promoted and left devising exact recipes up to each regional office.[62]

The account books survey (which was admittedly based on a sample of households that were already "orderly," because only these housewives kept the accounts in the kind of detail demanded by the Women's Bureau) also shows how tight the budgets of most households already were. As one analyst noted, in most of these households, the main breadwinner did not receive any wage raises during this period. Even before the Nazi Four-Year Plan, precious little waste was occurring in most of these families. Food expenditures accounted for about half of the total income, on average; among the poorer households, food took up to 70 percent of the money earned. Rent payments and heating accounted for about 25 percent of the household's money. As the Women's Bureau concluded, "the little that remains of these households' incomes has to cover all remaining expenses: household acquisitions, furniture, cleaning products, clothing, repairs ... money spent on newspapers, radio or cinema, luxury items or travel, etc. For all of these things very little can be spent." Only nine of these households managed to save any money on a regular basis.[63] Modest incomes, and the poverty of choice that these incomes entailed, were thus the most compelling forces of all operating on these households.

It was not surprising, therefore, that local Women's Bureau reporters sometimes wrote that working-class or lower-middle-class women in their audiences found the propaganda offered to them condescending because they knew how to be thrifty and were spending as little as possible already. Some of the advice offered to them insulted the intelligence of any experienced housewife, such as recipes that advised women to make jams or jellies out of the wild fruits and plants they had gathered using only astonishingly and unrealistically small amounts of sugar.[64]

---

[62] See the discussion of this account books survey in ibid.; see also Vorwerck, "Hauswirtschaft in Selbstverwaltung," 90–1. See also Thea Weber, "Forschungen im städtischen Haushalt," *Hauswirtschaftliche Jahrbücher* 11 (1940), 57–62.

[63] BA NS 44/45, Rundschreiben FW 96/37, Oct. 20, 1937.

[64] See the recipes attached to some of the memos in BA NS 44, vol. 49, which recommend making jellies with only one part sugar to five parts fruit (with no pectin added). Most fruit jellies or jams require at least equal parts sugar and fruit to gel.

As the Gelsenkirchen Home Economics Section leader admitted, many of the women she tried to recruit for meetings resisted coming, arguing that "what they tell us at those meetings, we already know, and we're already only just making ends meet."[65] At another meeting in Buer, Westphalia in 1936, Nazi Party women activists showed a film on *Kampf dem Verderb* that evoked similar protests. While the film was being shown, "voices were raised in the [darkened] auditorium that asked 'What! Are we in elementary school here? Any child knows that! etc.' These were not pampered ladies who said this; completely ordinary women enthusiastically joined in criticizing the film."[66] Thus, for women from poorer households, the Women's Bureau's advice was often perceived as superfluous; for bourgeois housewives, it was unwelcome.

Even worse, the Women's Bureau's attempts to promote dark bread, recycling, and the collection of wild fruits and herbs recalled the government propaganda of 1914–18 and made consumers fearful that similar privations lay ahead. A female Nazi Party volunteer in Dortmund noted in 1936 that many of the women were made uneasy by her propaganda efforts. "I have had to put off lectures on the recycling of used materials, in order to avoid creating unrest among those who are already anxious, who say that 'Germany is again so poor, that we have to collect everything, just like in the war.'" By the late 1930s, Berliners had invented mocking nicknames for the regime's most favored and heavily promoted products and *ersatz* products: *Pellkartoffeln* were called "Four Year Plan nuggets;" the *ersatz* coffee offered to consumers was derided as "nigger sweat" [sic]; while the bluish skimmed milk that the Women's Bureau touted as "healthy" was dismissed as "cadaver juice."[67]

Housewives' fears about what the consumption policies of the Nazi Four-Year Plan portended were vindicated after the war's outbreak in 1939. Rationing was immediately introduced, but because consumers

[65] NWSM NS-Frauenschaft Westfalen-Nord no. 60, monthly report from Kreis Gelsenkirchen, Oct. 1935.

[66] NWSM NS-Frauenschaft Westfalen-Nord, no. 378, Oct. 1936 report for Gau division of Volkswirtschaft/Hauswirtschaft.

[67] Bayles, *Postmarked Berlin*, 25. The translation is that of Bayles. The original saying in the first instance was undoubtedly *Negerschweiss*, which would be better translated as "Negro sweat."

were already accustomed to sporadic shortages of goods throughout the prewar years the transition was not an abrupt one except for German Jews and foreign workers, whose rations were soon cut back to almost starvation levels. Shortages of meat became somewhat worse, leading to the further proliferation of rumors and complaints. A 1940 memo sent from the Berlin office to all provincial Nazi Women's League bureaus urged them to contradict popular stories that dog meat was now being introduced into the ground meats sold in shops.[68] But the supply of substitute products and foods, along with the flow of resources back to Germany from the occupied territories, meant that in most areas, shortages were annoying but not drastic, at least through 1942. This is what some Nazi leaders had intended: the massive quantities of stolen goods funneled back to Germany were supposed to make the other burdens imposed by war on civilians more palatable.

After the initial flush of looted products, however, food shortages and price inflation became steadily worse: by 1945, weekly rations of bread, meat, and fat for consumers who were not in a special category (e.g., heavy laborers) had been cut down to about 50 percent of their 1939 levels.[69] The catastrophic food shortages of the "Turnip Winter" of World War I were evidently not repeated and consumer unrest never reached the levels seen during that war. In many areas, shortages indeed became most acute after the war's end, as food supplies simply dried up in some urban areas. The plight of millions of refugees who had fled to Germany to escape the advancing Soviet Army was often particularly acute.[70] In retrospect, those housewives who had been reminded of the earlier war when they had to buy margarine "through the back door" of shops during the late 1930s and who had feared what this might ultimately signify had proven prescient

---

[68] See memo FW 147/40, dated Nov. 29, 1940, in BA NS 44, vol. 49.

[69] Stibbe, *Women in the Third Reich*, 152. For an overview of the experiences of women within Germany during the war, see ibid.,150–69; Szepansky, *Blitzmädel, Heldenmutter, Kriegerwitwe*; Jill Stephenson, *Women in Nazi Society* (London: Barnes and Noble Books, 1975); and Maruta Schmidt and Gabi Dietz, eds., *Frauen uterm Hakenkreuz* (Berlin: Elefanten Verlag, 1983).

[70] For the position of civilians and particularly refugees in the immediate postwar period, see the individual accounts in Alison Owings, *Frauen. German Women Recall the Third Reich* (New Brunswick, NJ: Rutgers University Press, 1995); Wolfgang Samuel, *German Boy: A Refugee's Story* (Jackson: Mississippi University Press, 2000); Stibbe, *Women in the Third Reich*, 167–8.

Conclusion

The combination of enticement and deprivation, coercion and exhortation ultimately succeeded in dampening the growth of German household consumption through the 1930s, and redirecting demand to areas favored by the regime. The autarkic diet so strongly promoted by the Nazi Women's Bureau did gain ground under the Nazi Four-Year Plan. German families increased their consumption of dark breads and potatoes somewhat, while cutting back on the amount of wheat flour and bread that they ate. The amount of dietary fats consumed dropped as much as 20 percent and the amount of meat consumed per capita rose only slightly in spite of Germany's economic recovery, while fish consumption grew substantially. The Women's Bureau regularly promised housewives (falsely) that sugar contained many of the same nutritional elements as butter and fats and urged them to substitute sugar (made from German sugar beets) for imported fats: housewives were told to offer jam in place of butter as a bread spread. As a result – and doubtless because nothing better was available – per capita jam consumption tripled by 1938 (most of it made by housewives), while whipped cream and cream cakes were banned during the same year.[71]

The regime attempted to make women feel empowered (and reconciled to their increased work loads) by constantly stressing their importance to the Nazi Four-Year Plan and national economy. The leader of the Nazi Women's League, Gertrud Scholz-Klink, repeatedly invoked women's "cooking spoons" as weapons that could benefit the nation. The housekeeping and consumption strategies urged on German women during the late 1930s thus attributed power to them by arguing that women could reconcile the conflict between choosing "guns or butter." Guns were prioritized: but although families could not eat their fill of butter, they should at least enjoy a sufficiency of jams made by mother. Nazi leaders hoped that access to such cheaper but palatable substitutes would defuse consumers' resistance to or

---

[71] Hans Teuteberg, "Verzehr von Nahrungsmitteln," 346–47, concludes that fat consumption fell about 20 percent per capita during these years; meat consumption rose very slightly, from 51.4 to 53.5 kilos per capita; fish consumption rose as much as one-third; and rye bread and potato consumption increased modestly while wheat bread consumption fell almost 10 percent. See also Thamer, *Verführung und Gewalt*, 489; Berghoff, "Enticement and Deprivation," 180–1 discusses the banning of heavy cream products in 1938.

criticisms of the privations imposed by the Nazi Four-Year Plan and thus prevent, over the long run, the popular anger and revolts that Nazi leaders blamed for Germany's defeat in 1918. But many housewives apparently were not persuaded of their "national importance," and stubbornly insisted on focusing on the needs of their own households.

In designing their programs, Women's Bureau leaders took up, manipulated, and redeployed many preexisting practices and assumptions regarding housekeeping, diet, and consumption in German domestic culture, including popular or class-specific household management approaches based on thrift, health, nature, local foods, and the value of home-produced clothes or foods. As we have seen, these practices had long histories even before 1933 and would continue to evolve after 1945.

But these "threads" can be woven into entirely different political tapestries, and made to serve quite opposing political purposes. During the 1930s, the German housewife's thrift and management of her household's consumption was redefined. Her thrift was valued before 1933 primarily because it served her family's needs; but during the Nazi period, her choices regarding consumption – and the increased work some choices entailed for her – were depicted as a sort of national service. Under the Nazi Four-Year Plan, long-standing patterns of household management were strategically exploited by the Nazi Party and state in order to support a larger agenda that directly undermined consumers' choices, autonomy, and standard of living. The same approach to managing domesticity would be deployed in occupied Poland after 1939, as Nazi women's groups attempted to "Germanize" the homes and housekeeping of populations that were subjected to large-scale deportation, relocation, expropriation, and genocide.

6

Domesticity and "Germanization" in Occupied Poland

We don't want to train [the Poles] up to levels of German cleanliness in our new territories. Even if they began to scrub themselves and their houses daily, it wouldn't matter to us.

Adolf Hitler

What a burden they carry, if they are to give a German face to their formerly Polish homes.

NS "advisor," writing about "resettled" ethnic German women in occupied Poland, June 1941

Occupied Poland – and much of the Soviet Union after mid-1941 – became a macabre sort of terrain, where many of the most brutal or arbitrary aspects of both Nazi theory and practice flourished. Far from home, National Socialist bureaucrats attempted to "reorganize" Eastern Europe to fit an imagined racial hierarchy. Quite often their goals were simply unrealizable and they were repeatedly forced to chop and change their plans due to the restraints imposed by limited resources or the plan's own sheer impracticality. At the same time, the polycratic tendencies inherent in Nazi agencies reached full fruition in occupied Poland. Officials from a variety of Nazi Party and state organizations pursued both their personal and institutional interests, asserting competing and conflicting claims to jurisdiction over the land, businesses, and population of occupied Poland.[1] As a result, even though Poland

---

[1] The literature on NS bureaucracies and what became known as the "General Plan East" is too large to summarize here, and I will only cite the studies relevant to my particular

was occupied and administered by thousands Nazi Party officials, German civil servants, and the German Army, in some senses it was still chaotic because jurisdiction and authority over the occupied population were contested so often.

One of the Nazi organizations competing for control over occupied Poland was Heinrich Himmler's Commissariat for the Strengthening of Germandom (largely staffed by the SS), which had been charged by Hitler with the large-scale expropriation and deportation of much of the prewar Polish population. The commissariat's goal was to expel millions of Polish citizens (both Jews and gentiles) from the western part of Poland, which had been annexed by Germany proper and organized into new "German" provinces.[2] The deportees were to be dumped into central Poland – now designated the "General Government" – which was ruled by a German commandant, Hans Frank. The General Government was supposed to become a densely packed "reservation" for Jews, deported ethnic Poles, and other "undesirables."

---

topic. The competition between different Nazi agencies in occupied Poland, and the repeated changes in the grotesquely improvised, unrealistic planning of the "Final Solution" are documented in Götz Aly, *'Endlösung' Völkerverschiebung und der Mord an den europäischen Juden* (Frankfurt: S. Fischer Verlag, 1995). Some of the other accounts of the Nazis' massive resettlement of ethnic Germans from across Europe that I consulted included Doris L. Bergen, "The 'Volksdeutschen' of Eastern Europe, World War II, and the Holocaust: Constructed Ethnicity, Real Genocide," in Keith Bullivant, Geoffrey Giles, and Walter Pape, eds., *Germany and Eastern Europe: Cultural Identities and Cultural Differences* (Yearbook of European Studies 13) (Amsterdam: Rodopi, 1999); Bergen, "Sex, Blood, and Vulnerability: Women Outsiders in German-Occupied Europe," in Robert Gellately and Nathan Stolzfus, eds., *Social Outsiders in Nazi Germany* (Princeton: Princeton University Press, 2001), 273–93; Bergen, "Drawing Lines of Blood: Racial Categorization, Gender, War, and the Holocaust," paper presented at the Berkshire Conference on the History of Women, June 2005; Hans-Christian Harten, *De-Kulturation und Germanisierung. Die nationalsozialistische Rassen- und Erziehungspolitik in Polen 1939–1945* (Frankfurt: Campus, 1996); Robert Koehl, *RKFDV: German Resettlement and Population Policy, 1939–1945* (Cambridge, MA: Harvard University Press, 1957); Dietmut Majer, *"Fremdvölkische" im Dritten Reich* (Boppard am Rhein: Harald Boldt Verlag, 1981); Isabel Heinemann, *Rasse, Siedlung, deutsches Blut. Das Rasse- und Siedlungshauptamt der SS und die rassenpolitische Neuordnung Europas* (Göttingen: Wallstein, 2003); Bryant, "Making Czechs German"; and Valdis Lumans, *Himmler's Auxiliaries. The Volksdeutsche Mittelstelle and the German National Minorities of Europe, 1933–1945* (Chapel Hill: University of North Carolina Press, 1993).

[2] The two "new provinces" were dubbed the Wartheland and Danzig-West Prussia. Additional Polish territory swelled two preexisting German provinces, Upper Silesia and East Prussia.

Poland's former eastern provinces were then conquered and annexed by the Soviet Union in accordance the NS-Soviet Pact of 1939.

In the Wartheland and Danzig-West Prussia (the "new German provinces" carved out of western Poland) Himmler and Hitler planned to resettle millions of *Volksdeutschen*, ethnic Germans who came from across Europe, and particularly from areas controlled by the Soviets after the Soviet conquest of the Baltic republics and eastern Poland. The newcomers were to be added to a preexisting population of *Volksdeutschen* already present in Poland before 1939. Some Polish *Volksdeutschen* were people who had been German citizens before 1918, but who had been placed outside of Germany's boundaries by the Treaty of Versailles. But others were people whose ethnicity was more indeterminate; in some cases, a *Volksdeutscher* was anyone who could persuade a German official that he or she deserved the designation. All of these millions of *Volksdeutschen* – from Poland or elsewhere, with varying claims to "Germanness" and thus citizenship – were to be moved to the Wartheland and Danzig-West Prussia in order to form a "living wall" of German settlers, protecting Germany from the Slavic cultures to the east. Once there, National Socialist bureaucrats from a variety of organizations intended to Germanize those settlers who were seen as being not yet completely German in their language skills, life-style, or political attitudes.

Women from several Nazi organizations were prominent in these "Germanization" campaigns: they played a supporting role in the expropriation and deportation of Poles and Jews within the "new provinces," and assumed the lead in Germanizing *Volksdeusche* women and children after these families had been resettled on expropriated properties. As *Reich* German women saw their job, the Germanization of the *Volksdeutschen* often consisted of their resocialization as housewives. Nazi women's groups dispatched members to teach ethnic German women (or those thought to be of German ancestry) "proper" practices of German housekeeping: approaches to cooking, cleaning, hygiene, child care, washing, and holiday celebration that were presumed to be essentially German.

In occupied Poland, the intertwining of domestic practices and German national identity – in discourse, actual household management, and the application of Nazi policies – was constantly highlighted in the work of women from a variety of Nazi organizations.

The gendered, domestic nature of German identity shaped how these "missionaries" of Germanness defined themselves, and how they evaluated both the resettled *Volksdeutschen* and the displaced and deported population. Domestic notions of national identity determined how German women went about resocializing the resettled ethnic Germans in order to "strengthen" their Germanness, even as these same stereotypes about German housekeeping could help to determine who was granted German citizenship by the Commissariat for the Strengthening of Germandom and who was not.

"Polish Management," and Prewar Stereotypes of Polish and Ethnic German Households

When Nazi officials (male and female) arrived in Poland, they often perceived Polish homes and farms as they had expected to find them: as filthy, chaotic households that brought to life the old German expression "Polish management" (*Polnische Wirtschaft,* a byword for disorder and inefficiency that could be used to describe a home, business, or farm). German popular and scholarly literature on Poles and Polish culture had reflected this stereotype since the partition of Poland in the eighteenth century. Poles were usually described in German publications as being a passionate, courageous, and lively people, but also as being slovenly and often lazy, incapable of self-government or organization. Early-nineteenth-century German historians set the tone, writing that uncleanliness and disorganization had been a common trait among "Polish tribes" since the beginning of recorded history, and that in general their life-style and economy was always very primitive compared to that of neighboring Germanic tribes. German settlers arriving in the medieval period had been the "culture bearers" of the region and, according to these scholars, almost all cultural institutions and urban development in Poland had Germanic roots. But many earlier German settlements had allegedly been "overrun" by the more fertile Poles, who had "absorbed" the "most valuable" German blood into their own reproductive ranks.[3]

---

[3] For discussions of Polish stereotypes in German scholarship and popular culture, see Hubert Orlowski, "'Polnische Wirtschaft': Zum deutschen Polendiskurs der späten Neuzeit," in Karl-Günter Schirrmeister, ed., *Deutsch-Polnisches Symposium,* 22.–24.

Before 1914, German publications sometimes described ethnic Poles who lived in Prussia as superior to their counterparts in the Russian Empire, which was allegedly due to the influence of German culture. But after Poland's reconstitution in 1918, German images of Poles in *belles-lettres*, popular science publications, and theatrical productions became much more negative, as Germans sought to establish claims to territory that had been given to Poland under the Treaty of Versailles. A German geographer reflected this mood when he asserted (as a well-established fact) in a 1923 article that Poles "eat grubby food and live in dens."[4] German publications after 1933 carried forward these tropes and strengthened the anti-Semitic descriptions of Polish Jewish communities and homes that had been occasionally found in earlier accounts of Polish homes. A 1939 textbook reproduced photos of "primitive" Polish peasant dwellings next to images of tidy, more architecturally sophisticated ethnic German homes in the same region. Jewish Polish homes, the author noted, were even worse than those of their gentile counterparts because Polish Jews lived in "darkened dwellings that contain unbelievable dirt."[5]

But the work produced after 1918 about households of Jews, Poles, and ethnic Germans in Poland was only one category within a much broader scholarly and popular literature devoted to the *Auslandsdeutschen* or ethnic Germans, who lived in so-called *Sprachinseln* (islands of German language) across Eastern Europe. Eastern European *Auslandsdeutschen* were indeed a "hot" scholarly topic within Germany during the interwar period. These publications ranged from

Januar 1995 in Strausberg (Strausberg: Akademie der Bundeswehr für Information und Kommunikation, 1995); see also Wolfgang Wippermann, "Das Slawenbild der Deutschen im 19. und 20. Jahrhundert," in Geraldine Saherwala and Felix Escher, eds., *Slawen und Deutsche zwischen Elbe und Oder: vor 1000 Jahren, der Slawenaufstand von 983* (Berlin: Berliner Gesellschaft für Anthropologie, Ethnologie und Urgeschichte, 1983); and Angela Koch, *DruckBilder: Stereotype und Geschlechtercodes in den antipolnischen Diskursen der "Gartenlaube" (1870–1930)* (Cologne: Böhlau, 2002).

4 F. Braun, "Die polnische Geschichte in ihrer geographischer Bedingtheit" in the *Geographischer Anzeiger* quoted in Karl Fiedor, Janusz Sobczak, and Wojciech Wrzesinski, "The Image of the Poles in Germany and of the German in Poland in Inter-War Years and Its Role in Shaping the Relations between the Two States," *Polish Western Affairs* 19 (1978): 207.

5 From J. Müting, ed., *Heimat und Welt. Teubners Erdkundliches Unterrichtswerk für die höhere Schulen* (Leipzig: Teubner, 1939), 33 and 40.

heavy, serious academic tomes by geographers, historians, linguists, and ethnographers; to coffee table books or travel literature aimed at a popular audience; to amateur research of varying quality published by a host of local historical associations; to popular magazines from the interwar period, such as *der Auslandsdeutsche* and *der Volksdeutsche*. Almost certainly, most Germans who came to Poland after 1939 had been exposed to much of this literature and the stereotypes about ethnic Germans that it propagated. At the same time, German voluntary organizations created to support ethnic German communities abroad flourished, attracting millions of members.[6]

The expansion of organizations devoted to ethnic Germans in Eastern Europe, like the enormous increase during the interwar period in the number of publications devoted to these communities, was related to the change in the status of those who had lived within the Hapsburg Empire. Before 1918, ethnic German enclaves were scattered across East Central Europe and those in the Russian Empire were often seen as "outposts" in a Slavic environment. But within the Hapsburg Empire, Germans were the single most influential ethnic group and German was the language of both the civil service and military. After 1918, such ethnic Germans were now vulnerable ethnic minorities, whom metropolitan Germans perceived as "endangered" *Sprachinseln* and thus a much more interesting research subject.[7]

---

[6] For studies of the right-wing voluntary associations (e.g., the Verein für das Deutschtum im Auslande) and academic institutions that supported and promoted such publications, see Michael Burleigh, *Germany Turns Eastward. A Study of Ostforschung in the Third* Reich (Cambridge: Cambridge University Press, 1988); Gerhard Weidenfeller, *VDA. Verein für das Deuschtum im Auslande. Allgemeiner Deutscher Schulverein (1881–1918). Ein Beitrag zur Geschichte des deutschen Nationalismus und Imperialismus im Kaiserreich* (Berlin: Peter Land, 1976); Ernst Ritter, *Das Deutsche Auslands-Institut in Stuttgart 1917–1945: ein Beispiel deutscher Volkstumsarbeit zwischen den Weltkriegen* (Wiesbaden: Steiner, 1976); Walter v. Goldendach and Hans-Rüdiger Minow, *'Deutschtum Erwache!' Aus dem Innenleben des staatlichen Pangermanismus* (Berlin: Dietz,1994); Pieter Judson, *Exclusive Revolutionaries: Liberal Politics, Social Experience, and National Identity in the Austrian Empire, 1848–1914* (Ann Arbor: University of Michigan Press, 1996).

[7] For the change in the perceptions and self-definition of ethnic Germans who lived in the Hapsburg Empire after 1918, see Pieter Judson, "When is a Diaspora not a Diaspora? Rethinking Nation-Centered Narratives about Germans in Habsburg East Central Europe" in Krista O'Donnell, Renate Bridenthal and Nancy Reagin, eds., *Heimat Abroad: The Boundaries of Germanness* (Ann Arbor: University of Michigan Press, 2005). For a discussion of the varied relationships between ethnic German communities

At the same time, the purpose and focus of these publications shifted from economic boosterism to an openly *revanchist* focus on German claims in Eastern Europe, using such research to support the expansion of Germany's boundaries and influence in Central and Eastern Europe. Writers of both popular and scholarly literature devoted to the *Auslandsdeutschen* depicted the oppression of ethnic Germans in Eastern Europe arguing that, at best, *Auslandsdeutschen* faced pressures that might submerge their ethnic islands; at worst, they faced open persecution, even torture or rape.[8] Awareness of ethnic Germans abroad and the perils they allegedly faced were a core part of popular German nationalism after World War I, which in turn inspired enormous publicity about them and fund-raising for them. These ethnic Germans were incorporated into the larger nationalist vision of the "community of the *Volk*" during the interwar period.

Establishing claims meant surveying boundaries, and this literature used a variety of markers – deriving from agricultural, economic, religious, educational, and domestic life – to demarcate lines between the *Auslandsdeutschen* and surrounding host cultures. These works devoted considerable space to the crafts, guilds, and agricultural practices of ethnic German communities, including painstaking map after map of the layouts of fields and villages, which argued for the superior productivity, industriousness, and technological sophistication of ethnic German farmers and artisans. Ethnic German men were thus depicted as harder working, dedicated, and orderly than their non-German counterparts.

But intermingled with the discussion of masculine workplaces were discussions of domestic spaces and practices, which made analogous claims for ethnic German women and their families. Academic and especially popular publications were fascinated with the daily lives and homes of *Auslandsdeutschen*, and reproduced photographs, drawings, and elaborate descriptions of their clothing (*Trachten*), dialects, neighborhoods, domestic architecture, furniture, domestic decorative arts, holiday customs, and family life, including the division of work within the family and inheritance patterns.

from across Europe and the German Foreign Office and Nazi Party agencies during the 1930s and 1940s, see Valdis Lumans, *Himmler's Auxiliaries*.

[8] Goldendach, *VDA*, 51–5 and 131.

Interwar scholars of the *Auslandsdeutschen* argued that German settlements (which they sometimes referred to as *Volksboden*, landscapes that bore an intrinsically German stamp) were distinguished by their clean streets, laid out in straight lines. Ethnic German homes were supposedly characterized by elaborate gables and straight lines; they too were kept in good repair.[9] One ethnologist's 1933 description of ethnic German villages in the *Banat* region of Romania was typical: "the German settlements are distinguished by their exemplary cleanliness and order, as seen in the neat cobbled streets and their clean courtyards, which sharply sets them apart from the homes of the other ethnic groups."[10] Slavic families, on the other hand, invariably lived in irregular, badly kept "huts," sometimes smoky or infested by vermin. Many books simply reproduced photographs of supposedly "representative" ethnic German and Slavic houses, which formed a striking contrast. One ethnologist claimed that the homes of "natives" in the Balkans were

huts [which] consist of one, or at most two rooms.... [T]heir kitchens are blackened with smoke and covered with soot, because they are not designed to prevent the fires from smoking.... There is no furniture: chairs, benches, beds, and cabinets are unknown. One simply sleeps on a straw mat on the floor.... [When the Germans first came to this area] they were quartered in the dirty, smoky rooms of the Jews and Serbs, and became vermin-infested. Therefore they immediately built primitive huts for temporary use [until their houses were finished], which, according to their custom, they kept painstakingly clean.[11]

[9] See Burleigh, *Germany Turns Eastward*, 25–6. Lyrical descriptions of ethnic German fields and streets, which are always described as *schnurgerade* (laid out in very straight lines), abound in descriptions of ethnic German communities. See, e.g., Raimund Kaindl, *Die Deutschen in Galizien und in der Bukowina* (Frankfurt: H. Keller, 1916) 128–32; Irmgard Pohl, *Deutsche im Südosten Europas. Vorposten des Volkstums* (Leipzig: J. Klinkhardt, 1938), 55–7; Maria Kahle, *Deutsches Volk in der Fremde* (Oldenburg: Gerhard Stalling, 1933), 9–10.

[10] See Carl Petersen et al., eds., *Handwörterbuch des Grenz- und Auslandsdeutschtums* vol. 1 (Breslau: F. Hirt, 1933–35), 242.

[11] Pohl, *Deutsche im Südosten Europas*, 55 and 57. This description combines all the stereotypes about Slavs presented by earlier authors. For the inability of Slavs and Southeastern Europeans to get rid of vermin, see also "Leben der deutschen Frau im Orient," *Die Welt der Frau* (1909) Nr. 35; the prevalence of fleas and lice throughout Romania recurs in Ilse Obrig, *Guter Mucki, nimm auch mit. Eine Reise zu den Auslandsdeutschen in Rumänien* (Stuttgart: Union Deutsche Verlagsgesellschaft, n.d.). See also Raimund Kaindl, *Deutsche Art – treu bewahrt* (Vienna: W. Braumüller, 1924), 57.

In this literature, German housewives and their household management (especially their alleged penchant for order and sparkling white sheets, curtains, etc.) were used to define – in gendered terms – German national identity and superiority. One writer wrote that among the Volga Germans women maintained a bridge between the old *Heimat* and the new through such domestic rituals and symbols. Such housekeeping, he concluded, passed on to their children the values of "a love for order, cleanliness, and a higher standard of living," qualities that represented a uniquely German heritage.[12]

Across Eastern Europe, therefore, ethnic German homes were described as standing out from those in surrounding cultures by virtue of their cleanliness and the "snow white" linens and aprons produced by *Auslandsdeutsche* housewives. In Southeastern Europe, one writer described the parlor (*gute Stube*) of the typical ethnic German household:

On either side of the room are beds, each with its large down-filled quilt, covered with white duvets.... [B]y the window is a cabinet, which is covered with a snow-white cloth, produced by the housewife herself.... [T]he floor is wooden, and is thoroughly scoured once a week. Over the windows, we see small white, homemade embroidered curtains.[13]

German farms in Galicia, another wrote, "have lovely houses ... which are distinguished by an impressive degree of cleanliness.... [Even the local Poles acknowledge] that the Germans are thriftier and harder working than the Poles, and that their homes are cleaner."[14] These depictions take on a special irony when we consider the reaction that Nazi women had to actual Galician Germans, who came under these women's supervision after they were resettled to western Poland in 1939–40, as discussed in the following text. Another writer described a group of ethnic German young women going to church in Romania:

I watched the group of young women in their lovely traditional costumes. Sparkling white embroidered aprons fluttered around each tall, slim figure. Each one had tightly braided hair, and wore a satin *Borte* [a headdress] from

[12] Jakob Stach, *Die deutschen Kolonien in Südrussland* (Prischib: G. Schaad, ca. 1905), 97–9.

[13] Karl Kraushaar, *Sitten und Bräuche der Deutschen in Ungarn, Rumänien, und Jugoslavien* (Vienna: A. C. Trupp, 1932), 12–13.

[14] Kaindl, *Die Deutschen in Galizien*, 159 and 161.

which fell long silk ribbons, flowing over the pure white, heavily embroidered shirt.[15]

In Dobrudja, an ethnologist described the *gute Stube* (the parlor used to receive guests) of a typical ethnic German home:

[This room] contains the best furniture and linens . . . clean, bright curtains hang in the windows, and the walls are richly decorated with pictures, photographs, and framed sayings. . . . [There is invariably also] a large bed [*Paradebett*] which displays five feather pillows, each encased in a snow white, embroidered covering. . . . [A]lmost without exception, all houses and rooms are meticulously orderly and clean.[16]

Expressions such as *gute Stube, Paradebett,* and *Kachelofen* (tiled oven) were frequently used to describe *Auslandsdeutsche* homes in interwar publications. These were familiar, cozy domestic items and terms familiar to metropolitan Germans. And readers were assured that although much else might have changed in Eastern Europe over the centuries, domestic details had been relatively unchanging and hence were implicitly timeless. Many academic works, such as the multivolume, monumental *Handwörterbuch des Grenz- und Auslanddeutschtums,* documented change over time in various ethnic German communities' economic organizations, legal institutions, arts, and literary life, but argued that life-style and domesticity, in a broad sense, remained unchanged. Thus, the *Handwörterbuch* included successive sections for each community, chronologically organized for different periods, which traced historic change and development in the public sphere among ethnic Germans in each region. Private life was treated in an enormous section on *Hausform und Wohnweise* (Home and Lifestyle) in the very first chronological segment for each community (which might cover the early modern period or the nineteenth century). In subsequent segments, the information for each topic in the public sphere was updated, but for *Hausform und Wohnweise* readers were always referred back to the section in the opening segment.

---

[15] Kahle, *Deutsches Volk in der Fremde,* 34.
[16] Paul Träger, *Die Deutschen in der Dobrudscha* (Stuttgart: Ausland und Heimat Verlagsaktiengesellschaft, 1922), 146.

Private life thus evidently stood outside of historic change, even as the nations German communities were located in were divided and reorganized. According to this literature the roots of domestic practices could be traced back to the German-speaking parts of the Holy Roman Empire. Scholars claimed that *Trachten*, domestic architectural forms, and dialects could be clearly shown to derive from whatever section of the Holy Roman Empire these people's ancestors had come from. Costumes, expressions, and holiday customs from early modern Pflalz or Rhineland – swept away by modernization in Germany – still allegedly lived on in the ethnic German communities of Eastern Europe, preserved in isolation.

German occupation authorities after 1930 were therefore strongly predisposed to see the Polish population through the lens created by this vast and widely distributed set of publications, and tended to fit what they experienced into this template. Most ethnic German homes and farms were allegedly visibly superior to those of their Polish neighbors (or if they were not, this was due to "Polish oppression" during the interwar period). An orderly, flourishing Polish farm was characterized as exceptional. Helga Schmidt-Thrö, who headed the NS Women's League in the Wartheland during World War II, still embraced these stereotypes even decades later, when she flatly asserted in a 1984 letter that

[German settlers] produced enormous economic, cultural, legal and administrative accomplishments [in medieval and Early Modern Poland], and founded cities and villages. In the 13th and 14th centuries many cities [in Poland] were purely German ... but the Catholic Church bolstered the ethnic identity of the Poles and their biological strength [fertility] with the result that more and more German blood was soaked up into the Polish population, which lent creative powers to the Poles. ... [When we arrived in 1939] in the areas that were formerly Prussian, we could recognize the German farms and homes from a distance, because of their well-kept appearance ... disorderly German farms were the exception; by comparison, "Polish management" [in Polish homes and farms] but was not just a saying, but was real and widespread evil, which of course doesn't mean that there weren't some exceptions to this rule.[17]

---

[17] From the lengthy and tendentious apologia written by Schmidt-Thrö in 1984 in response to a historian's inquiry, in BA NS 44, vol. 63.

Expropriation, Deportation, and the Transfer
of Populations in Occupied Poland

The farms that Schmidt-Thrö saw – along with their inhabitants – were subjected to large-scale ethnic cleansing, which began almost as soon as the hostilities ended and the occupation began. The "General Plan for the East" developed by Himmler and his subordinates in the Commissariat for the Strengthening of Germandom envisioned the resettlement of millions, as prewar Polish citizens (ethnic Poles, Jews, and others) were to be deported from Western Poland to make room for both *Volksdeutschen* from Eastern Europe and Germans from the *Reich*. After the invasion of the Soviet Union in June 1941, the plan's proposed scope was extended to include the deportation of local populations and the resettlement of ethnic Germans in both Eastern Poland and the Soviet Union.[18]

Himmler's implementation of the plan resulted in the deportation of hundreds of thousands of prewar Polish citizens from Western Poland to the "new" provinces to central Poland, where most of the Jews and many of the ethnic Poles were later murdered. To replace those who were deported and murdered, the commissariat and another NS resettlement agency, the Liaison Office for *Volksdeutschen* (the *Volksdeutsche Mittelstelle*, which the commissariat oversaw along with several other subordinate agencies, such as the *Einwandererzentrale*) brought in hundreds of thousands of ethnic Germans from eastern Poland, the Baltic republics, and the Soviet Union.[19] Altogether, the Liaison Office and the commissariat relocated about four hundred thousand *Volksdeutschen* from their homes in the Baltic republics, Galizia, Volhynia, Dobrudja, Bessarabia, Bukovina, and other areas

---

[18] For the ongoing revisions to the plan, see Aly, *Endlösung*, 95 ff. Aly offers evidence that the pace and timing of the resettlement of ethnic Germans from Eastern Poland and the Soviet Union determined the scheduling and details of the ethnic cleansing of Poles and Jews from the "new provinces." See also Sybille Steinbacher, *"Musterstadt" Auschwitz. Germanisierungspolitik und Judenmord in Ostoberschlesien* (Munich: K. G. Saur, 2000), 82–8.

[19] The list of agencies that the *Reichkommissariat* oversaw, and the overlap between their jurisdictions and personnel is dicussed in Heinemann, *Rasse, Siedlung, deutsches Blut*. In practice, the "racial evaluators" employed by the agencies responsible for "sorting" and classifying both the resettled *Volksdeutschen* and the disposed Poles (who were sometimes evaluated to see whether they could be "re-Germanized") were lent to these agencies by the *Rasse- und Siedlungs-Hauptamt* of the SS.

of Eastern Europe to the "new" provinces in western Poland by 1944. Hundreds of thousands of other *Volksdeutschen* were taken from their homes to Germany or in some cases languished in Liaison Office transit camps for years. In most cases, these ethnic Germans had not had much choice about their relocation. Some (e.g., the settlers from the Baltic republics) had fled the Soviet invasion, while others had been rounded up and relocated by German authorities. In addition, about five hundred thousand Germans from the *Reich* settled in western Poland.[20]

The first waves of ethnic Germans came to western Poland as refugees from the Baltic republics (in October and November of 1939) and were followed shortly thereafter by *Volksdeutschen* from the parts of eastern Poland conquered by the Soviet Army (particularly Galicia and Volhynia). Officials from the commissariat (sometimes in accordance with agreements made with the Soviet Union) traveled to Bukovina, Dubrodja, and Bessarabia to oversee the transfer of *Volksdeutschen* from the Soviet Union in 1940–1. There, so-called flying detachments of racial experts from the commissariat sometimes screened families to see if they were sufficiently German to qualify for resettlement. Those who passed muster were rounded up for transport to western Poland, where they were placed in transit camps.[21] In other areas within the Soviet Union, entire communities were uprooted

---

[20] It is difficult to reach an exact total of the number of Jews and Poles deported from western and central Poland, and the number of *Volksdeutschen* relocated and resettled in western Poland in their place. This is because of incomplete prewar demographic information, and because different studies use different starting and ending dates, focus on different geographical areas, or include different categories of *Volksdeutschen*. There seems to be a consensus that about one million Jews and gentile Poles were expelled from western Poland by the end of 1943, and most were later murdered; another 300,000 Poles lost their farms, but were allowed to remain in western Poland. Altogether, about 6.1 million Poles (Jews and gentiles) were killed during the NS occupation, about 22 percent of the prewar population. See Koehl, *RKFDV*, 130–1 and 190; Harten, *De-Kulturation und Germanisierung*, 75 and 116. The number of *Volksdeutschen* who were resettled to a new location (but in many cases, no further than a Liason Office transit camp, where they languished) was at least 600,000 and may have been higher. See Koehl, *RKFDV*, 210–15 and Lumans, *Himmler's Auxiliaries*, 198; see also Aly, *Endlösung*, 167–8 and 321–3. Elizabeth Harvey gives slightly lower figures for the number of ethnic Germans resettled in western Poland, and the number of *Reichsdeutschen* who moved there; see Harvey, *Women and the Nazi East: Agents and Witnesses of Germanization*, 79.
[21] For the work of the "flying detachments," see Heinemann, *Rasse, Siedlung, deutsches Blut*, 238–40.

hurriedly from the Soviet sphere and dumped into Liaison Office transit camps in Poland, where they could be examined and sorted at leisure. The single largest transit camp was run by the Liason Office was in Litzmannstadt (Lódź) in Wartheland. There and in other camps, resettled populations were sorted and classified as potential German citizens. After screening, the *Volksdeutschen* in the camps waited while another branch of the commissariat expropriated the homes and farms of former Polish citizens (who were then usually deported). Then the resettled *Volksdeutsche* families would be assigned and transported to "their" new homes and farms.[22]

But before the commissariat and its subordinate agencies could relocate *Voksdeutsche* families from the Soviet Union or, (in the case of those not screened before they came to Poland) evaluate and classify them while they were in the transit camps, officials faced the often messy problem of determining who, exactly, qualified as an ethnic German. Social reality was much more blurred and open to interpretation than NS racial theory had admitted. Some of the individuals or families being evaluated were culturally hybrid; over centuries, some ethnic Germans had intermarried with Ukrainians, Poles, Russians, or others. Many of their descendents did not speak fluent German or any German at all. Some could not document their alleged German ancestry, while others felt no particular loyalty to or identification with Germany. Ethnic Germans varied enormously in their levels of education (ranging from urban professionals in the Baltics to illiterate peasants in Russia), degree of support for National Socialism and Germany, and willingness to be resettled.

The standards that the commissariat and Liaison Office personnel used to evaluate each person were often arbitrary and varied considerably, depending on circumstances and on the prejudices of the Nazi official involved. Examiners were concerned with physical "evidence" of Germanness, such as eye and hair color, and also with each person's ancestry, as far as this could be determined. Coloring was problematic because many Poles were blond-haired and blue-eyed. Race

[22] See Bergen, "Volksdeutschen," 72–4; Harten, *De-Kulturation und Germanisierung*, 211–13; Lumans, *Himmler's Auxiliaries*, 93–4; Benjamin Pinkus, *Die Deutschen in der Sowjetunion. Geschichte einer nationalen Minderheit im 20. Jahrhundert* (Baden-Baden: Nomos, 1987), 248ff.

assessors also considered a range of other factors, including the shape of the face, eyes, and eyelids, or each person's body type and height. But where evidence of ancestry was lacking, or the physical evidence was ambiguous, a variety of other factors might be used to determine ethnicity: German language fluency; education; political affiliations or memberships in voluntary associations; and the applicant's attitude toward Germany.[23]

If the evaluation was favorable, families might be granted German citizenship (either permanently or on a sort of probationary status). The commissariat and German occupation authorities ultimately developed a system of categorization dubbed the "German *Volk* list," which was used to classify individuals and assign citizenship and other legal rights. The list contained four categories. People who could persuasively prove a claim to Germanness were assigned to one of the first two categories and were granted German citizenship outright. Category 3 status was given to applicants whose Germanness was considered attenuated, but who were "capable of being re-Germanized." Such people were granted a sort of second-class citizenship on probation and were sometimes sent to Germany for further Germanization. Applicants assigned to category 4 were considered to have German ancestry, but to be "renegades" who had cast their lot with other nationalities; such people were to be forced to resettle in Germany or else sent to camps run by the SS.[24]

Because some officials evidently saw cleanliness as being tantamount to Germanness, the housekeeping of applicants was sometimes used as one criterion to determine ethnicity, and thus to grant German citizenship. The cleanliness and tidiness of entire families could be a determining factor in cases where other evidence of Germanness was ambiguous (although such considerations could never override or cancel out

---

[23] Generally, "racial examiners" were first and foremost concerned with physical appearance and evidence of ancestry; other factors came into play in borderline cases. For a detailed description of the entire examination process, see Heinemann, *Rasse, Siedlung, deutsches Blut*, 232–46. For the varied and sometimes conflicting criteria used by NS racial examiners, see Koehl, *RKFDV*, 100–9; Pinkus, *Die Deutschen in der Sowjetunion*, 248–53. Bergen, "Volksdeutsche," 74–5, offers astonishing and brutal examples of the outcomes that these arbitrary criteria could lead to.

[24] Harten, *De-Kulturation und Germanisierung*, 99ff; Koehl, *RKFDV*, 139–40; Lumans, *Himmler's Auxiliaries*, 184ff. See also Heinemann, *Rasse, Siedlung, deutsches Blut*, 260–1 and Steinbacher, *"Musterstadt" Auschwitz*, 221–2.

Jewish ancestry), both in Poland and elsewhere in the Nazi empire.[25] One memo that offered guidelines for classification to officials in the "flying detachments" showed how arbitrary and subjective criteria that related to life-style and domestic practices had become integrated into the selection process:

> The entire family should be evaluated on the basis of its members' racial and hereditary value (including their achievements in their professions, their social standing, no criminal record, clean housekeeping, etc.), to see if they would be a welcome addition to the [German] population.... [If they satisfy these criteria] even a Polish spouse can qualify [for probationary citizenship].[26]

On the other hand, borderline applicants who had a "good racial characteristics" (physical appearance), who been assigned to category 3 of the *Volksliste* because they were judged to be "capable of re-Germanization," and who had been sent to Germany as "probationary" members of the German community could be removed from this category if they demonstrated "antisocial" behavior in their private life. The Liaison Office decreed in 1942 that such people should be sent back to their place of origin if

> their inner value does not match their external racial appearance, for example if they prove themselves to be antisocial or work shy elements [refusing a work assignment], or if the intellectual level of the children is well below average, or if the housekeeping of the family is not clean.[27]

These criteria are strikingly reminiscent of those applied in Germany during the 1930s to "asocial families." Thus, life-style could override even a favorable initial "racial" classification. The end result, for many families, was the result of a calculation by Nazi Liaison Office officials that combined assessments of both life-style and physical appearance (along with other factors). In the cases of both the "asocial" families of

---

[25] For the use of household cleanliness as classification criteria, see Bergen, "Volksdeutschen," 74–5; and Harten, *De-Kulturation und Germanisierung*, 105–6; and Pinkus, *Die Deutschen in der Sowjetunion*, 248–50. For a similar usage of domestic order and cleanliness to determine Germanness and citizenship in the Nazi Protectorate of Moravia and Bohemia, see Bryant, "Making Czechs German," 216–17, 224, and 257.

[26] From BA R 69, vol. 302, 169–70, Einwandererzentralstelle Litzmannstadt, "Reglung von Staatsangehörigkeitsfragen . . . Richtlinien," dated July 31, 1944.

[27] From BA R 59, vol. 46, Volksdeutsche Mittelstelle, memo on "Behandlung von wiedereindeutschungsfähige Personen," dated Dec. 12, 1942.

the Hashude camp and the *Volksdeutschen* of occupied Poland, disorderly family life and poor housekeeping could lead to a family's being labeled "un-German," and excluded from the *Volksgemeinschaft*, an exclusion that often had serious consequences.

On the other hand, the incorporation of domestic skill and cleanliness as one factor that could lead to a "favorable" classification also carried forward prewar Nazi policies that measured "racial value" because this factor had been used by the SS to assess the "fitness" of the brides of SS men. Isabel Heinemann notes that SS racial evaluators had often undergone a similar process before the war, when they and their fiancés underwent an examination process in order to obtain permission to marry. The SS "marriage approval process" was intended to ensure that SS men married only similarly "racially valuable" German women in an effort to produce a racial elite. For both spouses, the marriage approval process relied primarily on proof of ancestry (which had to be given going back to the year 1800) and physical appearance. But the brides of SS men also had to bring two attestations by witnesses who would vouch for their domestic skills and personal characteristics.[28]

The prewar standards of "racial value" that underlay the German *Volk* list categories were used to classify not only the *Volksdeutschen* who were being uprooted from the Soviet sphere of influence and resettled, but were also applied to large parts of the non-Jewish Polish population. Indeed, the decision to sort through and classify the indigenous Polish population slowed down the drive to "clear" local farms for incoming ethnic Germans because farmers learned they could forestall deportation or retain property that might otherwise be expropriated if they applied for assignment to the German *Volk* list. The assignment of *Volk* list categories to applicants within Poland was often egregiously arbitrary and varied widely between the "new provinces," depending on the whims of the Nazi provincial leaders involved. *Gauleiter* Albert Foster, the head of the Nazi Party organization in Danzig-West Prussia, apparently had less patience with the process than his more fanatic counterpart in the Wartheland, and the Danzig-West Prussia administration became notorious for its tendency to apply the criteria quite loosely. In the Polish territory added to Upper Silesia, the majority of the non-Jewish Polish population was simply added to the *Volk* list and

---

[28] Heinemann, *Rasse, Siedlung, deutsches Blut*, 55–7.

thus in many Silesian public schools Polish teachers taught in Polish because few pupils understood German.[29]

Families and individuals did not always have to apply for *Volk* list categorization; in some instances, NS bureaucrats sought out new candidates. Some of these people did not want to be added to the list, even when they met the imaginary standards of NS officials. In the General Government (central Poland), SS teams fanned out in 1942 in an initiative "to seek German blood," searching for non-Jewish individuals whose ancestors might include Germans whose blood had been "absorbed" centuries before; building up the *Volksliste* in this fashion would (the SS hoped) buy off part of the local population.[30] Because German language fluency and documentation regarding ancestry was almost always lacking in such cases, SS officials were forced to rely on eye and hair color, or on even more subjective notions of Germanness that were grounded in domesticity and life-style. The results could be almost farcical, as shown in the report of one SS team:

In Walowice village we met a 70 year old named Greber, who at first claimed not to have any German ancestry. But in the course of the conversation he did come to remember that his father long ago had been called a "Swabian" by the Poles.... Swiecichow village made a particularly favorable impression on us. Both the buildings and the inhabitants themselves appeared to be quite orderly and clean. But the search for German blood was unfortunately fruitless here, as neither the mayor, nor the priest, nor any of the other inhabitants were able to recall that they had German ancestors.[31]

Eventually, about seven thousand persons in central Poland were identified by such means and categorized as "capable of re-Germanization."[32]

Domesticity and Re-Germanization

Women from a variety of Nazi organizations such as the BDM, the Land and the Labor Services, the Nazi People's Welfare, and the NS

---

[29] Harten, *De-Kulturation und Germanisierung*, 105–6 and 211–15.
[30] See Harvey, *Women and the Nazi East*, 234–37 for other examples of such "trawling for German blood."
[31] Quoted in Harten, *De-Kulturation und Germanisierung*, 118.
[32] Ibid., 277–9.

Women's League came from Germany to occupied Poland in order to speed the process of "re-Germanization" through the creation of German kindergartens, groups to teach German language and songs, youth groups, domestic sciences courses, and by working as "advisors" (*Betreuerinnen,* i.e., social workers) with ethnic Germans. Ultimately, several thousand women were sent from Germany to work with Polish *Volksdeutschen* and with families that had been relocated from the Soviet sphere of influence to western Poland. Their motives varied, as did the extent to which their posting to Poland had been voluntary. Some – such as the students who were fulfilling their mandatory period of service before starting university studies – were there on short-term assignments and had not asked to be sent to Poland. Others were activists and careerists within Nazi women's agencies who were motivated by feelings of comradeship, patriotism, the value of the work to be done in Poland, or simple opportunism because a posting to Poland might lead to personal advancement. Although the degree to which they were zealous varied, many saw themselves as "female missionaries" to the *Volksdeutschen* of the "German East."

The women sent to Poland tended to be in their twenties or early thirties, and many had gone through the BDM, Nazified schools and universities, and a year in the Labor Service. They thus tended to be younger, single, better-educated, and from a somewhat "better" social background than most of their "charges." Like Helga Schmidt-Thrö, before starting their assignments they had been exposed to education and orientation training that justified the expropriation of Polish or Jewish homes and farms and the deportation of their former owners. They had been told that they were to be advisors and models for ethnic German women in Poland, and were also expected to enforce "racial" boundaries between the *Volksdeutschen* and the Poles who remained. Some actively participated in the expulsion and deportation of Poles and Jews, assisting SS detachments in the roundups of Polish and Jewish families and the expropriation of their property. Most, however, tended simply to screen out or overlook the crimes of the German occupation, although the fate of the deported was widely shared information among the German occupiers.[33]

---

[33] Harvey's *Women and the Nazi East* offers a detailed examination of the backgrounds and deployment of German women in occupied Poland. She discusses the "imperial

As in their outreach program to ethnic German girls before 1939 (in which some young *Volksdeutsche* women had been recruited to come to Germany for a year at home economics schools), women from Nazi agencies in Poland often turned to domestic science training as a means to "strengthen Germanness" in families and individuals whose ethnic identity was shaky or unclear. Even before *Volksdeutschen* left Liaison Office transit camps in western Poland, the NS Women's League launched programs to reach housewives who were in the process of being resettled. "[We must] effect a complete re-education of these women in their daily work, for example in questions of diet and [household] economics," the Women's League leadership informed all provincial women's organizations, because resettled women "need not only infant care classes, but we must also teach them the most basic knowledge of domestic science through courses in housekeeping, cooking, mending, and sewing." The NS Women's League also intended to mount classes in the transit camps to teach *Volksdeutsche* women the most common German Christmas celebration practices; the Berlin office promised to supply songs, printed texts, and recipes for Christmas baking.[34] In transit camps in the Wartheland, camp administrators tried to ensure that girls from families that had been assigned to categories 3 and 4 on the *Volksliste* (whose ethnicity was seen as particularly dubious or "threatened") were compelled to attend home economics courses in camps run by the Hitler Youth. One young woman who worked with such girls complained that the pupils preferred to speak Polish, even during lessons. "Order and cleanliness are almost unknown to them," she concluded angrily.[35]

viewpoint" shared by German women and men in Poland, and examines in detail the degree to which these German women were involved in the deportation of Jews and Poles, what they saw, and how they chose to remember their involvement. Harvey's study is invaluable for any history of occupied Poland, but she is largely concerned with the women and their knowledge of and complicity in German war crimes. I am more interested here in the hands-on details of the resocialization that German women were pursuing, and the ways in which their work carried forward prewar notions of a nationalized and racialized German domesticity. For the backgrounds, motives, and organizational affiliations of the women sent to Poland, see Harvey, *Women and the Nazi East*, 93–118.

[34] From memo FW 144/40, sent by the NS Women's League headquarters to all provincial offices working with resettled women, dated Nov. 15, 1940, in BA NS 44 vol. 49.

[35] Quoted in Harten, *De-Kulturation und Germanisierung*, 283.

Often, the work of women from Nazi organizations began even before the resettled ethnic Germans arrived at "their" new homes, when women from the NS Women's League or BDM were called in by the SS to assist in the deportation of Poles or Jews who were being "cleared" from their farms or homes. Once the former owners had been forcibly removed by the SS (often in the middle of the night), German women set to work, cleaning and Germanizing the homes for the *Volksdeutschen* who would soon arrive. Their role resembled the work of Nazi women volunteers who were called into the Saar region during the summer of 1940 to "clean away" the traces of French occupation from German homes.[36] The seizure of Polish and Jewish property in Poland had been foreshadowed, moreover, by the wholesale expropriation and public auctions of German Jewish homes and household goods within Germany before the war. Unlike their former owners, German Jewish and Polish household goods could be "cleansed," severed from their previous histories, and then "naturalized" within German homes.

Women from the BDM or Nazi Women's League sometimes traveled with teams of SS men to the homes and farms that were being expropriated and waited until the former owners had been rounded up, before moving in with their soap, buckets, and brooms to clean the homes before *Volksdeutsche* families arrived the next day. In the reports they filed with their superiors, and the press releases they wrote for newspapers back home, these women invariably described Polish and Jewish homes as "filthy," little more than pigsties. One woman who participated in several such "cleaning actions" filed a typical report in which she commented that "our most important task is to clean out the unbelievable dirt from the former Polish homes, which the Volhynian

---

[36] Some areas on Germany's western border had been occupied during the opening months of the war, but German troops drove out French forces by the summer of 1940. Thereafter, thousands of women volunteers were bussed in by the SS to erase the traces of French occupation. One press release gushed over the women's work, declaring that

> the traces that the 'grand nation' left behind in these homes, the devastation of these homes, is unimaginable ... and yet, these industrious women are able to repair the worst damages, to order and clean these homes. ... [The women's work] is the appropriate complement to the deeds of the Army. The villages, which were protected in armed struggle by German troops, are now brought into order and beautified by the women.
>
> From a press release, dated Aug. 1940, in BA NS 44, vol. 7, 15–18.

or Galizian German women are often struck dumb by, when they arrive [and see these homes] and compare them with the snug, clean homes in their old villages."[37] All such reports emphasized the necessity of cleaning the households (if circumstances allowed) before the resettled families arrived in order to remove traces of foreignness and make it more German by putting out flowers, hanging clean white curtains, and so forth.[38] In many cases, German volunteers could "obtain" additional furniture or other goods for the new families by simply walking in and seizing items from other Polish homes or from stockpiles of goods that had been taken from deported Jews.[39]

One report, filed in November 1940 by a German woman assigned by the Nazi Women's League to the Scharnikau district in the Wartheland, contained almost all of the tropes typical of such descriptions of Germanizing the homes of the deported (and will therefore be quoted at length):

[We were called by the SS] to Penskowo, where evacuations [*sic*] had just taken place. . . . [W]e entered the homes and were puzzled by how we were to overcome so much dirt [but then asked the SS to order some Polish women from the village to help the Germans scrub] . . . [W]hen the resettled families arrived at 2 p.m. the next day, they found clean homes, decorated with flowers. . . . [A few days later] 20 of us were again called in to help. . . . When we came into the

---

[37] From a report by an advisor in Kreis Leslau in the summer of 1940, in BA R 49, vol. 3045, 36. For additional reports on volunteers' involvement in such "cleaning actions" see BA R 49, vol. 3045, 94, 98–100, and 148; BA R 49, vol. 3046, 73–7. Some of these reports (particularly those in R 49, vols. 3045 and 3046) were written as press releases for German newspapers, and must be read as such. Others (e.g., the reports in NS 44, vol. 3133 or R 49, vols. 3062 and 3060) were written as internal monthly reports for these women's superiors or were kept in the form of diary entries (although presumably intended for others to read). These latter reports are considerably more frank and open in their admissions of frustration or failures, complaints, and discussions of limitations on advisors' work.

[38] See, e.g., the press release entitled "The Youth Group Tackles the Job," in BA R 49, vol. 3045, 83, in which teams of young women from the BDM are depicted as whitewashing the walls of Polish homes and hanging clean white curtains, while other young women "obtain" additional furniture from an unnamed location.

[39] For additional examples of such theft of Polish and Jewish property by NS women volunteers (sometimes for their own use, sometimes for their *Volksdeutsche* charges), see Harvey, *Women and the Nazi East*, 254–5. Melita Maschmann, who supervised BDM members assisting in the expulsions of Polish families, and the subsequent "cleaning actions" and theft of Polish household goods, notes that she told "her girls" to avoid turning their backs on the furious Poles. See Melita Maschmann, *Account Rendered. A Dossier on My Former Self* (London: Abelard-Schuman, 1965), 118–21.

homes left by the Poles during the early hours of the morning, we would have preferred to simply turn around and walk out again, since we had never seen so much filth, dirt, and stink.... [T]he Poles had tried to destroy at the last minute, whatever they could ... [after hours of cleaning, the resettled *Volksdeutschen* arrived] and I was shocked to find that none of them spoke a word of German.... [T]hey told me [in Polish] that their ancestors had come from Holland to Galizia [in eastern Poland] three to four hundred years ago ... and that in the course of the years, they had forgotten their native tongue because of Russian and Polish oppression and were now Polonized [*verpolonisiert*] ... but they have kept their blood lines pure.... [O]ur first assignment will be to teach these people the German language, and gradually to introduce them to German culture, which won't be so easy, since they hold fast to their own customs and traditions.[40]

The Poles, knowing that their homes were to be taken from them, had resisted by breaking and throwing out household objects; the German advisor had merely interpreted this as malice and additional evidence of "Polish management." Her involvement, however, had served only to help one group of Polish speakers displace another group of Polish speakers. Still, she saw her charges as capable of being "re-Germanized"; ethnic identity was evidently created through a complex interaction between "blood" and environment or life-style.

In many reports written for press releases, however, women advisors comforted their readers (and themselves) by concluding that within a short period of time, the stolen homes had been successfully Germanized. When she visited a recently "cleared" village a few months later, one German woman wrote in 1942, she now noticed the extreme cleanliness of these homes: "the beds were now covered with sparkling white sheets, and everywhere, we saw quite pretty curtains hanging in the windows."[41] Another advisor ended her report by noting that after the resettled *Volksdeutschen* moved into another village, "many farms quickly assumed a German appearance; the windows were washed, and everywhere, one noticed that a [woman's] hand had brought order."[42]

---

[40] From BA R 49, vol. 3045, 91–2. For an overview of the "evacuations" of Polish and Jewish families in the Warthegau during this period, see Heinemann, *Rasse, Siedlung, deutsches Blut*, 220–3.

[41] From the report on a follow-up visit by an NS Women's League advisor who had organized a "cleaning action" in Dobberschütz, in the Wartheland, dated May 1942 in BA R 49, vol. 3045, 103.

[42] The report is in BA R 49, vol. 3045, 148.

Reassuring before-and-after stories – about filthy homes that were "made German" through being scrubbed and outfitted with white curtains and sheets – were usually reserved for press releases, however. Internal reports filed by women from the NS Women's League or NS People's Welfare were generally more open about the complexities and difficulties inherent in trying to re-Germanize families whose ethnic identity was ambiguous. In public statements, therefore, the Germanization of formerly Polish or Jewish homes was presented as something that was "natural" and innate: as soon as the resettled *Volksdeutschen* moved in, these households allegedly became cleaner and more orderly as flowers were planted and white curtains were hung. But German women advisors were well aware that Germanization was a process of resocialization.

Resettled housewives had to be taught "*Reich* German" styles of cooking, cleaning, home décor, child care practices, standards of personal hygiene, and much more. As in the United States a few decades earlier – where social workers had attempted to promote the "Americanization" of immigrant women through altering their household management – German advisors believed that they could bring *Volksdeutsche* women into the "national community" by standardizing and modernizing their housekeeping and child care practices. Their work with resettled women therefore combined instruction in newer technologies and approaches (teaching them to use thermometers to measure a child's fever or to use coal stoves in place of wood-burning ovens) with the teaching of German popular culture (songs, recipes, holiday practices) and the more stylized aspects of housekeeping.

But although women from Nazi organizations saw the approach to domesticity that they were promoting as a *Reich* German one, in fact it was implicitly a bourgeois style. The advisors were generally from middle-class backgrounds (often urban) and were speaking to their "charges" across both a class and cultural divide. The roots of the sort of household management that women advisors were trying to impart could be traced to the German bourgeoisie, particularly in urban areas. Thus, at heart, the attempts to Germanize the housekeeping of ethnic German women could also be seen as a project of the modernization and *embourgeoisement* of rural housewives. This fact was reflected in many of the conflicts that German women had with ethnic German housewives, such as the campaign mounted by some advisors to persuade *Volksdeutsche* in some communities to stop wearing "old-fashioned" headscarves or the frequent attempts of (often Protestant) women from Nazi groups to persuade Catholic ethnic German housewives to take down the "kitschy" images of the Virgin or small religious statues that decorated their homes.[43]

Many (but not all) of the changes that German women were pushing on ethnic German housewives were identical to those pursued by German social workers in their work with poor or even "asocial" families back home. The work of women sent by Nazi organizations to Poland combined the job descriptions of the social worker, nurse, teacher, and mother. The German women who came to the East had to "procure" food, clothing, and household goods for their charges (sometimes by stealing these items from others); clean or prepare homes for them; obtain medical care in some cases, or do the nursing themselves; grease the wheels of German bureaucracies for them, often filling out their paperwork; instruct them in new ways of cooking, cleaning, and decorating, along with popular German folk songs and customs; persuade them to stop giving their children wine, or to bathe their babies more often; indoctrinate them politically with an NS world view; and teach some of them to speak German.

In their reports for superiors back in Germany, some women advisors sought to win recognition by claiming that theirs was an entirely new "women's profession," whose creation was the result of unique historical circumstances. One argued for her audience back home that "nowhere else can one see the colossal importance of [Nazi] women's work as well as one can here, in these territories, where the clean, *tastefully decorated* German home and its inhabitants, who are aware of their Germanness…must raise themselves above other peoples through superior behavior and achievements."[44] In a 1942 press release written for newspapers back home, another woman expanded on the novelty and significance of German women's work with the *Volksdeutschen*, claiming that the woman advisor's job

is to bring the resettled members of the *Volk* [*Volksgenossen*] closer to a National Socialist style of life and thus to lead them into the great National

---

[43] For the attempts of some German women to discourage head scarves, see Harvey, *Women and the Nazi East*, 161.

[44] From a May 1941 report in BA R 49, vol. 3046, 15–16. The italics are mine.

Socialist racial community. Of course this means attention not only to the family, but also to their household – after all, a German can only really feel at home and begin to sink roots in a place, when he has a clean and orderly home. . . . [Building up farms and households in this way will ensure] that the Wartheland becomes a strong, firm bridge of Germanness, leading further East . . . thus the practical work of the NS advisor . . . focuses on instruction in practical housekeeping, ranging from how to keep the home clean to infant care.[45]

Successful German colonization, as these women saw it, thus hinged on the thorough "domestication" (and implicit *embourgeoisement*) of the *Volksdeutschen*.

The various agencies that claimed jurisdiction over women's issues apparently worked hard at the resocialization of *Volksdeutsche* women in the "new provinces," persuading tens of thousands of women to enroll in courses on sewing, nursing, practical hygiene, home décor, how to prepare for Christmas, cooking, thrift and food preservation, and infant care. In 1941 alone, the Mother's Service and the Section on Home Economics claimed that they had held a total of 2,266 courses in Wartheland province alone, which attracted 35,498 participants. By the end of 1942, the NS Women's League had placed between three and ten advisors in each district in the Wartheland, and claimed that these advisors were "caring for" and monitoring about forty-five thousand households.[46] It is unclear how welcome German advisors' attentions (and courses) were, however. Resettled *Volksdeutsche* families, after all, were without local networks of support or connections, and were thus often dependent on women from Nazi organizations for material assistance of all sorts. In many cases, ethnic German housewives might have hesitated to directly contradict or ignore advice given by a *Reichs* German advisor, no matter how much she might have disdained it.[47]

---

[45] From a report written for distribution in Württemberg – which had been designated the "sister province" for the Wartheland – dated Apr. 29, 1942, in BA R 49, vol. 3045, 16.

[46] These numbers are taken from BA R 49, vol. 3060, 18, "Ansiedlerbetreuerinnen der NS-Frauenschaft Gau Wartheland, Jahresbericht vom 1.12.1940–1.12.1941," and from the second annual report, 20.

[47] For an example of a resettled housewife who simply refused to speak with German women advisors (and who left all interactions with such *Reich* German women to her husband), see Harvey, *Women and the Nazi East*, 166.

In their internal reports, the women who worked with *Volks-deutschen* often described their charges as being "primitive," or "simple," as these largely middle-class women came into contact with the realities of rural family life. Their experiences indeed echoed the reactions of women from Nazi groups who had been sent to German rural areas bordering on Poland before 1939, who had also recoiled from the "backwardness" of peasant households.[48] Some German advisors complained that "their" women knew very little about washing or cleaning, and that they had to repeatedly nag these housewives to keep cleaner homes. One German woman, assigned to the Welun district in the Wartheland in 1942 wrote that "I regret that I must repeatedly admonish these women about their lack of cleanliness . . . but one seldom has much impact. . . . [M]ost of them simply say that their children will grow up anyway, even if they are not so clean." In one surprise household inspection, she had found a girl playing with her mother's combed out hair; she rebuked the mother sharply, saying that this was not hygienic.[49] But because the German advisors were younger than the *Volksdeutsche* women they were assigned to and were in most cases childless, many ethnic German housewives might not have seen their assigned advisors as authoritative sources of advice on child rearing.

But although these families were "primitive," most German women claimed that *Volksdeutsche* housewives and their children were almost childishly eager to hear learn about how things were done at home in Germany. One young kindergarten teacher reported that she had been able to persuade her charges to gradually begin to wash themselves and brush their teeth daily, and taught their mothers how to put up fruits and vegetables, "just as they do in the *Reich*."[50] Other advisors told their superiors that they had introduced ethnic German housewives to the foods that Germans ate back home, including the potato (evidently unknown to some *Volksdeutschen*), spinach, asparagus, and cauliflower. One advisor added that she had taught housewives from Bukovina to make fruit juice out of blueberries and red currants; before, she said, they had only known how to make wine

[48] See, e.g., the difficulties that activists from Nazi women's groups had with German rural housewives before 1939 in ibid., 65–6.
[49] From BA R 49, vol. 3062, 176, monthly report from Kreis Welun, dated Dec. 17, 1942.
[50] From BA R 49, vol. 3046, 22.

out of these berries. She persuaded them that juice was better for their children.[51] The emphasis on health, hygiene, and "modern" life-styles would have been familiar to many social workers within Germany. And women sent as advisors to the ethnic Germans in Poland enjoyed particular advantages (compared to well-meaning bourgeois women back home) in persuading their charges because the resettled *Volksdeutsche* families were often dependent on their German advisors' largesse or connections with local German authorities.

German advisors and teachers were often appalled by the house-keeping skills of resettled women from eastern Poland in particular. These *Volksdeutschen* were usually uneducated peasants and German women found them to be often stubbornly "primitive." One cooking instructor from the Samter district in the Wartheland reported that many Volhynian women simply refused to include vegetables in their cooking. "It is hard to grasp," she wrote, "how a woman who has six or eight children, in other words a housewife who has been cooking daily for at least twelve years, can know so little about cooking. We cannot assume that they know anything, but rather must teach them the simplest rules of cooking and most basic recipes."[52] Other advisors reported that Volhynian mothers in particular cherished numerous "superstitious" beliefs regarding child care and personal hygiene, which were hard to eradicate.[53]

Many *Volksdeutsche* women had never seen food preserved in glass jars with rubber rings, which seemed odd to them. But German advisors were able to procure the necessary equipment to teach them, and one reported proudly in June 1941 that she had been able to persuade local ethnic German housewives to learn to make gooseberry jam (which was for them an entirely new food). At first, they had resisted, but now when she visited their homes she was shown rows of filled glass jars on their shelves. She added that she always brought German newspapers and other publications with her so that she could teach them about what was going on "back home."[54] By discussing "back home" with her families this German advisor (like many others)

---

[51] From reports in BA R 49, vol. 3046, 90 and R 49, vol. 3062, 133.

[52] BA R 49, vol. 3046, 93. For similar complaints, see also Harvey, *Women and the Nazi East*, 167.

[53] BA R 49, vol. 3046, 103–5.

[54] BA R 49, vol. 3045, 150–1. This report purported to be (presumably edited) excerpts from an advisor's diary, prepared for publication in the *NS Frauenwarte*.

was in effect redefining what "back home" was; she was also helping ethnic Germans to construct a set of expectations about the German "homeland."

Some resettled *Volksdeutschen* resented the insistence of German authorities that children must attend school and Nazi youth groups. They wanted their children at home, helping out on the farm, and complained that they now "got little from their children."[55] German advisors and teachers insisted that children attend school and the Hitler Youth or BDM meetings nevertheless, and in some cases also carried on a tug-of-war with *Volksdeutsche* housewives over home décor. Many German advisors disliked the *Volksdeutsche* preference for what German women characterized as "kitschy Polish pictures" (presumably, pictures of saints or the Madonna), which the deported Poles had left behind, and which their *Volksdeutsche* replacements (who were often Catholic) apparently also liked. The tastes and life-style of the resettled families evidently resembled that of their Polish predecessors, at least in some respects. One advisor, who was assigned to work with resettled Galician Germans and who expressed some affection for her charges, was nonetheless exasperated by their taste for these pictures. She was able to gradually persuade some of them, however, to replace the "Polish images" with "pretty prints and framed German proverbs," akin to those displayed by people from her own social stratum.[56]

German women from a variety of agencies also worked to teach the *Volksdeutschen* how to celebrate a "real" German Christmas, along with the new, pseudo-Germanic solstice customs that the Nazi Party was promoting in Germany. Women from NS organizations taught their charges how to make the same small toys and decorations that German women often made at Christmas, provided texts for popular Christmas and NS solstice songs, and offered courses on how to bake traditional German Christmas cookies and treats. They noted that sometimes these celebrations were difficult to organize because many *Volksdeutsche* women spoke only broken German, and thus could not sing along with Christmas carols.[57] But others claimed that they had organized quite successful Christmas parties. One German teacher assigned to a village in Galicia reported in 1944 that

[55] BA R 49, vol. 3062, 194.
[56] From BA R 49, vol. 3045, 150–1.
[57] From BA R 49, vol. 3062, 71 and vol. 3046, 114–16.

thirty-eight *Volksdeutsche* mothers had attended her Christmas party, where an SS man had appeared dressed as Santa to distribute presents. The teacher concluded that the whole celebration had been something new and pleasant for these mothers.[58]

How German *Were* They? Degrees of Germanness

When German female teachers, advisors, or other volunteers from Nazi affiliate groups met new *Volksdeutschen* in Poland, they invariably assessed the degree of Germanness that each family or housewife still "retained." Their assessments were often complex and varied, and reflected their own *Reichs* German class-based standards and preconceptions. The *Volksdeutsche* households they entered could serve to confirm or challenge the prejudices and stereotypes that German women brought to their work. One of the most important preconceptions that many women who came from Germany brought to their work was the expectation that they would find an essential, timeless domestic Germanness in their charges who allegedly had "German blood." In the enormous body of popular publications on Eastern European *Volksdeutschen* (and in Nazi training materials for women advisors), ethnic German communities had been depicted as premodern bastions of authentic Germanness: remote and isolated, they had been preserved from the cosmopolitan contaminations of modernity.[59] Sometimes, these preconceptions were confirmed by actual contact with resettled ethnic Germans; but other times they were not, because the markers and practices they were looking for were sometimes bourgeois or urban in origin.

Resettled women from Bessarabia or Dobrudja still spun linen thread or wove their own blankets and curtains in "quaint" patterns, which some advisors found enchanting. German women assigned to work with Dobrudja Germans in Krotoschin and Welun districts in the Wartheland repeatedly praised the clothes, curtains, and other "charming" textiles that their charges wove.[60] Another German woman, assigned to work with ethnic German women from Bessarabia, wrote in her diary that she enjoyed watching these women at their spinning.

[58] From Harvey, *Women and the Nazi East*, 251.
[59] Such *Volksdeutsche* communities indeed resembled the mythical "lost" Scottish village of Brigadoon.
[60] From BA R 49, vol. 3062, 23–4.

They gave her spinning lessons and in exchange she taught them *Reichs* German folk songs. She concluded approvingly that "these are magnificent people. They have preserved their Germanness, and it is so pure that we 'Germans from the interior' must sometimes stand ashamed before them."[61] The "preservation" of German "purity" – which exceeded even that of metropolitan German advisors – seems to be equated with the preservation of chastity or virtue, proving these people's worthiness to receive support and citizenship.

In some cases, German female advisors were thus able to confirm their preconceptions about ethnic Germans, but in other instances they were disappointed in their charges. German women tended to evaluate the Germanness of the families assigned to them in the first analysis by how well their *Volksdeutschen* spoke German. Their second criterion for German identity was invariably the housekeeping of each *Volksdeutsche* household. The cleaner and more orderly a family was, the more likely a German advisor was to perceive them as having "kept" their Germanness. Somewhat surprisingly, German women rarely if ever commented on the "racial" characteristics – skin tone, facial shape, height, or eye color – that some SS commissariat examiners considered evidence of German ancestry. In the eyes of many German female advisors, a scrubbed floor and white sheets were evidently more important markers than "Aryan" coloring. For them, the domestic environment was both a marker of ethnicity and a factor that could help to reproduce it in the next generation.

Measured by these standards, the Baltic Germans tended to stand out as the most unambiguously German according to the metropolitan German standards of women from Nazi organizations. The Baltic Germans tended to be more urbanized, bourgeois, and educated than other groups of ethnic Germans, and usually spoke German as their first language (albeit with a particular regional accent). Nazi officials therefore generally accepted the resettled Baltic Germans easily, and Baltic Germans quickly assumed a prominent role in local administration and businesses in occupied Poland. Their ready acceptance by the German officials, however, was an ironic commentary on the regime's *Blut und Boden* ideology, which asserted that "authentic" Germanness was most likely to be found in populations untouched by modernity.

[61] BA R 49, vol. 3045, 150–1.

The language skills and cultural "purity" of other resettled groups varied. Resettled *Volksdeutschen* from eastern Poland were usually ranked at the bottom of this hierarchy: uneducated and "dirty," they were usually more comfortable speaking in Polish and sometimes drove the German women assigned to resocialize them to despair.

Ethnic Germans from Bessarabia, Dobrudja, and Bukovina might not all speak German perfectly, but German advisors generally saw them as being "clean" and hard working, and often compared them favorably with indigenous Polish *Volksdeutschen*. One German woman who went to visit a recently resettled group of families from Bukovina noted with relief that they "are clean and willing to learn. In four weeks they have accomplished more with their [new] farms than the Volhynian families have in a year. It is much easier to work with them than with the Volhynians and *Volksdeutschen* of this district."[62] Other women from the NS Women's League assigned to work with families from Dobrudja, again linking household order and German-ness, were pleased to report that "these families speak good German and also make a very German impression. These families are a joy to work with. In all their homes, they value cleanliness and order." Another German woman assigned to work with the Dobrudja Germans noted with pleasure that not only did these women keep very clean houses, but that they had also begun to pressure their *Volksdeutsche* neighbors (who were native to the district) to keep their houses cleaner.[63]

When German women paid their first visit to *Volksdeutsche* families, their relief could be almost palpable if they found that their "charges" spoke fluent German. One woman assigned by the NS Women's League to work with resettled families in a district in eastern Wartheland wrote for newspapers back home about her first visit to the village of Neudorf in the summer of 1940.

Mothers and children wait for us in front of the schoolhouse. They greet us with a smiling "Heil Hitler." Here, we are in the most German part of the district. Everyone here speaks German as something natural, as a matter of course. How happy we are! The schoolhouse is clean and friendly-looking,

---

[62] From BA R 49, vol. 3046, 91.
[63] The reports on the Dobrudja Germans can be found in BA R 49, vol. 3062, 22–3 and 44.

just like the homes that we passed. In their gardens, peonies, irises and jasmine are blooming.[64]

Polish *Volksdeutschen* – both "locals" who had been assigned to the German *Volk* list and those resettled from eastern Poland – often did not speak German very well (or even at all). Still, German advisors found that some of these families kept clean homes and tended to see these families as more worthy because they were at least trying to maintain a proper German home. One advisor, assigned to Milowka district in the Wartheland, reported in the spring of 1943 on a visit to the home of a local *Volksdeutsche* woman who spoke very little German, and whose husband was in the German army:

When I dropped by unexpectedly, I was amazed by the extreme cleanliness of the house, which was a model in its orderliness, and by this young woman's willingness to learn... even though she finds it difficult to express herself in German, she still makes every effort to give the home a German appearance.[65]

The homes could thus apparently be German, even where the housewife's ethnicity was ambiguous.

More often, however, German women found both the housekeeping and German fluency of Polish *Volksdeutsche* families to be disappointing. One kindergarten teacher assigned to Galicia commented sourly that "one seldom sees such filth as I saw [in a *Volksdeutsche* home] in the *Reich*, no matter how poor the people there might be."[66] Advisors also frequently complained that indigenous Polish *Volksdeutschen* had no sense of racial superiority: they did not maintain a proper social distance from their Polish neighbors and persisted in preferring to speak Polish rather than German. German women advisors reprimanded *Volksdeutsche* housewives for "chatting" with their Polish neighbors about child care advice; going to see Polish doctors; or eating together with their Polish maids or field workers. One German advisor was horrified to see a resettled ethnic German woman sharing a bottle of beer

---

[64] BA R 49, vol. 3045, 26. This writer did not mention this fact, but during the same months, the remaining Jewish inhabitants of this district were being deported to ghettos in the General Government. See Aly, *Endlösung*, 354.

[65] BA NS 44, vol. 3133, 12.

[66] Quoted in Harvey, "Man muss bloss," 111–12. Germans in other districts complained about the cleanliness of Polish *Volksdeutschen*. See Harten, *De-Kulturation und Germanisierung*, 117.

with a Polish woman and complained angrily that the *Volksdeutschen* in her district simply didn't understand why they should sever their social ties with Polish friends or acquaintances.[67] The attempt to sever long-standing links between local *Volksdeutschen* and their neighbors were intended not only to speed the "modernization" of ethnic Germans but also to sever those placed on the *Volksliste* from other Polish speakers, and thus to "re-Germanize" them by effectively deracinating them as Poles.

But although German women were sometimes disappointed by the *Volksdeutsche* families they worked with, many German advisors still developed a powerful personal investment in and identification with those they saw as their families. One German woman noted that after just one month, she now thought of the resettled families in her district as "'*my* resettled Germans.' I already feel as though I belong to them.... [O]ne simply has to be the leader for these people in every way."[68] In their reports, German women usually depicted resettled families as unsophisticated, almost childlike: dependent upon and looking up to their German advisors, who were depicted as these families' chief link to the authorities, the main source of all material support and (sometimes) news of the outside world.

Toward the end of the war, when many *Volksdeutsche* men had been drafted into the German army, a German female advisor was sometimes the sole remaining authority figure in a village, enjoying far more autonomy and power than she could have back home. It was an odd sort of "emancipation" for some German women, achieved within the framework of Nazi conquest and racism, in which they developed a sort of patronizing maternal relationship with the resettled ethnic Germans they oversaw, infantilizing the housewives assigned to them. The relationship also confirmed the authority of the German advisors, which derived from their provenance as *Reich* Germans.

After early 1943 (and particularly after Stalingrad), internal reports filed by advisors showed that morale among ethnic Germans soured and declined steadily throughout 1944 as the Soviet army advanced through Poland. Many resettled ethnic Germans complained that the

---

[67] From reports in BA R 49, vol. 3062, 90–1, 100, 102, 106–9, and 184–5.
[68] From BA R 49, vol. 3045, 150–1. Both the United States and Great Britain acquiesced in this policy.

Polish farms assigned to them were not equal to what they had left behind. They were unhappy with the life-style and property that they'd been given in exchange for their confiscated former homes and now destroyed communities, and they were more vulnerable than local indigenous *Volksdeutschen* because they lacked local connections and resources. German women assigned to work with these settlers reported that some openly said that they would leave the "new provinces" after the war was over. A few, relocated far from their relatives or friends in the "old homeland" (and perhaps fearing the Soviet Army), hanged themselves in despair. One advisor noted that she dealt with the worst complainers "by threatening to have them sent as workers to the *Reich*, which often works wonders."[69]

But by 1944, German advisors noted that Poles were becoming increasing "lazy and insolent," Polish bandits (partisans) were attacking *Volksdeutsche* families in the district, and some Poles had even come back to their old homes and simply taken their animals and other household goods.[70] Hundreds of thousands of *Volksdeutsche* families fled with their German advisors to Germany (where they were absorbed after 1945 into the German population) when the Soviets finally did arrive at the beginning of 1945. Those who stayed in Poland often took their turn at being subjected to ethnic cleansing, as both Poles and the Soviet Army took revenge on the ethnic Germans who remained.[71] Nazi Germany's grandiose efforts at massive ethnic cleansing, genocide, and the creation of a "German East" came to an abrupt end.

Conclusion

The "General Plan East" (in all its iterations and actual implementation) attempted to redraw the ethnographic map of Europe during World War II by deporting and murdering millions of Jews, Poles,

---

[69] From BA R 49, vol. 3062, 3 and 7.
[70] From BA NS 44, vol. 3133, 1–5 and 8–12.
[71] For the history of ethnic Germans both inside and outside of Germany after 1945, see Stefan Wolff, "The Politics of Homeland. Irredentism and Reconciliation in the Policies of German Federal Governments and Expellee Organizations towards Ethnic German Minorities in Central and Eastern Europe, 1949–1999," in Krista O'Donnell, Renate Bridenthal and Nancy Reagin, eds., *The Heimat Abroad*; see also David Rock, ed., *Coming Home to Germany?: The Integration of Ethnic Germans from Central and Eastern Europe in the Federal Republic* (New York: Berghahn Books, 2002).

Ukrainians, Russians, and others; uprooting and bringing in *Volks-deutsche* settlers in their place; and subjecting hundreds of thousands of people with putative German ancestry to "re-Germanization." In uprooting, incarcerating, classifying, and disposing over the lives of hundreds of thousands of candidates for German citizenship, German bureaucrats (male and female) applied a variety of yardsticks to "measure" the Germanness of the individuals in front of them. The personal qualities being used to determine Germanness varied, depending on the whims of the official involved. While some criteria were grounded in social reality (e.g., German language fluency), others were more subjective and reflected widely shared but imagined notions of Germanness: religious practices, skin tone or facial shape, social affiliations, lifestyle, personal hygiene, and standards of household cleanliness and order that had their roots among the German bourgeoisie.

In the transit camps and during the classification process applied by "flying detachments" of racial experts, applicants' domestic practices had been only one factor among many used in the assignment of German citizenship. Generally speaking, domesticity came into play only where other evidence regarding German ancestry was lacking or ambiguous. But in the "new provinces," domestic practices and standards assumed a crucial role in the evaluation of *Volksdeutschen* by German female advisors and in these women's efforts to re-Germanize those with questionable ancestry. As in their work before 1939 with ethnic German girls from Eastern Europe or with "asocial" housewives, NS women's agencies assumed that German identity could be "strengthened" through training in domestic science. In effect, they were applying established social welfare and educational policies – which incorporated long-standing bourgeois German domestic norms and practices – to new populations.

Nazi women's groups had not invented any of the banal traditions that they espoused: domestic symbols such as "sparkling clean" curtains and sheets; high standards for household cleanliness and order; rows of glass jars with homemade jams or preserved produce in the pantry; careful thrift and recycling of household resources; or particular Christmas recipes, carols, and forms of holiday rituals. These domestic markers of German national identity had been developed before 1914 and had helped define the identity of generations of housewife-activists before 1933. But although they had not created these practices, activists from Nazi women's groups had worked hard to spread these traditions to new populations, and thus gave them added weight. In so doing, they took norms that had previously served to further the *embourgeoisement* of poorer Germans and used them to support more sinister goals, such as the creation of a "living wall" of ethnic Germans in occupied Poland, as one part of a massive campaign of ethnic cleansing.

A particular approach to domesticity was central to their vision of Germanness (as it was to the national identity of many Germans) and they therefore concluded that if *Volksdeutsche* housewives – who were candidates for German citizenship – could be taught these domestic practices they then would be absorbed more readily into the national community. The domestic assistance that NS women offered was thus meant to be more than merely a practical support (to improve their charges' living standards). The NS women were also destined "to strengthen the Germanness of the resettled...to help them all to find a *Heimat* [in their new homes], and to be a living model of German nature, this is the great and beautiful task" of NS women in the Wartheland, as one 1942 press release concluded.[72]

In German popular culture, cleanliness had been next to Germanness long before 1933. But in occupied Poland, cleanliness (along with order and thrift) also became a bridge to Germanness, as NS women's groups placed domestic practices at the heart of Germanization. Their decision to do so exploited and played upon long-established notions of German national identity, which had always been rooted in the daily practices of private life. In their work, NS women were acknowledging that Germanness had always begun at home. But now, "home" could be located many hundreds of miles further to the East.

---

[72] From BA R 49, vol. 3046, 59.

Conclusion

"Order must be, but not in our house," said the indolent housewife.
From the 1876 edition of the Brockhaus Lexicon of German Sayings

Holidays and traditions sometimes become entrenched within a few years of their creation, as happened in the case of Mother's Day.[1] Domestic practices, however, evolve over decades, linked to changes in social conditions and household technology. German identity altered substantially during the period covered by this book and its domestic aspects continued to evolve after 1945. National identity is still rooted at least in part in the private sphere in Germany today, but many of the particular norms and practices of housekeeping discussed in this book have since disappeared in the face of political, technological, and social changes. More German housewives today purchase frozen foods, for example, than put up their own supplies of fruits and vegetables each fall.

This book has argued that in Germany, a model of household management – defined through particular symbols, practices, and

[1] For the origins of Mother's Day, see Karin Hausen, "Mütter zwischen Geschäftsinteresse und kultischer Verehrung. Der 'Deutsche Muttertag' in der Weimarer Republik," in Gerhard Huck, ed., *Sozialgeschichte der Freizeit*, (Wuppertal: Hammer, 1980), 249–80; see also Hausen, "Mothers, Sons and the Sale of Symbols and Goods. The German 'Mother's Day'," in Hans Medick and David W. Sabean, eds., *Interest and Emotion. Essays on the Study of Family and Kinship*, (London and New York: Cambridge University Press, 1984), 371–413.

objects – developed among the bourgeoisie during the second half of the nineteenth century. These standards and practices had much in common with the life-style developed among the bourgeoisie in other nations because these practices were markers of class identity throughout the West. In Germany, the particular values and practices associated with this style of domesticity became integral to national identity. After 1914, household norms and practices also became part of partisan political debates, as housewives' groups were rapidly absorbed into the world of nationalist politics after 1918. And during the Weimar period, the domestic norms of the bourgeoisie increasingly formed the starting point for a variety of public policies, a trend that accelerated after 1933. The domestic and gendered aspects of German identity were further racialized under the Nazi regime, as a particular approach to homemaking and family life became integral to the Nazi ideal of the *Volksgemeinschaft*.

Particular aspects of household management were associated with national identity in other contemporary nations, no doubt: but the objects and practices might vary considerably. In a broader sense, domestic values and objects became integral to all European imperialist rhetoric and practices: many domestic norms (cleanliness, modest clothing and orderly homes) became symbols of and justifications for European hegemony around the world.[2] Marjory Morgan's research on nineteenth-century travelers from Great Britain suggests that – when confronted with the life-styles and domestic values of other cultures – English travelers tended to associate such objects as teapots and hearths with Englishness.[3] German identity was associated with somewhat different objects and rituals.

But in Germany, practices and rituals used to define the nation within the public sphere (e.g., a national flag, holiday, or patriotic songs) were only partially successful for a variety of reasons. And such public

---

[2] See Chapter 2 for a discussion of the role that domesticity played in imperialist rhetoric regarding European superiority.

[3] Morgan's book examines travel literature to discuss how ordinary British travelers used the "others" they encountered abroad to define Englishness, Scottish identity, etc. Domesticity does not seem to have played such a key role as in Germany, but she does find that some domestic practices (particularly associated with tea-drinking rituals) and the notion of "comfort" (achieved through carpets, plenty of fires, etc.) were often invoked to define English identity. See Marjorie Morgan, *National Identities and Travel in Victorian Britain* (New York: Palgrave, 2001), 123 and 143.

symbols were changeable, or even not yet determined, during the first half of the twentieth century, as Germany's borders and political systems underwent repeated changes. By contrast, domestic practices and norms were seen as stable and unchanging, and also as essentially German. Domesticity thus provided an "unchanging" foundation for German national identity, an integral part of the repertoire of identities available to Germans (which could also be confessional, regional, or class based) in the late nineteenth and twentieth centuries.

The power and appeal that the private sphere had as a basis for identity was grounded precisely in its normalcy. And in their unobtrusiveness and their apparently non-partisan nature, the norms of bourgeois domesticity resembled the other social and cultural accomplishments of the Imperial German bourgeoisie. These included more public phenomena such as the zoological garden or the revised civil code, which also enjoyed widespread support. But unlike some of the other silent victories of the bourgeoisie, the success of the urban bourgeois approach to household management was largely the accomplishment of women, not men.

It was bourgeois women like Lina Morgenstern or Mrs. Sidgwick, after all, who supported and promoted demanding standards for housekeeping and then celebrated the resulting domestic order as being akin to what manufacturers referred to as *deutsche Qualitätsarbeit*. Explaining German home life to an English-speaking audience, Mrs. Sidgwick underscored repeatedly that the domesticity fundamental to German national character was a female accomplishment. Her pride in this showed, for example, in her description of a Berlin acquaintance's home: "She showed me each cupboard and corner of the flat," she wrote after her friend gave her a tour of the apartment, "and I saw everywhere the exquisite order and spotlessness the notable German housewife knows how to maintain."[4]

It was bourgeois leaders of housewives' groups who began to assert during the Weimar period (and even sometimes before) that housewives were a *Stand*, a profession. Bourgeois women's groups began to create domestic science courses in many German cities long before 1914, and began to argue (with some success) that the state should

---

[4] Sidgwick, *Home Life in Germany*, 135–6. For an additional discussion of the symbolic importance of "snow white" linens, see Wiedemann, *Herrin im Hause*.

make this training mandatory for young women and that employers should offer such instruction to their female employees. By the Weimar period, housewives' leaders were pushing for some sort of state certification or recognition for their work. They were not successful in this before 1933, but did persuade government authorities at many levels to include representatives from housewives' organizations on a variety of government commissions, advisory agencies, and chambers. All of this is evidence that the men of their class were at least partially persuaded of the importance of "quality" household management, and were willing to tacitly concede the validity of bourgeois women's standards for domestic life.

And just as women had pushed domestic science training and the notion of quality housekeeping into public discussions and policy during the Weimar period, they were also instrumental in the implementation of many Nazi social policies that sought to evaluate or intervene in German women's household management after 1933. Nazi female block wardens, female social workers, and district nurses processed the millions of applications for the Mother Cross, flagging those whose housekeeping did not pass muster. Women from a variety of Nazi organizations offered the lush spread of domestic science training courses for women of every age and social background created during the 1930s, and later administered the mandatory "year of service" for German girls. Activists from the Nazi Women's League helped to create and disseminate the enormous propaganda campaigns that sought to reshape German women's shopping and cooking in order to support the Nazi Four-Year Plan. Social workers and activists from the local Nazi Women's League in Bremen helped select disorderly housewives and their families for referral to the Hashude Educational Settlement and oversaw these inmates' daily housekeeping. The massive scope and sometimes compulsory nature of Nazi social policies that intervened in Germans' homes would not have been possible without the support and involvement of tens of thousands of women activists for various Nazi women's affiliate groups.

The enormous programs of classification, expropriation, incarceration, resettlement, deportation, and Germanization undertaken in Poland and the Soviet Union after 1939 also depended on German women's involvement. As Elizabeth Harvey has shown, how voluntary their presence in Poland was varied considerably. Students sent there to serve a term of service might only be in Poland for a few months and might be unenthusiastic about their work. Others, activists sent by the Nazi People's Welfare or BDM, might have requested assignment to Poland for ideological or opportunistic reasons and stayed there for years. Regardless of their original motives or the length of their assignment, Harvey argues persuasively that there was a widely shared awareness of the fate of deported Jews and Poles among the members of the German occupation, and that many German women had firsthand exposure to Jewish ghettos; some joined in the process of roundups, deportation, and expropriation of the prewar Polish population.[5] Women from Nazi organizations were also instrumental in programs that tried to Germanize formerly Polish or Jewish homes and the ethnic Germans who had been resettled on these properties.

The work of German women sent to Poland went beyond the important sorts of familial support for Nazi men already examined in the work of historians such as Claudia Koonz, Gudrun Schwarz, and Sybille Steinbacher. These scholars and others have examined the ways in which women provided a backdrop of domestic normalcy that supported the careers of Nazi Party members engaged in racial persecution and genocide. Wives or sisters of SS men and others with the occupation forces kept house near or even in the midst of concentration camps, provided emotional and domestic support for those committing atrocities, and were exposed to the information about the fate of the deported Jews and Poles, which was widely shared knowledge among the occupiers. Some of these women also often benefited personally from their privileged positions as members of the SS *Sippengemeinschaft* ("tribal community") or merely as part of the "ruling race."[6] But the social policies examined here (both in Poland and Germany) entailed the engagement of a much larger number of German women, acting in their own right and not as male surrogates: employees of various Nazi women's

---

[5] Harvey, *Women in the Nazi East*, 294–301.

[6] See Gudrun Schwarz, *Eine Frau an seiner Seite: Ehefrauen in der 'SS-Sippengemein-schaft'* (Hamburg: Hamburger Ed., 1997), 99–169. See also Steinbacher, *"Muster-stadt" Auschwitz*, 243–5. See also Claudia Koonz, *Mothers in the Fatherland. Women, the Family, and Nazi Politics* (New York: St. Martin's Press, 1987); and for discussions about the debates over female "perpetrators" vs. bystanders, see Adelheid v. Saldern, "Victims or Perpetrators? Controversies about the Role of Women in the Nazi State," in David Crew, ed., *Nazism and German Society, 1933–1945.* (New York: Routledge, 1994)

bureaucracies (e.g.,. the BDM, or the agencies under the leadership of the Nazi Women's League), Nazi women's groups chapter activists across Germany, block wardens, social workers, nurses, teachers, and other professionals.

The involvement of women in creating and implementing Nazi family policy was much more sustained and less dependent on personal familial connections or chance circumstances than any complicity shared by female relatives of the SS or Nazi Party bureaucrats. But this involvement was also lower key, attracting less attention both then and now than that of the "profile" positions occupied by wives and family members of leading Nazi officials. Most of the Nazi programs and initiatives discussed in this book (such as the Mother Cross or the plethora of domestic science courses) were hardly controversial. Like the Hashude camp, however, some could be quite aggressive or coercive. But whether popular or coercive, Nazi policies that sought to reshape private households were extending and manipulating standards of household management that had come to seem normative and desirable long before 1933. The template of domesticity that originated among the urban bourgeoisie had become integral to many Germans' understanding of their national identity even before 1914 and for Nazi officials it was an assumed part of membership in the *Volksgemeinschaft*. Cleanliness, order, thrift, and the other household practices discussed were key to Nazi women's (and many other Germans') understanding of what it meant to be German, and thus became crucial to their efforts to Germanize those resettled under the General Plan East.

German perceptions of the *Volksdeutschen* and their households during World War II were yet another demonstration that domestic standards and practices were central to German identity, but also reflected the fact that these standards evolved over a long period of time. Housekeeping and domestic life continued to change after 1945. Today, a life-style that would have embodied the essence of Germanness to one generation now seems old-fashioned and even (to people on the left) unattractive. This reflects the reality that under every political system, the "public" and the "private" are engaged in an intricate minuet: each helps to define the other and the nation as a whole. And like the nation, German domesticity is still a work in progress.

Bibliography

Primary Sources

Archival Sources

Archiv des Katholischen Deutschen Frauenbundes, Cologne
  Bestand *Reichshausfrauenvereinigung*
Bundesarchiv, Berlin
  NS 5/VI *Deutsche Arbeitsfront, Zeitungsausschnitt-Sammlung*
  NS 44 *Reichsfrauenführung/NS Frauenschaft und Deutsches Frauenwerk*
  R 49 *Reichskommisar für die Festigung deutschen Volkstums*
  R 59 *Volksdeutsche Mittelstelle*
  R 69 *Einwandererzentralstelle Litzmannstadt*
  R 8083 *Bestand Reichsgemeinschaft deutscher Hausfrauen*
Niedersächsisches Hauptstaatsarchiv, Hanover
  Hann 320 I, *Bestand Reichsverband Deutscher Hausfrauenvereine, Hannover* (records for both Hanover municipal and provincial chapters)
Nordrhein-Westfälisches Staatsarchiv Münster
  Bestand *NS-Frauenschaft Westfalen-Nord*
Staatsarchiv, Bremen
  S0–7-C.X.1.C *Zeitungsausschnitte*
  4.29/1–859 *Senator für das Bauwesen*
  4.13/1 W.3 *Senator für die innere Verwaltung*
  4.124/1 F.3.b.10
  4.130/1 K.I.2 Staatliches Gesundheitsamt Akte betreffend Wohnungsfürsorge Hashude
  3-W.11 Senats-Registratur. Akte betreffend Errichtung einer Asozialen-Kolonie für Bremen

Periodicals

Das Deutsche Frauenwerk
Deutsche Kolonialzeitung
Die Deutsche Hausfrau
Die Deutsche Hausfrauen-Zeitung
Die Frau im Osten
Die Welt der Frau (supplement to *Gartenlaube*)
Frauenland
Fürs Haus. Praktisches Wochenblatt für alle Hausfrauen
Hannoverscher Kurier
Hauswirtschaftliche Jahrbücher
Jahrbuch des Reichsverbandes Deutscher Hausfrauenvereine
Kolonie und Heimat
Mitteilungen des Hausfrauenvereins Hannover
Neue Hauswirtschaft
NS-Frauenwart

Published Primary Sources

Ackermann, Ernst and Hein Brewer. *Der Deutsche in Böhmen*. Berlin: Julius Beltz Verlag, 1935.

Adelung, Margarete. "Der 'Kampf dem Verderb' im Haushalt mit sparsamen Mittlen," Ph.D. diss., University of Munich, 1940.

Aubel, Cilli van. "Bedeutung und Aufgabe der Frau als Verbraucherin in der Wirtschaft," in Katholischer Deutscher Frauenbund, ed., *Frau und Wirtschaft. Vorträge der 11. Generalversammlung des KDF in Breslau.* Cologne: Katholischer Deutscher Frauenbund, 1931.

Bayles, William. *Postmarked Berlin*. London: Jarrolds Limited, 1942.

Beyer, Karl. *Familie und Frau im neuen Deutschland*. Berlin: Julius Beltz Verlag, 1936.

Brace, Charles Loring. *Home Life in Germany*. New York: C. Scribner, 1860.

Brockmann, Clara. *Die deutsche Frau in Südwestafrika. Ein Beitrag zur Frauenfrage in unseren Kolonien*. Berlin: Siegfried Mittler and Sons, 1910.

Browne, Maggie. *Chats about Germany*. London: Cassel and Co., 1884.

v. Bülow, Frieda. *Im Lande der Verheissung. Ein Kolonialroman um Carl Peters*. 3rd ed. Berlin: Oswald Arnold Verlag, 1943.

Burgdörfer, Friedrich. *Familie und Volk*. Berlin: Deutscher Schriftenverlag, 1936.

Cramer, Ada. *Weiss oder Schwarz. Lehr- und Leidensjahre eines Farmers in Südwest im Lichte des Rassenhasses*. Berlin: Deutscher Kolonial-Verlag, 1913.

Davidis, Henriette. *Die Hausfrau. Praktische Anleitung zur selbständigen und sparsamen Führung von Stadt- und Landhaushaltungen*. 6th ed. Leipzig: E. A. Seemann Verlag, 1872.

———. Revised and edited by Hedwig Voss. *Praktisches Kochbuch für die Deutschen in Amerika*. Milwaukee: Brumder's Verlag, 1897.

Der Haushalt als Wirtschaftsfaktor. Ergebnisse der Ausstellung Heim und Technik. Munich: Georg Callwey Verlag, 1928.

Deutsche Kolonialgesellschaft. *10 Jahre Frauenbund der Deutschen Kolonialgesellschaft.* Berlin: "Kolonie und Heimat" Verlagsgesellschaft, 1918.

v. Eckenbrecher, Margarethe. *Was Afrika mir gab und nahm. Erlebnisse einer deutschen Frau in Südwestafrika.* Rev. ed. Berlin: E. S. Mittler, 1940.

v. Eckenbrecher, Margarethe, Helene v. Falkenhausen, Stabsarzt Dr. Kuhn, and Oberleutnant Stuhlmann. *Deutsch-Südwestafrika. Kriegs- und Friedensbilder.* Leipzig: E. S. Mittler, 1907.

v. Falkenhausen, Helene. *Ansiedlerschicksale. Elf Jahre in Deutsch-Südwestafrika 1893–1904.* Berlin: Dietrich Reimer, 1905.

Fittbogen, Gottfried. *Was jeder Deutsche vom Grenz- und Auslandsdeustchtum wissen muss.* 3rd ed. Munich and Berlin: R. Oldenbourg Verlag, 1924.

———. *Was jeder Deutsche vom Grenz- und Auslandsdeutschtum wissen muss.* 9th ed. Munich and Berlin: R. Oldenbourg Verlag, 1938.

Frauenwirken in Haus und Familie. Die Ausstellung der Düsseldorfer Frauenverbände. Rückblick und Ausblick. Düsseldorf: E. D. Lintz, 1930.

Gauamtsleitung der NS-Frauenschaft. *Vom Wollen und Schaffen der NS-Frauenschaft, Gau Thüringen.* Thüringen: n.p., 1935.

Gauss, Paul, ed. *Das Buch vom deutschen Volkstum. Wesen-Lebensraum-Schicksal.* Leipzig: F. A. Brockhaus, 1935.

Heyl, Hedwig. *Ratgeber. Das ABC der Küche.* 4th ed. Berlin: Carl Habel Verlag, 1897.

Kahle, Maria. *Deutsches Volk in der Fremde.* Oldenburg: Gerhard Stalling, 1933.

Kaindl, Raimund. *Die Deutschen in Galizien und in der Bukowina.* Frankfurt: H. Keller, 1916.

———. *Deutsche Art – treu bewahrt,* Vienna: W. Braumüller, 1924.

Karow, Maria. *Wo sonst der Fuss des Kriegers Trat. Farmerleben in Südwest nach dem Kriege.* Berlin: E. S. Mittler, 1909.

Katholischer Deutscher Frauenbund. *Frau und Wirtschaft. Vorträge der 11. Generalversammlung des KDFs in Breslau.* Cologne: Katholischer Deutscher Frauenbund, 1931.

Katterfeld, Anna. *Vom Ich zu Wir. Eine Großstadtpfarrfrau erlebt den Umbruch der Zeit.* Bad Blankenberg: Harfe Verlag, 1936.

Kirkpatrick, Clifford. *Nazi Germany. Its Women and Family Life.* New York: Bobbs-Merrill, 1938.

Knorr, Wolfgang. *Vergleichende erbbiologische Untersuchungen an drei asozialen Grossfamilien.* Berlin: Walter de Gruyter and Co., 1939.

Kraushaar, Karl. *Sitten und Bräuche der Deutschen in Ungarn, Rumänien, und Jugoslavien.* Vienna: A. C. Trupp, 1932.

Kreyenberg, Gotthold. *Mädchenerziehung und Frauenleben im Aus- und Inlande. Neudruck der Ausgabe Berlin 1872 mit Einleitung von Ruth Bleckwann.* Paderborn: Hüttemann Verlag, 1990.

Lüders, Marie-Elisabeth. *Das unbekannte Heer. Frauen kämpfen für Deutschland, 1914–1918.* Berlin: E. S. Mittler and Sohn, 1936.

Maschmann, Melita. *Account Rendered. A Dossier on My Former Self.* London: Abelard-Schuman, 1965.

Mayer, August. *Deutsche Mutter und deutscher Aufstieg.* Munich: Lehmanns Verlag, 1938.

Meyer, Erna. *Der neue Haushalt. Ein Wegweiser zur wirtschaftlicher Hausführung.* 2nd ed. Stuttgart: Franckh'sche Verlagshandlung, 1926.

——. *Hausfrauen Taschen-Kalender 1928.* Stuttgart: Franckh'sche Verlagshandlung, 1928.

Munske, Hilde, ed. *Mädel im Dritten Reich.* Berlin: Freiheitsverlag, 1935.

Müting, J., ed. *Heimat und Welt. Teubners Erdkundliches Unterrichtswerk für die höhere Schulen.* Leipzig: Teubner, 1939.

Neundörfer, Klara. *Haushalten.* Königstein im Taunus: Verlag der Eiserne Hammer, 1929.

Neundörfer, Ludwig. *Wie Wohnen?* Königstein im Taunus: Verlag der Eiserne Hammer, 1928.

Obrig, Ilse. *Guter Mucki, nimm auch mit. Eine Reise zu den Auslandsdeutschen in Rumänien.* Stuttgart: Union Deutsche Verlagsgesellschaft, n.d.

Petersen, Carl et al., eds. *Handwörterbuch des Grenz- und Auslandsdeutschtums.* Breslau: F. Hirt, 1933–5.

Pfannes, Fini. *So will ich sparen! Das Wirtschaftsbuch der Hausfrau.* Stuttgart: Franckh'sche Verlagshandlung, 1930.

Pohl, Irmgard. *Deutsche im Südosten Europas. Vorposten des Volkstums.* Leipzig: J. Klinkhardt, 1938.

Reichsfrauenführung. *Beiträge zur Wirtschaftslehre des Haushalts.* Stuttgart: Franckh'sche Verlagshandlung, 1941.

Rez, Heinrich. *Bibliographie zur Volkskunde der Donauschwaben.* Munich: Ernst Reinhardt Verlag, 1935.

Rudorff, Margarethe. *Die Normung in der Hauswirtschaft.* Berlin: Reichskuratorium für Wirtschaftlichkeit, n.d.

Scherer, Anton. *Donauschwäbischer Bibliographie 1935–1955.* Munich: Verlag des Südostdeutschen Kulturwerks, 1966.

Schiller, Friedrich. *Gedichte/ Schiller.* Berlin: Aufbau Verlag, 1980.

Schirmacher, Käthe. *Völkische Frauenpflichten.* Charlottenberg: Augustin and Co., 1917.

Scholtz-Klink, Gertrud. *Die Frau im Dritten Reich. Eine Dokumentation.* Tübingen: Grabert Verlag, 1978.

Seminar der Koch- und Haushaltungsschule "Hedwig Heyl." *Lehrgang des Pestalozzi-Fröbel-Hauses II.* Berlin: Carl Habel, 1905.

Sidgwick, Mrs. Alfred. *Home Life in Germany.* London: Methuen and Co., 1908.

Sonnenberg, Else. *Wie es am Waterberg zuging. Ein Beitrag zur Geschichte des Hereroaufstandes.* Berlin: W. Süsserott, 1905.

Stach, Jakob. *Die deutschen Kolonien in Südrussland.* Prischib: G. Schaad, ca. 1905.

Tiling, Magda ed., *Grundfragen Pädagogischen Handelns. Beiträge zur neuen Erziehung.* Arbeitsbund für wissenschaftliche Pädagogik auf reformatorischer. Grundlage: Stuttgart, 1934.

Träger, Paul. *Die Deutschen in der Dobrudscha.* Stuttgart: Ausland und Heimat Verlagsaktiengesellschaft, 1922.

Villwock, G. *Hausarbeit leicht gemacht.* 3rd ed. Berlin: Reichskuratorium für Wirtschaftlichkeit, n.d.

Vorwerck, Else. "Hauswirtschaft in Selbstverwaltung. Ein erster grosser Versuch, 1934–1945." Unpublished manuscript, 1948.

Wander, Karl Friedrich Wilhelm *Deutsches Sprichwörter-Lexikon.* Vols. 1–5. Leipzig: Brockhaus, 1876.

Wylie, Ida A. R. *The Germans.* Indianapolis: Bobbs-Merrill, 1911.

Zuberbier, Eva. "Die nationalsozialistische Auffassung vom häuslichen Dienst der deutschen Frau und ihre praktische Verwirklichung." Ph.D. diss., University of Leipzig, 1939.

Secondary Literature

Abusch-Magder, Ruth. "Matzo Balls and Matzo Kleis: A Comparative Study of Domestic Life in the United States and Germany, 1840–1914," Ph.D. diss., Yale University, 2006.

Aly, Götz. *"Endlösung" Völkerverschiebung und der Mord an den europäischen Juden.* Frankfurt: S. Fischer Verlag, 1995.

Andersen, Arne. *Der Traum vom guten Leben. Alltags- und Konsumgeschichte vom Wirtschaftswunder bis heute.* Frankfurt: Campus, 1997.

Anderson, Benedict. *Imagined Communities. Reflections on the Origins and Spread of Nationalism.* Rev. ed. New York: Verso, 1991.

Applegate, Celia. *A Nation of Provincials: The German Idea of Heimat.* Berkeley and Los Angeles: University of California Press, 1990.

Applegate, Celia and Pamela Potter, eds. *Music and German National Identity.* Chicago: University of Chicago Press, 2002.

Auslander, Leora. "Citizenship Law, State Form, and Everyday Aesthetics in Modern France and Germany, 1920–1940," in Martin Daunton and Matthew Hilton, eds., *The Politics of Consumption. Material Culture and Citizenship in Europe and America.* New York: Berg, 2001.

Baranowski, Shelley. "Strength through Joy: Tourism and National Integration in the Third Reich," in Shelley Baranowski and Ellen Furlough, eds., *Being Elsewhere: Tourism, Consumer Culture, and Identity in Modern Europe and North America.* Ann Arbor: University of Michigan Press, 2001.

Barkai, Avraham. *Nazi Economics. Ideology, Theory, and Policy.* New Haven, CT: Yale University Press, 1990.

Becker, Franziska. *Gewalt und Gedächtnis: Erinnerungen an die nationalsozialistischen Verfolgung einer jüdischen Landgemeinde.* Göttingen: V. Schmerse, 1994.

Belgum, Kirsten. "A Nation For the Masses: Production of the German Identity in the Late-Nineteenth-Century Popular Press," in Scott Denham, Irene Kacandes, and Jonathan Petropoulos, eds., *A User's Guide to German Cultural Studies.* Ann Arbor: University of Michigan Press, 1997.

———. *Popularizing the Nation. Audience, Representation, and the Production of Identity in Die Gartenlaube, 1853–1900.* Lincoln: University of Nebraska Press, 1998.

Benninghoff-Lühl, Sibylle. "'Ach Afrika! Wär ich zu Hause!' Gedanken zum Deutschen Kolonialroman der Jahrhundertwende," in Renate Nestvogel and Rainer Tetzlaff, eds., *Afrika und der deutsche Kolonialismus. Zivilisierung zwischen Schnapshandel und Bibelstunde.* Berlin: D. Reimer, 1987.

Benz, Wolfgang, ed. *Die Vertreibung der Deutschen aus dem Osten: Ursachen, Ereignisse, Folgen.* Frankfurt: Fischer Verlag, 1985.

Bergen, Doris L. "The 'Volksdeutschen' of Eastern Europe, World War II, and the Holocaust: Constructed Ethnicity, Real Genocide," in Keith Bullivant, Geoffrey Giles, and Walter Pape, eds., *Germany and Eastern Europe: Cultural Identities and Cultural Differences* (Yearbook of European Studies 13). Amsterdam: Rodopi, 1999.

———. "Sex, Blood, and Vulnerability: Women Outsiders in German-Occupied Europe," in Robert Gellately and Nathan Stolzfus, eds., *Social Outsiders in Nazi Germany.* Princeton: Princeton University Press, 2001.

———. "Drawing Lines of Blood: Racial Categorization, Gender, War, and the Holocaust." Paper presented at the Berkshire Conference on the History of Women, June 2005.

Berghoff, Hartmut. "Konsumgüterindustrie im Nationalsozialismus. Marketing im Spannungsfeld von Profit- und Regimeinteressen," *Archiv für Sozialgeschichte* 36 (1996): 293–322.

———. ed. *Konsumpolitik. Die Regulierung des privaten Verbrauchs im 20. Jahrhundert.* Göttingen: Vandenhoeck and Ruprecht, 1999.

———. "Enticement and Deprivation: The Regulation of Consumption in Prewar Nazi Germany," in Martin Daunton and Matthew Hilton, eds., *The Politics of Consumption. Material Culture and Citizenship in Europe and America.* New York: Berg, 2001.

Bessel, Richard. *Life in the Third Reich.* Oxford: Oxford University Press, 1987.

Betts, Paul. "The Nierentisch Nemesis: Organic Design in West German Pop Culture," *German History* 19 (2001): 185–217.

Beuys, Barbara. *Familienleben in Deutschland. Neue Bilder aus der deutschen Vergangenheit.* Reinbek bei Hamburg: Rowohlt, 1980.

Beyer, Horst and Annelies. *Sprichwörterlexikon. Sprichwörter und sprichwörtliche Ausdrücke aus deutschen Sammlungen vom 16. Jahrhundert bis zur Gegenwart.* Munich: Verlag C. H. Beck, 1985.

Billig, Michael. *Banal Nationalism.* London: Sage Publications, 1995.

Blackbourne, David and Geoff Eley. *The Peculiarities of German History: Bourgeois Society and Politics in Nineteenth Century Germany.* Oxford: Oxford University Press, 1985.

Heidi Blöcher. "Zellwolle und Kunstseide, die neuen Spinnstoffe," in Almut Junker, ed., *Frankfurt Macht Mode, 1933–1945.* Frankfurt: Jonas Verlag, 1994.

Bluth, Siegfried. *Der Hausfrau gewidmet. Ein Beitrag zur Kulturgeschichte der Hausfrau.* Weil der Stadt: Hadecke, 1979.

Bock, Giesela. *Zwangssterilisation im Nationalsozialismus: Studien zur Rassenpolitik und Frauenpolitik.* Opladen: Westdeutscher Verlag, 1986.

Bourdieu, Pierre. *Language and Symbolic Power.* Cambridge: Cambridge University Press, 1991.

Bourke, Joanna. *Husbandry to Housewifery. Women, Economic Change, and Housework in Ireland 1890–1914.* Oxford: Clarendon Press, 1993.

Boydston, Jeanne. *Home and Work. Housework, Wages, and the Ideology of Labor in the Early Republic.* New York: Oxford University Press, 1990.

Breuilly, John. *Nationalism and the State.* New York: St. Martin's Press, 1982.

Bridenthal, Renate. "Class Struggle around the Hearth: Women and Domestic Service in the Weimar Republic," in Michael Dobkowski and Isidor Walliman, eds., *Towards the Holocaust: Anti-Semitism and Fascism in Weimar Germany.* Westport, CT: Greenwood Press, 1983.

———. "'Professional Housewives': Stepsisters of the Women's Movement," in Renate Bridenthal, Atina Grossmann, and Marion Kaplan, eds., *When Biology Became Destiny: Women in Weimar and Nazi Germany.* New York: Monthly Review Press, 1984.

———. "Organized Rural Women in the Conservative Mobilization of the German Countryside in the Weimar Republic," in Larry E. Jones and James N. Retallack, eds., *Between Reform, Reaction, and Resistance. Studies in the History of German Conservatism from 1789 to 1945.* New York: Berg, 1993.

Brubaker, Rogers. *Citizenship and Nationhood in France and Germany.* Cambridge, MA: Harvard University Press, 1992.

———. *Nationalism Reframed. Nationhood and the National Question in the New Europe.* Cambridge: Cambridge University Press, 1996.

Bryant, Chad Carl. "Making Czechs German: German Nationality and Nazi Rule in the Protectorate of Bohemia and Moravia, 1939–1945," Ph.D. diss., University of California, Berkeley, 2002.

Burke, Timothy. *Lifebuoy Men and Lux Women. Commodification, Consumption, and Cleanliness in Modern Zimbabwe.* Durham and London: Duke University Press, 1996.

Burleigh, Michael. *Germany Turns Eastward. A Study of Ostforschung in the Third Reich.* Cambridge: Cambridge University Press, 1988.

Burleigh, Michael and Wolfgang Wippermann. *The Racial State: Germany, 1933–1945.* New York: Cambridge University Press, 1991.

Burton, Antoinette. *Burdens of History. British Feminists, Indian Women, and Imperial Culture, 1865–1915.* Chapel Hill: University of North Carolina Press, 1994.

Bussemer, Herrad U., Sibylle Meyer, Barbara Orland, and Eva Schulze. "Zur technischen Entwicklung von Haushaltsgeräten," in Gerda Tornieporth, ed., *Arbeitsplatz Haushalt. Zur Theorie und Ökologie der Hausarbeit.* Berlin: D. Reimer, 1988.

Canning, Kathleen. *Languages of Labor and Gender. Female Factory Work in Germany, 1850–1914*. Ithaca: Cornell University Press, 1996.

Chickering, Roger. *We Men Who Feel Most German. A Cultural Study of the Pan-German League, 1866–1914*. Boston: Allen and Unwin, 1984.

———. "'Casting Their Gaze More Broadly': Women's Patriotic Activism in Imperial Germany," *Past and Present* 118 (1988): 156–85.

Childers, Thomas. *The Nazi Voter: The Social Foundations of Fascism in Germany, 1919–1933*. Chapel Hill: University of North Carolina Press, 1983.

Chodera, Jan. *Die deutsche Polenliteratur 1918–1939. Stoff- und Motivgeschichte*. Poznan: University of Poznan Press, 1966.

Coetzee, Marilyn Shevin. *The German Army League. Popular Nationalism in Wilhelmine Germany*. New York: Oxford University Press, 1990.

Comaroff, Jean and John Comaroff. "Homemade Hegemony: Modernity, Domesticity, and Colonialism in South Africa," in Karen T. Hansen, ed., *African Encounters with Domesticity*. New Brunswick, NJ: Rutgers University Press, 1992.

Confino, Alon. *The Nation as Local Metaphor. Württemberg, Imperial Germany, and National Memory, 1871–1918*. Chapel Hill: University of North Carolina Press, 1997.

Connelly, John. "Nazis and Slavs: From Racial Theory to Racist Practice," *Central European History* 32 (1999): 1–33.

Conze, Werner and Jürgen Kocka. *Bildungsbürgertum im 19. Jahrhundert*. 4 vols. Stuttgart: Klett-Cotta, 1985–1992.

Cott, Nancy. *Public Vows: A History of Marriage and the Nation*. Cambridge, MA: Harvard University Press, 2000.

Czarnowski, Gabrielle. "'Der Wert der Ehe für die Volksgemeinschaft': Frauen und Männer in der nationalsozialistischen Ehepolitik" in Kirsten Heinsohn, Barbara Vogel, and Ulrike Weckel, eds., *Zwischen Karriere und Verfolgung. Handlungsräume von Frauen in nationalsozialitischen Deutschland*. Frankfurt: Campus Verlag, 1997.

Dammer, Susanne. "Kinder, Küche, Kriegsarbeit – die Schulung der Frauen durch die NS-Frauenschaft," in Frauengruppe Faschismusforschung, ed., *Mutterkreuz und Arbeitsbuch. Zur Geschichte der Frauen in der Weimarer Republik und im Nationalsozialismus*. Frankfurt: Fischer Verlag, 1981.

Dann, Otto. "Nationale Fragen in Deutschland: Kulturnation, Volksnation, Reichsnation," in Etienne Francois, Hannes Siegrist, and Jakob Vogel, eds., *Nation und Emotion. Deutschland und Frankreich im Vergleich, 19. und 20. Jahrhundert*. Göttingen: Vandenhoeck and Ruprecht, 1995.

Daunton, Martin and Matthew Hilton, eds. *The Politics of Consumption. Material Culture and Citizenship in Europe and America*. New York: Berg, 2001.

Davidoff, Leonore and Catherine Hall. *Family Fortunes. Men and Women of the English Middle Class, 1780–1850*. Chicago: University of Chicago Press, 1987.

Davidson, Caroline. *A Woman's Work Is Never Done. A History of Housework in the British Isles, 1650–1950*. London: Chatto and Windus, 1982.

Davis, Belinda. *Home Fires Burning: Politics, Identity, and Food in World War I Berlin*. Chapel Hill: University of North Carolina Press, 2000.

Dick, Jutta and Marina Sassenberg, eds. *Jüdische Frauen im 19. Und 20. Jahrhundert*. Reinbek bei Hamburg: Rowohlt, 1993.

Dobat, Klaus-Dieter. "O Tannenbaum, O Tannenbaum . . ." Wie der Siegeszug eines deutschen Weihnachtssymbols begann," *Damals* 21 (1989): 1093–101.

Einfeldt, Anne-Katrin. "Auskommen – Durchkommen – Weiterkommen. Weibliche Arbeitserfahrungen in der Bergarbeiterkolonie," in Lutz Niethammer, ed., *Die Jahre weiss man nicht, wo man die heute hinsetzen soll. Faschismus-Erfahrungen im Ruhrgebiet*. Berlin: Dietz, 1983.

Eley, Geoff. *Reshaping the Germany Right. Radical Nationalism and Political Change after Bismarck*. New Haven, CT: Yale University Press, 1980.

Fahlbusch, Michael. *Wissenschaft im Dienst der nationalsozialistischen Politik? Die 'Volksdeutschen Forschungsgemeinschaften' von 1931–1945*. Baden-Baden: Nomos, 1999.

Fiedor, Karol, Janusz Sobczak, and Wojciech Wrzesinski. "The Image of the Poles in Germany and of the German in Poland in Inter-War Years and Its Role in Shaping the Relations Between the Two States," *Polish Western Affairs* 19 (1978): 202–28.

Fllmer, Moritz. "Die bürgerliche Ordnung der Nation. Zur Diskursgeschichte von Industriellen und hohen Beamten in Deutschland und Frankreich 1900–1930." Ph.D. diss., Humboldt University of Berlin, 2000.

Fox, Richard and Jackson Lears, eds. *The Culture of Consumption*. New York: Pantheon Books, 1983.

Frauengruppe Faschismusforschung. *Mutterkreuz und Arbeitsbuch. Zur Geschichte der Frauen in der Weimarer Republik und im Nationalsozialismus*. Frankfurt: Fischer Verlag, 1981.

Freudenthal, Margarete. *Gestaltwandel der städtischen, bürgerlichen, und proletarischen Hauswirtschaft zwischen 1760 und 1910*. Berlin: Ullstein Verlag, 1986 (reprint ed.).

Frevert, Ute. "Fürsorgliche Belagerung. Hygienebewegung und Arbeiterfrauen im 19. und frühen 20. Jahrhundert," *Geschichte und Gesellschaft* 11 (1985): 420–46.

Frey, Manual. *Der reinliche Bürger. Entstehung und Verbreitung bürgerlicher Tugenden in Deutschland, 1760–1860*. Göttingen: Vandenhoek and Ruprecht, 1997.

Fritzsche, Peter. *Germans into Nazis*. Cambridge, MA: Harvard University Press, 1998.

Frost, Robert. "Machine Liberation: Inventing Housewives and Home Appliances in Interwar France," *French Historical Studies* 18 (1993): 109–30.

v. Goldendach, Walter and Hans-Rüdiger Minow, *'Deutschtum Erwache!' Aus dem Innenleben des staatlichen Pangermanismus*. Berlin: Dietz, 1994.

Goltermann, Svenja. *Körper der Nation: Habitusformierung und die Politik des Turnens.* Göttingen: Vandenhoeck and Ruprecht, 1998.

Gordon, Jean and Jan McArthur. "American Women and Domestic Consumption, 1800–1920: Four Interpretive Themes," in Marilyn Ferris Motz and Pat Browne, eds., *Making the American Home. Middle-Class Women and Domestic Material Culture, 1940–1940.* Bowling Green, OH: Bowling Green State University Press, 1988.

Gray, Marion. "Prescriptions for Productive Female Domesticity in a Transitional Era: Germany's Hausmütterliteratur, 1780–1840," *History of European Ideas* 8 (1987): 413–26.

———. "Bourgeois Values in the Rural Household, 1810–1840: The New Domesticity in Germany," *The Consortium on Revolutionary Europe, 1750–1850,* 23 (1994): 449–56.

de Grazia, Victoria and Ellen Furlough, eds. *The Sex of Things. Gender and Consumption in Historical Perspective.* Berkeley: University of California Press, 1996.

Green, Abigail. *Fatherlands: State-Building and Nationhood in Nineteenth-Century Germany.* Cambridge: Cambridge University Press, 2001.

Greenfeld, Liah. *Nationalism: Five Roads to Modernity.* Cambridge, MA: Harvard University Press, 1992.

Grunberger, Richard. *A Social History of the Third Reich.* London: Weidenfeld and Nicolson, 1971.

Guenther, Irene. "Nazi 'Chic'? German Politics and Womens' Fashions, 1915–1945," *Fashion Theory* 1 (1997): 29–58.

Guttmann, Barbara. "'in nie erlebter Leibhaftigkeit zum 'Volke' vereint': Frauenbewegung und Nationalismus im Ersten Weltkrieg," in Frauen und Geschichte Baden-Württemberg, ed., *Frauen und Nation.* Tübingen: Silberberg, 1996.

Hagemann, Karen. *Frauenalltag und Männerpolitik. Alltagsleben und gesellschaftliches Handeln von Arbeiterfrauen in der Weimarer Republik.* Bonn: Dietz, 1990.

———. *"Männlicher Muth und Teutsche Ehre": Nation, Militär und Geschlecht zur Zeit der Antinapoleonischen Kriege Preussens.* Paderborn: F. Schöningh, 2002.

Hardyment, Christina. *From Mangle to Microwave. The Mechanization of Household Work.* New York: Polity Press, 1988.

Harker, Richard, Cheleen Mahar, and Chris Wilkes. *An Introduction to the Work of Pierre Bourdieu. The Practice of Theory.* New York: St. Martin's Press, 1990.

Harten, Hans-Christian. *De-Kulturation und Germanisierung. Die nationalsozialistische Rassen- und Erziehungspolitik in Polen 1939–1945.* Frankfurt: Campus, 1996.

Hartwig, Wolfgang. "Bürgertum, Staatssymbolik und Staatsbewusstsein 1871–1914," *Geschichte und Gesellschaft* 16 (1990): 269–95.

Harvey, Elizabeth. "'Die deutsche Frau im Osten': 'Rasse,' Geschlecht, und öffentlicher Raum im besetzten Polen 1940–1944," *Archiv für Sozialgeschichte* 38 (1998): 191–214.

———. "'Pilgrimages to the 'Bleeding Border': Gender and Rituals of Nationalist Protest in Germany, 1919–1939," *Women's History Review* 9 (2000): 201–29.

———. "'We Forgot All Jews and Poles': German Women and the 'Ethnic Struggle' in Nazi-Occupied Poland," *Contemporary European History* 10 (2001a): 447–61.

———. "'Man muss bloss einen unerschütterlichen Willen haben' Deutsche Kindergärtnerinnen und der nationalsozialistische 'Volkstumskampf' im 'Distrikt Galizien,' 1941–1944," *L'Homme* 12 (2001b): 98–123.

———. *Women and the Nazi East. Agents and Witnesses of Germanization.* New Haven, CT: Yale University Press, 2003.

Hausen, Karen. "Mütter zwischen Geschäftsinteresse und kultischer Verehrung. Der 'Deutsche Muttertag' in der Weimarer Republik," in Gerhard Huck, ed., *Sozialgeschichte der Freizeit.* Wuppertal: Hammer, 1980.

———. "Family and Role Division: The Polarization of Sexual Stereotypes in the Nineteenth Century – An Aspect of the Disassociation of Work and Family Life," in Richard Evans and W. R. Lee, eds., *The German Family.* London: Croom Helm, 1981.

———. "Mothers, Sons and the Sale of Symbols and Goods. The German 'Mother's Day'," in Hans Medick and David W. Sabean, eds., *Interest and Emotion. Essays on the Study of Family and Kinship.* London and New York: Cambridge University Press, 1984.

———. "Grosse Wäsche. Technischer Fortschritt und sozialer Wandel in Deutschland vom 18. bis ins 20. Jahrhundert," *Geschichte und Gesellschaft* 13 (1987): 273–303.

Hebert, Ulrich. "Good Times, Bad Times: Memories of the Third Reich," in Richard Bessel, *Life in the Third Reich.* Oxford: Oxford University Press, 1987.

Heineman, Elizabeth. *What Difference Does a Husband Make? Women and Marital Status in Nazi and Postwar Germany.* Berkeley: University of California Press, 1999.

Heinemann, Isabel. *Rasse, Siedlung, deutsches Blut. Das Rasse- und Siedlungshauptamt der SS und die rassenpolitische Neuordnung Europas.* Göttingen: Wallstein, 2003.

Heinsohn, Kirsten, Barbara Vogel, and Ulrike Weckel, eds. *Zwischen Karriere und Verfolgung. Handlungsräume von Frauen in nationalsozialitischen Deutschland.* Frankfurt: Campus Verlag, 1997.

Hellmann, Ullrich. *Künstliche Kälte. Die Geschichte der Kühlung im Haushalt.* Geissen: Anabas-Verlag, 1990.

Henning, Hansjoachim. *Das westdeutsche Bürgertum in der Epoche der Hochindustrialisierung 1860–1914 Teil I: Das Bildungsbürgertum in den preussischen Westprovinzen.* Wiesbaden: F. Steiner, 1972.

Herminghouse Patricia, and Magda Mueller, eds. *Gender and Germanness. Cultural Productions of Nation.* Oxford: Berghahn Press, 1997.

Hervé, Florence, ed. *Namibia. Frauen mischen sich ein.* Berlin: Orlanda Frauenverlag, 1993.

Hessler, Martina. "Die Einführung elektrischer Haushaltsgeräte in der Zwischenkriegszeit – Der Angebotspush der Produzenten und die Reaktion der Konsumentinnen," *Technikgeschichte* 65 (1998): 297–311.

Hobsbawm, Eric and Terence Ranger, eds. *The Invention of Tradition.* Cambridge: Cambridge University Press, 1983.

———. *Nations and Nationalism since 1780. Programme, Myth, Reality.* Cambridge: Cambridge University Press, 1990.

Hoffmann, Walther. *Das Wachstum der deutschen Wirtschaft seit der Mitte des 19. Jahrhunderts.* Berlin: Springer-Verlag, 1965.

Holborn, Hajo. *A History of Modern Germany.* Princeton: Princeton University Press, 1982.

Hroch, Miroslav. *Social Preconditions of National Revival in Europe.* Cambridge: Cambridge University Press, 1985.

Hunt, Nancy Rose. "Colonial Fairy Tales and the Knife and Fork Doctrine in the Heart of Africa," in Karen T. Hansen, ed., *African Encounters with Domesticity.* New Brunswick, NJ: Rutgers University Press, 1992.

Hunt, Nancy Rose, Tessie Liu, and Jean Quataert, eds., *Gendered Colonialisms in African History.* London: Blackwell, 1997.

Jacobeit, Sigrid. "Clothing in Nazi Germany," in Georg Iggers, ed., *Marxist Historiography in Transformation.* New York: Berg, 1991.

Jacobsen, Hans-Adolf. "Vom Wandel des Polenbildes in Deutschland (1772–1972)," *Aus Politik und Zeitgeschichte* 21 (1973): 3–21.

James, Harold. *A German Identity, 1770–1990.* New York: Routledge Press, 1989.

Jarausch, Konrad. *Students, Society, and Politics in Imperial Germany: The Rise of Academic Illiberalism.* Princeton: Princeton University Press, 1982.

Jones, Elizabeth Bright. "Gender and Agricultural Change in Saxony, 1900–1930." Ph.D. diss., University of Minnesota, 2000.

Judson, Pieter. "Inventing Germans: Class, Nationality and Colonial Fantasy at the Margins of the Hapsburg Monarchy," *Social Analysis* 33 (1993): 47–67.

———. "Deutschnationale Politik und Geschlecht im Österreich, 1880–1900," in David Good, Margarete Giandrer, and Mary Jo Maynes, eds., *Frauen im Österreich. Beiträge zur ihrer Situation im 19. und 20. Jahrhundert.* Vienna: Böhlau Verlag, 1994.

———. "Frontiers, Islands, Forests, Stones: Mapping the Geography of a German Identity in the Habsburg Monarchy, 1848–1900," in Patricia Yaeger, ed., *The Geography of Identity.* Ann Arbor: University of Michigan Press, 1996.

———. *Exclusive Revolutionaries: Liberal Politics, Social Experience, and National Identity in the Austrian Empire, 1848–1914.* Ann Arbor: University of Michigan Press, 1996.

Junker, Almut. "Das Frankfurter Modeamt" in Almut Junker, ed., *Frankfurt Macht Mode, 1933–1945.* Frankfurt: Jonas Verlag, 1994.

Kaplan, Marion. *The Making of the Jewish Middle Class. Women, Family, and Identity in Imperial Germany.* New York: Oxford University Press, 1991.

———. *Between Dignity and Despair: Jewish Life in Nazi Germany*. New York: Oxford University Press, 1998.

Kater, Michael. *The Nazi Party: A Social Profile of Members and Leaders, 1919–1945*. Cambridge, MA: Harvard University Press, 1983.

Kennedy, Kathleen D.. "Lessons and Learners: Elementary Education in Southern Germany, 1871–1914." Ph.D. diss., Stanford University, 1981.

———. "Domesticity (Hauswirtschaft) in the *Volksschule*: Textbooks and Lessons for Girls, 1890–1914," *Internationale Schulbuchforschung* 13 (1991): 5–21.

Kerchner, Brigitte. *Beruf und Geschlecht: Frauenberufsverbände in Deutschland, 1848–1908*. Göttingen: Vandenhoek and Ruprecht, 1992.

Klinksiek, Dorothee. *Die Frau im NS-Staat*. Stuttgart: Deutsche Verlags-Anstalt, 1982.

Knoblauch, Heinz. *Die Suppenlina. Wiederbelebung einer Menschenfreundin*. Berlin: Hentrich, 1997.

Koch, Angela. *DruckBilder: Stereotype und Geschlechtercodes in den antipolnischen Diskursen der "Gartenlaube" (1870–1930)*. Cologne: Böhlau, 2002.

Koehl, Robert. *RKFDV: German Resettlement and Population Policy, 1939–1945*. Cambridge, MA: Harvard University Press, 1957.

Koonz, Claudia. *Mothers in the Fatherland. Women, the Family, and Nazi Politics*. New York: St. Martin's Press, 1987.

———. *The Nazi Conscience*. Cambridge, MA: Belknap Press of Harvard University Press, 2003.

Koshar, Rudy. *Social Life, Local Politics, and Nazism: Marburg, 1880–1935*. Chapel Hill: University of North Carolina Press, 1986.

Kuhn, Bärbel. "Und herrschet weise im häuslichen Kreise. Hausfrauenarbeit zwischen Disziplin und Eigensinn," in Richard van Duelmen, ed., *Verbrechen, Strafen, und soziale Kontrolle*. Stuttgart: Fischer, 1990.

———. *Haus-Frauen-Arbeit 1915–1965. Erinnerungen aus fünzig Jahren Haushaltsgeschichte*. St. Ingbert: Roehrig Universitätsverlag, 1994.

Lacey, Kate. *Feminine Frequencies. Gender, German Radio, and the Public Sphere, 1923–1945*. Ann Arbor: University of Michigan Press, 1996.

Link, Jürgen and Wulf Wülfing, eds. *Nationale Mythen und Symbole in der zweiten Hälfte des 19. Jahrhunderts. Strukturen und Funktionen von Konzepten nationaler Identität*. Stuttgart: Klett-Cotta Verlag, 1991.

Loehlin, Jennifer. *From Rugs to Riches. Housework, Consumption, and Modernity in Germany*. New York: Berg, 1999.

Lumans, Valdis. *Himmler's Auxiliaries. The Volksdeutsche Mittelstelle and the German National Minorities of Europe, 1933–1945*. Chapel Hill: University of North Carolina Press, 1993.

Macgregor, Miriam. *Etiquette and Elbowgrease. Housekeeping in Victorian New Zealand*. Wellington: A. H. and A. W. Reed, 1976.

Majer, Dietmut. *"Fremdvölkische" im Dritten Reich*. Boppard am Rhein: Harald Boldt Verlag, 1981.

Marenk, Gisela and Gisela Framke ed. *Beruf der Jungfrau. Henriette Davidis und bürgerliches Frauenverständis im 19. Jahrhundert.* Oberhausen: Graphium Press, 1988.

Mason, Timothy. *Sozialpolitik im Dritten Reich.* Opladen: Westdeutscher Verlag, 1977.

McDonald, Kenneth. "Fascist Fashion: Dress, the State, and the Clothing Industry in the Third Reich." Ph.D. diss., University of Califoria, Riverside, 1998.

Merkl, Christoph. "Die Nationalsozialistische Tabakpolitik," *Vierteljahreshefte für Zeitgeschichte* 46 (1998): 19–42.

Meyer, Sibylle. *Das Theater mit der Hausarbeit. Bürgerliche Repräsentation in der Familie der wilhelminischen Zeit.* Frankfurt: Campus, 1982.

Morgan, Marjorie. *National Identities and Travel in Victorian Britain.* New York: Palgrave, 2001.

Mörth, Ingo and Gerhard Fröhlich, eds. *Das symbolische Kapital der Lebensstile. Zur Kultursoziologie der Moderne nach Pierre Bourdieu.* Frankfurt/Main: Campus, 1994.

Mosse, George. *Nationalism and Sexuality. Respectability and Abnormal Sexuality in Modern Europe.* New York: Howard Fertig, 1985.

———. *Nationalization of the Masses: Political Symbolism and Mass Movements in Germany from the Napoleonic Wars through the Third Reich.* Ithaca: Cornell University Press, 1991.

Nestvogel, Renate and Rainer Tetzlaff, eds. *Afrika und der deutsche Kolonialismus. Zivilisierung zwischen Schnapshandel und Bibelstunde.* Berlin: Dietrich Reimer Verlag, 1987.

Niethammer, Lutz, ed. *Die Jahre weiss man nicht, wo man die heute hinsetzen soll. Faschismus-Erfahrungen im Ruhrgebiet.* Berlin: Dietz, 1983.

Nolan, Mary. *Visions of Modernity. American Business and the Modernization of Germany.* New York: Oxford University Press, 1994.

Münch, Paul. *Ordnung, Fleiss, und Sparsamkeit. Texte und Dokumente zur Entstehung der "bürgerlichen Tugenden."* Munich: DTV, 1984.

O'Donnell, Krista. "The Colonial Woman Question: Gender, National Identity, and Empire in the German Colonial Society Female Emigration Program, 1896–1914." Ph.D. diss., SUNY Binghamton, 1996.

O'Donnell, Krista, Renate Bridenthal, and Nancy Reagin, eds. *The Heimat Abroad: The Boundaries of Germanness.* Ann Arbor: University of Michigan Press, 2005.

Orland, Barbara. "Emanzipation durch Rationalisierung? Der 'rationelle Haushalt' als Konzept institutionalisierter Frauenpolitik in der Weimarer Republik," in Dagmar Reese et al., eds., *Rationale Beziehungen? Geschlechterverhältnisse im Rationalisierungsprozess.* Frankfurt: Suhrkamp, 1993.

Orlowski, Hubert. "'Polnische Wirtschaft': Zum deutschen Polendiskurs der späten Neuzeit," in Karl-Günter Schirrmeister, ed., *Deutsch-Polnisches Symposium, 22.–24. Januar 1995 in Strausberg.* Strausberg: Akademie der Bundeswehr für Information und Kommunikation, 1995.

Overy, R. J. *War and Economy in the Third Reich*. Cambridge: Cambridge University Press, 1994.

———. *The Nazi Economic Recovery, 1932–1938*. 2nd ed. Cambridge: Cambridge University Press, 1996.

Owings, Alison. *Frauen. German Women Recall the Third Reich*. New Brunswick, NJ: Rutgers University Press, 1995.

Palmer, Phyllis. *Domesticity and Dirt. Housewives and Domestic Servants in the United States, 1920–1945*. Philadelphia: Temple University Press, 1989.

Pelz, Anegret. *Reisen durch die eigene Fremde: Reiseliteratur von Frauen als autogeographische Schriften*. Cologne: Bölau Verlag, 1993.

Perry, Joseph. "The Private Life of the Nation: Christmas and the Invention of Modern Germany." Ph.D. diss., University of Illinois at Urbana-Champaign, 2001.

Peterson, Brent O. "The Fatherland's Kiss of Death. Gender and Germany in Nineteenth-Century Historical Fiction," in Patricia Herminghouse and Magda Mueller, eds., *Gender and Germanness. Cultural Productions of Nation*. Oxford: Berghahn Press, 1997.

Peukert, Detlev. *The Weimar Republic*. New York: Hill and Wang, 1989.

Pine, Lisa. *Nazi Family Policy, 1933–1945*. New York: Berg, 1997.

Pinkus, Benjamin. *Die Deutschen in der Sowjetunion. Geschichte einer nationalen Minderheit im 20. Jahrhundert*. Baden-Baden: Nomos, 1987.

Planert, Ute, ed. *Nation, Politik, und Geschlecht. Frauenbewegungen und Nationalismus in der Moderne*. Frankfurt/Main: Campus, 2000.

Proctor, Robert. *The Nazi War on Cancer*. Princeton: Princeton University Press, 1999.

Pundt, Helen. *AHEA. A History of Excellence*. Washington, DC: American Home Economics Association, 1980.

Quataert, Jean. *Staging Philanthropy. Patriotic Women and the National Imagination in Dynastic Germany, 1813–1916*. Ann Arbor: University of Michigan Press, 2001.

Reagin, Nancy. "Die Werkstatt der Hausfrau: Bürgerliche Frauenbewegung und Wohnungspolitik im Hannover der Zwanziger Jahre," in Adelheid v. Saldern and Sid Auffahrt, eds., *Altes und neues Wohnen: Linden und Hannover im frühen 20. Jahrhundert*. Hanover: Seelze-Velber, 1992.

———. *A German Women's Movement: Class and Gender in Hanover, 1880–1933*. Chapel Hill: University of North Carolina Press, 1995.

———. "Comparing Apples and Oranges: Housewives and the Politics of Consumption in Interwar Germany," in Susan Strasser, Charles McGovern, and Matthias Judt, eds., *Getting and Spending. European and American Consumer Societies in the Twentieth Century*. Cambridge: Cambridge University Press, 1998.

———. "The Imagined *Hausfrau*: National Identity, Domesticity, and Colonialism in Imperial Germany," *Journal of Modern History* 73 (March 2001a): 54–86.

————. "*Marktordnung* and Autarkic Housekeeping: Private Households under the Nazi Four Year Plan," *German History* 19 (May 2001b): 162–84.

————. "Recent Work on German National Identity: Regional? Imperial? Gendered? Imaginary?" in *Central European History* 37 (June 2004): 245–71.

————. "German Brigadoon? Domesticity and Metropolitan Perceptions of *Auslandsdeutschen* in Southwest Africa and Eastern Europe" in Krista O'Donnell, Renate Bridenthal, and Nancy Reagin eds., *The Heimat Abroad: The Boundaries of Germanness*. Ann Arbor: University of Michigan Press, 2005.

Reese, Dagmar. "Bund Deutscher Mädel – Zur Geschichte der weiblichen deutschen Jugend im Dritten Reich" in Frauengruppe Faschismusforschung, ed. *Mutterkreuz und Arbeitsbuch. Zur Geschichte der Frauen in der Weimarer Republik und im Nationalsozialismus*. Frankfurt: Fischer Verlag, 1981.

Rendall, Jane. *Women in an Industrializing Society: England, 1750–1880*. Oxford: Basil Blackwell, 1990.

Rentschler, Eric. *The Ministry of Illusion. Nazi Cinema and Its Afterlife*. Cambridge, MA: Harvard University Press, 1996.

Rieke-Müller, Annelore and Siegfried Müller. "Konzeptionen der Kulturgeschichte um die Mitte des 19. Jahrhunderts: Das Germanische Nationalmuseum in Nürnberg und die Zeitschrift für Deutsche Kulturgeschichte," *Archiv für Kulturgeschichte* 82(2) (2000): 345–75.

Ritter, Ernst. *Das Deutsche Auslands-Institut in Stuttgart 1917–1945: ein Beispiel deutscher Volkstumsarbeit zwischen den Weltkriegen*. Wiesbaden: Steiner, 1976.

Rock, David, ed. *Coming Home to Germany?: The Integration of Ethnic Germans from Central and Eastern Europe in the Federal Republic*. New York: Berghahn Books, 2002.

Roerkohl, Anne. *Hungerblockade und Heimatfront*. Stuttgart: F. Steiner, 1991.

Ruhl, Klaus-Jörg. "Die nationalsozialistische Familienpolitik (1933–1945)," *Geschichte in Wissenschaft und Unterricht* 8 (1991): 479–89.

Ryan, Mary P. *Cradle of the Middle Class. The Family in Oneida County, New York, 1790–1865*. Cambridge: Cambridge University Press, 1981.

Sachse, Carole. *Siemens, der Nationalsozialismus und die moderne Familie. Eine Untersuchung zur sozialen Rationalisierung in Deutschland im 20. Jahrhundert*. Hamburg: Rasch und Röhring Verlag, 1990.

Saherwala, G. and F. Escher. *Slawen und Deutsche zwischen Elbe und Oder: Vor 1000 Jahren, der Slawenaufstand von 983*. Berlin: Berliner Gesellschaft für Anthropologie, Ethnologie und Urgeschichte, 1983.

v. Saldern, Adelheid. "Victims or Perpetrators? Controversies about the Role of Women in the Nazi State," in David Crew, ed., *Nazism and German Society, 1933–1945*. New York: Routledge, 1994.

————. "Social Rationalization of Living and Housework in Germany and the United States in the 1920s," *History of the Family* 2 (1997): 73–97.

Samuel, Wolfgang. *German Boy: A Refugee's Story.* Jackson: Mississippi University Press, 2000.

Scheck, Raffael. "German Conservatism and Female Political Activism in the Early Weimar Republic," *German History* 15 (1997): 34–55.

———. *Mothers of the Nation: Right-Wing Women in Weimar Germany.* New York: Berg, 2004.

Schlegel-Matthies, Kirsten. *"Im Haus und am Herd." Der Wandel des Hausfrauenbildes und der Hausarbeit 1880–1930.* Stuttgart: F. Steiner, 1995.

Schmidt, Alexander. *Reisen in die Moderne. Der Amerika-Diskurs des deutschen Bürgertums vor dem Ersten Weltkrieg im europäischen Vergleich.* Berlin: Akademie Verlag, 1997.

Schmidt, Maruta and Gabi Dietz, eds., *Frauen unterm Hakenkreuz.* Berlin: Elefanten Verlag, 1983.

Schmidt-Waldherr, Hiltraud. *Emanzipation durch Professionalisierung? Politische Strategien und Konflikte innerhalb der bürgerlichen Frauenbewegung während der Weimarer Republik und die Reaktion des bürgerlichen Antifeminismus und des Nationalsozialismus.* Frankfurt: Materialis, 1987.

———. "Rationalisierung der Hausarbeit in der zwanziger Jahren," in Gerda Tornieporth, ed., *Arbeitsplatz Haushalt: zur Theorie und Ökologie der Hausarbeit.* Berlin: D. Reimer, 1988.

Schwarz, Gudrun. *Eine Frau an seiner Seite: Ehefrauen in der 'SS-Sippengemeinschaft'.* Hamburg: Hamburger Ed., 1997.

Siebert, Ulle. "Reise. Nation. Text. Repräsentationen von 'Nationalität' in Reisetexten deutscher Frauen, 1871–1914," in Frauen und Geschichte Baden-Württemberg, ed., *Frauen und Nation.* Tübingen: Silberberg, 1996.

Smith, Bonnie. *Ladies of the Leisure Class: The Bourgeoises of Northern France in the Nineteenth Century.* Princeton: Princeton University Press, 1984.

Smith, Helmut Walser, ed. *German Nationalism and Religious Conflict. Culture, Ideology, Politics, 1870–1914.* Princeton: Princeton University Press, 1995.

———. ed. *Protestants, Catholics and Jews in Germany, 1880–1914.* New York: Berg, 2002.

Smith, Woodruff. *The German Colonial Empire.* Chapel Hill: University of North Carolina Press, 1978.

Sneeringer, Julia. *Winning Women's Votes: Propaganda and Politics in Weimar Germany.* Chapel Hill: University of North Carolina Press, 2002.

Sperber, Jonathon. *Popular Catholicism in Nineteenth-Century Germany.* Princeton: Princeton University Press, 1984.

Speth, Rudolf. *Nation und Revolution. Politische Mythen im 19. Jahrhundert.* Opladen: Leske and Budrich, 2000.

Steinbacher, Sybille. *"Musterstadt" Auschwitz. Germanisierungspolitik und Judenmord in Ostoberschlesien.* Munich: K. G. Saur, 2000.

Stephenson, Jill. *Women in Nazi Society.* New York: Barnes and Noble Books, 1975.

———. "'Reichsbund der Kinderreichen': The League of Large Families in the Population Policy of Nazi Germany," *European Studies Review* 9 (1979): 351–75.

———. *The Nazi Organization of Women*. London: Croom Helm, 1980.

———. "Propaganda, Autarky, and the German Housewife," in David Welch, ed., *Nazi Propaganda. The Power and the Limitations*. London: Croom Helm, 1983.

Stibbe, Matthew. *Women in the Third Reich*. London: Oxford University Press, 2003.

Stoler, Ann L. "Carnal Knowledge and Imperial Power: Gender, Race, and Morality in Colonial Asia," in Micaela di Leonardo, ed., *Gender at the Crossroads of Knowledge. Feminist Anthropology in the Post-Modern Era*. Berkeley: University of California Press, 1991.

Stoler, Ann L. and Frederick Cooper, eds. *Tensions of Empire. Colonial Cultures in a Bourgeois World*. Berkeley: University of California Press, 1997.

Strasser, Susan. *Never Done. A History of American Housework*. New York: Pantheon Books, 1982.

Strasser, Susan, Charles McGovern, and Matthias Judt, eds. *Getting and Spending. European and American Consumer Societies in the Twentieth Century*. Cambridge: Cambridge University Press, 1998.

Strobel, Margaret. *Western Women and the Second British Empire*. Bloomington: Indiana University Press, 1991.

Süchtig-Hänger, Andrea. *Das 'Gewissen der Nation.' Nationales Engagement und politisches Handeln konservativer Frauenorganisationen 1900 bis 1937*. Düsseldorf: Droste Verlag, 2002.

Szepansky, Gerda. *Blitzmädel, Heldenmutter, Kriegerwitwe. Frauenleben im Zweiten Weltkrieg*. Frankfurt: Fischer Verlag, 1986.

Tacke, Charlotte. *Denkmal im sozialen Raum. Nationale Symbole in Deutschland und Frankreich im 19. Jahrhundert*. Göttingen: Vendenhoeck and Ruprecht, 1995.

———. "Nation und Geschlechtscharaktere" in Frauen and Geschichte Baden-Württemberg, eds., *Frauen und Nation*. Tübingen: Silberberg, 1996.

Teuteberg, Hans J. "Der Verzehr von Nahrungsmitteln in Deutschland pro Kopf und Jahr seit Beginn der Industrialisierung (1850–1975)," *Archiv für Sozialgeschichte* 19 (1979): 331–88.

Thamer, Hans-Ulrich. *Verführung und Gewalt. Deutschland 1933–1945*. Berlin: Siedler Verlag, 1986.

Tornieporth, Gerda. *Arbeitsplatz Haushalt. Zur Theorie und Ökologie der Hausarbeit*. Berlin: Dietrich Reimer Verlag, 1988.

Treibel, Armin. *Zwei Klassen und die Vielfalt des Konsums. Haushaltsbudgetierung bei abhängig Erwebstätigen in Deutschland im ersten Drittel des 20. Jahrhunderts*. Berlin: Max Plank Institute, 1991.

———. "Vom Konsum der Klasse zur Vielfalt der Stile: Haushaltsbudgetierung seit der ersten Hälfte des 20. Jahrhunderts," *Historical Social Research* 22 (1997): 81–102.

Vanchena, Lorie A. *Political Poetry in Periodicals and the Shaping of German National Consciousness in the Nineteenth Century*. New York: Peter Lang, 2000.

Verk, Sabine. *Geschmacksache. Kochbücher aus dem Museum für Volkskunde*. Berlin: Staatliche Museen zu Berlin, 1995.

Warmbold, Joachim. *Germania in Africa. Germany's Colonial Literature.* New York: Peter Lang, 1989.

Warth, Eva Maria. "The Reconceptualization of Women's Roles in War-Time National Socialism: An Analysis of *Die Frau meiner Träume,*" in Brandon Taylor and Wilfried van der Wall, eds., *The Nazification of Art. Art, Design, Music, Architecture, and Film in the Third Reich.* Winchester, UK: The Winchester Press, 1990.

Weber-Kellermann, Ingeborg. *Die Familie. Geschichte, Geschichten, und Bilder.* Frankfurt: Insel Verlag, 1977.

———. *Das Weihnachtsfest: Eine Kultur- und Sozialgeschichte der Weihnachtszeit.* Munich: C. J. Buchner, 1987.

Weidenfeller, Gerhard. *VDA. Verein für das Deutschtum im Ausland. Allgemeiner Deutscher Schulverein (1881–1918). Ein Beitrag zur Geschichte des deutschen Nationalismus und Imperialismus im Kaiserreich.* Berlin: Peter Lang, 1976.

Weismann, Anabella. *Froh erfülle deine Pflicht. Die Entwicklung des Hausfrauenleitbildes im Spiegel trivialer Massenmedien in der Zeit zwischen Reichsgründung und Weltwirtschaftskrise.* Berlin: Schelzky and Jeep, 1989.

Weyrather, Irmgard. *Muttertag und Mutterkreuz. Der Kult um die 'deutsche Mutter' im Nationalsozialismus.* Frankfurt: Fischer Verlag, 1993.

Wiedemann, Inga. *Herrin im Hause. Durch Koch- und Haushaltsbücher zur bürgerlichen Hausfrau.* Pfaffenweiler: Centarus-Verlagsgesellschaft, 1993.

Wiggershaus, Renate. *Frauen unterm Nationalsozialismus.* Wuppertal: Hammer Verlag, 1984.

Wildenthal, Lora. *German Women for Empire, 1884–1945.* Durham, NC: Duke University Press, 2001.

Wildt, Michael. *Am Beginn der "Konsumgesellschaft."* Hamburg: Erbgenisse Verlag, 1994.

Wippermann, Wolfgang. "Das Slawenbild der Deutschen im 19. und 20. Jahrhundert," in Geraldine Saherwala und Felix Escher, eds., *Slawen und Deutsche zwischen Elbe und Oder: vor 1000 Jahren, der Slawenaufstand von 983.* Berlin: Berliner Gesellschaft für Anthropologie, Ethnologie und Urgeschichte, 1983.

Wolff, Stefan. "The Politics of Homeland. Irredentism and Reconciliation in the Policies of German Federal Governments and Expellee Organizations towards Ethnic German Minorities in Central and Eastern Europe, 1949–1999," in Krista O'Donnell, Renate Bridenthal, and Nancy Reagin, eds., *The Heimat Abroad: The Boundaries of Germanness.* Ann Arbor: University of Michigan Press, 2005.

Yuval-Davis, Nira and Floya Anthias, eds. *Woman-Nation-State.* New York: St. Martin's Press, 1989.

———. *Gender and Nation.* London: Sage, 1997.

Zantrop, Susanne. *Colonial Fantasies. Conquest, Family, and Nation in Precolonial Germany, 1770–1870.* Durham and London: Duke University Press, 1997.

Index

Printed in Great Britain
by Amazon

32177068R00148